D0416593

BACK FROM THE BRINK

HOUSE OF COMMONS LIBRARY		
LOCATION	Research 8p	
AUTHOR	CLARK	
Acc DATE	17 NOV 1998	

TO BE
DISPOSED
BY
AUTHORITY

BACK FROM THE BRINK

Transforming the Ridings School – and our children's education

Peter Clark

metro

First published in paperback in Great Britain in 1998
by Metro Books (an imprint of Metro Publishing Limited), 19 Gerrard
Street, London W1V 7LA

All rights reserved: no part of this publication may be reproduced,
stored in a retrieval system, or transmitted in any form or by any means,
electronic, mechanical, photocopying or otherwise, without the prior
written consent of the publisher.

Copyright © 1998 Peter Clark

Peter Clark is hereby identified as the author of this work in accordance
with Section 77 of the Copyright, Designs and Patents Act 1988.

British Library Cataloguing in Publication Data. A CIP record of this
book is available on request from the British Library.

ISBN 1 900512 49 1

10 9 8 7 6 5 4 3 2 1

Typeset by Wakewing, High Wycombe, Buckinghamshire.

Printed in Great Britain by CPD Group, Wales.

CONTENTS

DEDICATION

To the students and staff of the Ridings School who together made the difference.

ACKNOWLEDGEMENTS

To those who read early drafts and advised me, particularly Morton Roberts and Alan Flux, and also to my wife, Carol, who spent many hours helping to re-draft and correcting my work.

To the students, staff and governors of Rastrick High School without whose efforts the opportunity for me to work at the Ridings School would not have arisen.

1

THE BIRTH OF THE RIDINGS SCHOOL

'Hello Peter. How do you fancy the career opportunity of a lifetime?'

It was 8.45a.m. on the Friday before the October half-term break in 1996, and I was in my office at Rastrick High School where I took a phone call from Peter Bartle, Chief Adviser of Calderdale Local Education Authority (LEA), the authority for the Halifax area. He told me that Karen Stansfield, the Head of the Ridings School in Halifax, had resigned, and that the LEA was looking for a short-term replacement. This call was to be the start of nine months in which my life would be turned upside down.

I was staggered. Of course it was common knowledge that there were problems at the Ridings, but I had not realized they were so bad that the Head would be driven to resign. Just three weeks before, I had had a snatched conversation with Karen in a car park in Huddersfield. She had told me about her troubles with the pupils and staff: how she felt that she had been set adrift to cope on her own, with little back-up from the local authority. The Ridings was created by merging two schools, and had inherited the problems of both.

There were at least 60 very difficult children: tribal rivalries dominated their lives outside school, and their behaviour in school mirrored this, occasionally breaking into outright warfare in the classroom. Vandalism was part of daily life: toilet rolls set on fire, toilets damaged, fire hoses used to flood areas of the school and windows smashed, especially out of school hours. A hard core of older pupils flouted authority and swaggered around the corridors at breaks and lunchtimes, bullying other pupils and extorting money from them. These youths were regarded as mini-emperors on the estates where they lived, and their domination continued at school.

Another, larger group of pupils copied the behaviour of this hard core. Although not quite so brazen, they intimidated others through sheer numbers. Inevitably the situation deteriorated, with teachers repeatedly on the receiving end of disrespectful behaviour, abusive language and even damage to their cars.

There had been attempts to halt the spiral of decline. The authority had provided additional support staff and £7,000 worth of computer and other equipment. Some months previously, a group of senior officers had been set up to work with Karen, the Chairman of Governors and a member of the teaching staff to try to improve the situation. However, councillors had insisted on being involved and meetings were soon dominated by characteristic mutual recriminations. Another attempt – the LEA's bid for substantial funds to address the problems of social deprivation and educational underachievement in the surrounding area – was turned down by central government. The authority also eventually removed a unit catering for disaffected youngsters from other schools who were adding to the chaos, although even this attempt at remedial action faced strong internal opposition.

Unsurprisingly, staff morale was at an all-time low. Sometimes it seemed as though teachers were having to fight battles on all fronts, not just at school. One councillor accused the teachers of incompetence. 'I've worked in inner London. I learned that taking abuse from children was part of the job. Why can't you accept it?' The staff were underwhelmed by this lack of support – reinforced by the LEA's limiting the exclusions of difficult pupils and continuing to admit more disruptive children to the school. So what was already a volatile situation grew steadily worse, culminating in Karen's resignation.

I tried to be encouraging and supportive towards Karen. 'If you keep working through and manage each situation as it arises, things will eventually get better,' I told her. 'Just as you think things can't get any worse, be prepared for another crisis – but they invariably improve after that.'

I told her about my time as the Acting Head of Reins Wood School, my first experience as a Head, and a 'failing school' of its day. Until May 1984, I had been happily settled in my role as Deputy Head of Brooksbank School, near Halifax. It was a large school – nearly 1,800 pupils and 100 teachers – and I was mainly responsible for the management of the curriculum. Out of the blue Calderdale Education Authority asked me if I would be seconded to Reins Wood School, a small secondary modern of just over 500 pupils. The Headteacher had resigned, and it was thought inappropriate for the Deputy Head to take over temporarily because the staff were split into warring camps. Fate intervened: almost to the day I took over, the then Secretary of State for Education, Sir Keith Joseph, agreed to the reorganization of six secondary schools in the Brighouse area into three comprehensives. Reins Wood was to merge with a small voluntary-aided grammar school for boys, Rastrick Grammar. Reins Wood was run and controlled by Calderdale Education Authority, but the grammar school, dating back to the 1620s, had the same management independence many church schools had, despite the LEA paying the majority of the running costs. The new comprehensive was to be 'voluntary controlled' – halfway between the two.

So the role immediately changed from that of merely keeping the place ticking over until a new Head was appointed. When, six months later, I was appointed Head of Rastrick High School, as the new school was to be known, my task was to build a school from scratch out of two schools with very different characteristics. Reins Wood had very poor examination results: for example, in the summer before my secondment, only one pupil out of over a hundred gained the equivalent of the higher grades of A* to C at GCSE (General Certificate of Secondary Education) level. Although this was very poor for the mid-1980s, education did not then have such a high political profile as it has now, and society's expectations of schools were lower. (Today it would be a national scandal; even at the start, the Ridings was achieving far higher standards than this.) The general acceptance that the children who attended Reins Wood needed to be 'cared for' rather than educated resulted in an emphasis on pastoral care above teaching, and the use of syllabuses that did not allow children to achieve higher grades, whatever their ability. Rastrick Grammar had a much better reputation but, due to the large number of grammar school places in Calderdale at that time, took in pupils with a much wider range of ability than is usual in a selective school. Consequently, some pupils were daunted and demotivated by the level of work expected of them, while some teachers were demoralized by dealing with the less able pupils. In fact, the combined results of the two schools in the summer before the amalgamation were worse than those of many failing schools in today's league tables.

At that time, I was given considerably more help by Calderdale LEA than Karen later received, but essentially we faced similar situations: the challenge of creating a vibrant and successful school by making the whole greater than the sum of the parts. From the very start, I was determined to build an excellent comprehensive school catering for the individual needs of all the students, setting high expectations and seeking to help pupils to fulfil their intellectual potential and achieve their ambitions. In the early days, we felt pretty insecure as a staff. The original staff were conscious of their lack of expertise in dealing with the pupils from different ends of the ability range, while those appointed from outside did not know the pupils and were mostly either newly promoted or in their first teaching jobs.

I found the ensuing round of appointing staff, planning the curriculum, policies and procedures, and convincing parents to trust their children to an untried and untested team both extremely rewarding and exhausting. It certainly concentrated my mind, and many of the problems of Reins Wood disappeared in the process. Before the merger was announced, the two groups of staff felt isolated from mainstream education. The reorganization changed all that: now teachers could look forward, enthusiastic about what we all hoped would become a successful comprehensive school. We managed to enlist the co-operation of the majority of the students, who saw the new school as an improvement. It had something for both sets of students: much better access for the grammar school pupils to facilities for science, design technology and PE, and as far as the Reins Wood pupils were concerned it was no longer a secondary modern. Their attitude was summed up by one senior pupil who said to his mother, 'Does this mean I can write Rastrick High School instead of Reins Wood on my job application form?'

As the school grew and became a united community, the educational divisions imposed by the previous system began to be exposed. By the end of our first year, for example, when we re-jigged the sets in Maths and English, we found that the top sets contained a number of ex-Reins Wood pupils who had made dramatic progress under our new regime. The pupils responded positively, and we grew more confident as staff, which in turn resulted in a positive spiral: a steady improvement in the quality of teaching, reflected in higher grades in external examinations, wider educational and extra-curricular opportunities and increased popularity with local parents. This positive trend continued. In 1993 the school opted out of the financial control of the LEA to become grant maintained, later becoming a specialist Technology College. I believe the government's specialist school initiative is an excellent scheme for supporting and reinforcing success; with the funds generated from grants and businesses, schools like Rastrick can pursue improvement plans knowing that they can be financed. Over the next 12 years Rastrick High School became a well-regarded school attracting children from a wide area of Brighouse and North Huddersfield.

So I could sympathize with Karen's hopes and expectations for the Ridings as well as her difficulties. As she was a new and inexperienced Headteacher, I thought all she needed was a little encouragement and the offer of further help; despite my similar experience, I did not appreciate the extent of the problems she faced. I only realized later that the last year had probably been the worst in her life.

Eighteen months before, Karen had been the successful Deputy Head of one of Bradford's biggest Upper Schools, catering for 13–18 year olds. Like many Bradford teachers, she regarded the schools in Halifax as part of 'the badlands' over the hill; Calderdale LEA had a reputation for in-fighting amongst the councillors. However, when the headship of the new secondary school in Calderdale was advertised, it was just at the point in Karen's career when she really needed to make the move to a headship. 'I was thrilled when I got the job; it was the big career break (but) I was completely out of my depth,' Karen admitted some time later. 'I felt totally under siege. I'd had 19 years of successful teaching and after one nightmare year it was all down the pan.'

The last decade has seen dramatic developments in the role of headteacher, resulting from the array of changes brought in since the 1988 Education Reform Act. One key change is the introduction of 'formula funding', where schools look after their own budgets, based on their pupil numbers. Previously, all decisions on the numbers of staff, their level of pay, short- and long-term maintenance, purchase of furniture, and so on, were taken by LEA officers, with schools being responsible only for spending on books and other teaching resources. Today, Rastrick High School has a budget of over £3 million and directly employs around 150 staff. Strategic planning, personnel management, financial control and marketing have been added to the traditional responsibilities of headteachers, requiring them to be in effect managing directors as well as senior teaching professionals. Open enrolment – which allows parents to choose schools outside the traditional, rigid catchment areas – reinforces the link between funding and the number of children, further increasing the pressure on headteachers to market their schools to attract sufficient pupils (and consequently funding) to maintain them. Wider parental choice and the quest for higher standards have inevitably led to a need for more accessible information on individual schools: hence league tables, inspections by the Office for Standards in Education (Ofsted), and much greater public accountability for heads and governing bodies.

Overall, this has been a positive development, freeing heads from the burden of the bureaucratic and inflexible decision-making procedures that often held back innovative schools. I believe that the delegation of responsibility to schools has done more to improve educational standards in the last few years than all the league tables and inspections put together. Providing the best for all children is now the top priority; in spite of the current political emphasis on 'life-long learning', school is the main opportunity for most young people to achieve their ambitions.

Like many aspiring headteachers, Karen welcomed this increased responsibility and the greater opportunity for real leadership. When she read the advertisement for the headship of the new Ridings School, which sought someone with 'the enthusiasm and skills to establish and develop the school as a major provider of secondary education in the authority', and the 'vision to motivate', who could 'work in partnership with the governors, the Authority, parents and the community', she was excited at the prospect. Although she was not interviewed initially in April, when no appointment was made, she was called in May and appointed to start as the Head of the newly amalgamated school in September 1994.

Like many LEAs, Calderdale had entered the 1980s with more schools than it needed, due to the falling birth-rate. In my opinion, small schools are uneconomic in both educational and financial terms – especially in an era of declining public spending. Larger schools have economies of scale, and so can afford specialist teachers, small classes in minority subjects, and individual attention for pupils. The policy of most LEAs was to merge or close schools where necessary, but Calderdale had been slow to act, with each attempt to rationalize meeting strong opposition. Then the government introduced an incentive in the form of a programme that paid LEAs a bounty to take out surplus places: Calderdale amalgamated two schools to the north of Halifax, Ovenden and Holmfield, to form the Ridings. This would attract an increase of over £4 million in the Calderdale Capital Programme – the money available for building and major maintenance projects throughout the borough.

Ovenden Secondary School was built in the 1930s – its solid, pre-war brick architecture providing a focus at the heart of a densely populated council estate. The school had won a place in the affections of the local community and over the years pupil numbers remained consistently high – some 700 – despite exam results that were often disappointing. Educational qualifications were not considered as essential as they are today at a time when school leavers found it relatively easy to gain employment in the area. However, by the early 1990s United Biscuits and Crossley Carpets, the largest local employers, were long gone. With the increased importance of results and surplus places in nearby comprehensive schools, the number of pupils declined to around 300.

Holmfield High School's roots lay in a different era of educational expansion. The original buildings were rather soulless, flat-roofed, late-1950s constructions, extended in the 1960s. It was one of four schools built on a 'school base' on the edge of the town; all had undergone reorganization during the intervening years, leaving a sprawling site. Holmfield itself had been formed in 1985 from a merger of two schools. With a capacity of 1,600 pupils, like Ovenden it suffered from competition from other schools, and its pupil numbers declined steadily, from 1,100 in 1985 to around 300 by the mid-1990s. With numbers falling, the high maintenance costs of a very large building caused the school severe financial difficulties. The Head had retired over a year before the amalgamation with Ovenden and was not replaced. While the local authority decided what to do, Deputy Head Andrew Bateman had been promoted to Acting Head. Not surprisingly, the uncertainty over the future of both Ovenden and Holmfield led increasing numbers of parents to transfer their children – many of the more able and well-behaved amongst them – to other schools.

When Calderdale announced they were applying to the Secretary of State for Education for permission to amalgamate the two schools, new problems arose. The Ovenden community rallied round its school. Parents and staff organized a media campaign arguing that the schools should not be amalgamated, but if that was a *fait accompli*, the new school should be sited at the Ovenden building. The Holmfield community, in contrast, seemed to accept the amalgamation; their only concern was that the new school should be sited at Holmfield. They knew their school building had problems, but it was a much larger and better-equipped site.

In spite of the need for urgent action, Calderdale's Education Committee decided that they should apply for permission not only to amalgamate the schools, but also to establish a sixth form at the new school. This led to a more exhaustive consultation process involving not only all the 11–18 schools in the area but also the Further Education Funding Council, which wanted to protect recruitment to colleges of further education and sixth-form colleges in nearby LEAs. It took 18 months for the final approval to come back from the Department for Education and Employment (DfEE). Meanwhile, anxieties intensified and the number of pupils at both schools plummeted still further – what parent would send their child to a school that was likely to shut next year if they had any other choice?

The governors of each school put their case, as rumours flew around the communities. The Chairman of the Ovenden governors was a Labour councillor and ex-alderman of Halifax, whilst the Chairman of Holmfield was a Labour councillor from the Illingworth ward. It was thought that Ovenden's Chairman would have the greater clout when it came to the final fight. When it was announced that the new Ridings School would be at Ovenden, the authority sugared the pill by announcing that £4.8 million, including £3 million from the government bounty, would be used to extend and equip the new school.

Although Karen had been appointed to open the new school in September 1994, the various delays meant a postponement until early in the spring term of 1995. A temporary governing body was set up, with members from both Ovenden and Holmfield. The Holmfield faction was particularly annoyed when told that the renovation and building work would start on the day the school opened, so disrupting the start of the new school. The earlier arguments about location were revived, deepening the split. Meanwhile, as Pauline Nicel, Head of Ovenden School for nearly 20 years, was to retire that summer, both schools would be run by Acting Heads who would oversee the move. Karen's brief was to concentrate on preparing for the start of the first term in January.

At first Karen was to be based in the local authority's offices. With hindsight, this was a mistake. Being exiled in the outpost of the Education Department at this formative stage in the school's development meant that she was less accessible and found it hard to break down barriers and work directly with the staff of the two schools. Without day-to-day involvement in the running of both schools it was difficult to form those relationships crucial for the future. From Karen's point of view the new job was beginning to seem like a poisoned chalice. She felt she had to bend over backwards to be seen to be fair: the smallest attention could be interpreted as favouritism. So whenever she needed to visit one of the schools, for example, she always made sure she visited the other, even if there was no reason to go. 'I had to be careful to visit each on the same days, the same number of times – otherwise their noses were put out of joint.'

The initial optimism turned sour. Karen felt she was a victim of a 'whispering campaign' from the 'misguided and embittered individuals' who acted as a cabal with a hidden agenda, resentments and ulterior motives, seeking to show she was the wrong choice. 'They (the staff) never bonded. In front of me they were polite to each other and there was a superficial bonhomie. But the moment there was any strain they would retreat to their separate camps. There was almost a conspiracy of silence borne of niceness. Teachers would sidle up to me and tell me to watch my back. The school became a cauldron of escalating tension.'

In an attempt to limit the animosity, Karen devised different management structures from those which already existed in the schools. For example, where Holmfield operated 'Heads of Year' and Ovenden 'Heads of Upper and Lower School', at the Ridings Karen decided to establish two 'Key Stage Co-ordinators' based on the stages of the National Curriculum. These co-ordinators would look after Key Stage 3 (Years 7 to 9) and Key Stage 4 (Years 10 and 11), overseeing pastoral care and some aspects of the curriculum. This overwhelming desire to avoid copying existing systems dogged the establishment of the new school's management structures and procedures, even extending to staff acronyms used for internal administration. When I joined I was referred to as *PCI*, simply because the more natural abbreviations – *CLA* and *PDC* – had already been used in the two old schools.

However, these were cosmetic changes which did not begin to address the underlying issues – poor staff morale and dissatisfaction with the appointment process. Before the merger was agreed, the LEA had negotiated an agreement with the unions on the appointment of staff and salary protections for those who could not be appointed to a post equal in status to their current one. Teachers are paid on a scale linked to their responsibility within a school. The starting point is the basic grade of classroom teacher, with five further grades (known as responsibility points) depending on the teacher's duties. Typically, a Head of English would receive four points, a Head of History two or three points, and responsibility for organizing some aspect of a subject would result in one or two points. Before Local Management – the policy of formula funding and delegating decisions – schools were allocated a total number of points depending on their size and the generosity of the LEA; now governors decide on a school's management and staffing structure within national guidelines. When schools are merged, LEAs usually agree to protect salaries so that, even if a teacher accepts a job that is graded lower, their salary remains the same.

Holmfield and Ovenden had a total of 16 members of staff in relatively senior grades. Inevitably, given the reduced number of senior posts, many could not be appointed to a post of similar responsibility; and so on down the scale. Under the union agreement, all were to be paid at their previous, higher level. These 'protections' cost approximately £100,000, not to mention the less quantifiable costs of jealousy and non-co-operation. Staff who failed to get senior posts were seen by some to be 'overpaid' for the jobs they were doing, while they in turn resented their 'demotion', some taking retribution by referring problems to their more successful colleagues: 'They're getting paid to do the job now, let *them* sort it out.'

A number of teachers were old enough to retire, which should have made matters easier: their retirement would have created an opportunity to bring in 'new blood' with different specialisms and interests. In all previous amalgamations in Calderdale, staff had been offered substantial inducements to retire early, but this merger was to be different. Calderdale's policy was: 'No retirement enhancements and the legal minimum redundancy payment' (about £5,000). The unions tried to persuade councillors to reverse this decision, but they would not budge, saying that everyone who wanted a job would get one, so there would be no need to worry. This policy created further feelings of injustice: the number of teachers might equal the number of jobs, but they did not necessarily have the relevant experience for the posts available.

The prospect of applying for a job after so many years was another point of contention. Teachers were presented with a list of the required personnel, based on the curriculum of the new school and the finance available. All teachers had to decide which jobs they suited, then apply and be interviewed. The appointment panels were made up of Karen, one or two of the governors, senior members of staff as they were appointed, Peter Flower (the LEA officer overseeing the process), and a subject adviser. However, the LEA was adamant: all the posts were to be filled from the two existing staffs; no other teachers could be drafted in.

Of the three deputies at the two amalgamating schools – David Bond and Jeanette Wallace from Ovenden, and Holmfield's Acting Head, Andrew Bateman – David and Andrew were appointed Deputy Heads while Jeanette became Head of Sixth Form. Andrew had applied for the headship of the Ridings but, despite being long-term Acting Head of one of the schools, had not been considered suitable for interview, because he had no experience in schools with Sixth Forms.

The number of available responsibility posts was severely limited by the tight budget – the maximum number of points per post was three – so even staff successful in their applications knew they would find themselves on protected salaries with a consequent loss of status and self-esteem. Others who had thought they had it made found it difficult to cope when they were not appointed to the job of their choice.

Filling the vacant post for a French teacher degenerated into farce. Only one member of staff applied: a maths teacher who had no experience of speaking French, let alone teaching it. He insisted that he was qualified for the post, so an interview was held which Karen conducted partly in French. It was clear that he was unsuitable, and the LEA agreed to advertise the post nationally. However, there were only two applicants, a newly qualified teacher and a retired policeman who lacked a teaching qualification. The unqualified person was appointed and the other taken on a temporary basis to cover the long-term sickness of the head of department.

Between September and the end of November 1994, Karen interviewed 83 people, and filled all but one of the new posts. Meanwhile, levels of staff sickness in the two schools were rising dramatically – two teachers had nervous breakdowns – as the impossibility of satisfying everyone reinforced the bitterness and frustration.

The schools closed for the Christmas holidays after Karen had taken a last assembly at each school, talking abut the future and telling the pupils how wonderful the new school would be. The pupils went off happily enough. Whether they were more impressed by the red, white and blue school ties they had all been given or the prospect of an extra four days of holiday is anybody's guess. It had also been agreed to give each pupil a new school jumper in the interest of promoting the wearing of uniform, but – perhaps as an omen of what was to come – the jumpers did not arrive until well into the first term.

For some reason, the Authority assumed that the teachers themselves would organize the movement of the books and equipment from Holmfield to Ovenden, and had provided no budget to pay for the removal expenses. This oversight resulted in the great DIY move – an operation in which Karen bought 1,000 cardboard boxes and the staff transported everything to Ovenden by car, using up much of the extra time intended for vital preparation for the new term. The sheer physical effort required to pack and load hundreds of boxes of heavy books and equipment into private cars, drive the mile or so up to Ovenden, unload and re-sort them all, was tremendous.

All this work diverted the teachers from their priority of planning the new courses and programmes of study – presumably the LEA felt that the teachers were better occupied as furniture removers – but at least it had the positive effect of uniting many by fostering a 'Dunkirk spirit'. 'It was one of the few times we all worked together', one teacher said, 'for the first time we shared, and successfully overcame, problems co-operatively.' Unfortunately this was short-lived, and soon it was back to coping with the huge backlog of work necessary to prepare the lessons and curriculum for the new classes, to minimize the disruption to education. This was especially important as the opening date was midway through the academic year, inevitably disturbing the Year 11 students' GCSE courses.

January 1995, and the Ridings opened fairly quietly, with most of the pupils sporting their new ties. All the teachers were there as well – even those who had been on long-term sick leave. Karen felt more optimistic than she had for weeks. Things were going to be all right: the school was buzzing with activity – the pupils in their classrooms, the workmen on the roof and the dinner ladies in the canteen. But the honeymoon period was over almost as soon as it began: later that day, the fights started.

For about a month after the school opened, the older, dominant boys took on all comers. Apart from excluding them for anything up to the maximum 15 school days allowed by law, Karen could only exhort them to behave acceptably. The pastoral staff spent hours trying to calm the situation in school and persuade parents to take more responsibility for their children, but the mayhem only ended once the pupils had established a pecking order.

This lack of discipline was exacerbated by having an LEA scheme for disaffected pupils, the Learning By Achievement (LBA) programme, based at a youth club situated in the main teaching block. This attempted to provide a relevant education to the 20 or so most disaffected pupils of all Calderdale's secondary schools. These were disruptive children, often with a truculent attitude to authority, many of whom had been permanently excluded from other schools. The decision to locate the unit at Ovenden School some years previously had been taken on grounds of cost and convenience. Under fairly loose control, the youths attending LBA felt they could ignore any instructions from the Ridings staff with impunity. They would roam around the school smoking and, in some instances, taking drugs. All newly amalgamated schools need time and space to establish an ethos and corporate identity; this situation put unnecessary pressure on those trying to create a purposeful atmosphere, and helped undermine the fragile discipline that existed. Karen did not succeed in having the Unit removed until, in one of its few positive moves, the Liaison Group recommended its relocation.

The problems of establishing a disciplined environment seemed to be intractable. Over the years, one of the major contentions between the LEA and its schools was the issue of pupil exclusions. A sub-committee of the Education Committee, minuted by a council clerk, discussed each and every permanent exclusion – whether or not the parents appealed. It is highly unusual to have such a formally constituted body looking at exclusions, and it caused no end of problems. Commonly referred to by local schools as the 'Star Chamber', in reference to Charles I's arbitrary, secret court, the sub-committee consistently overturned the decisions of governors, returning excluded pupils to their schools, sometimes even against the wishes of the parents. One of their decisions to reinstate resulted in the resignation of John Hanson, Chairman of Governors, from September 1995 to July 1996, both as chairman and from the governing body, because he felt 'unable to instruct the headteacher to reinstate a pupil who had been permanently excluded by governors, as ordered by the appeals panel'. Calderdale's reluctance to allow schools to exclude disruptive pupils permanently, compounded the limited alternatives they allowed schools to deal with disruptive pupils, only exacerbated the discipline problems.

So Karen was given little practical support to cope with the fights and disruptive classroom behaviour.

A number of staff on protected salaries volunteered to 'bolster' the pastoral system by acting as Heads of Year. At about the same time a section of the staff suggested that the Discipline for Learning (DFL) approach should be adopted. 'You must do something to sort out our problems,' they told Karen. Strategies similar to DFL have worked successfully in schools. Central to this approach are two basic principles: that children should be faced with the consequences of their actions and given the chance to modify their behaviour, being given three checks before the next level of sanctions was reached; and that there should be an equally strong system to reward good behaviour. The policy as employed at the Ridings laid out clear sanctions for different levels of misbehaviour. When pupils misbehaved they were 'checked', and after three checks put into 'isolation' – an area continually supervised by two teachers.

Unfortunately, although the pupils of both schools had effectively merged into one student body after the first term, the teachers were still divided. The atmosphere in the old Ovenden staffroom had changed overnight. Instead of the friendly banter of shared experiences and relationships that had endured over many years, there was a clash of cultures. The staff formed two groups, one coalescing around the old Ovenden philosophy of supportive pastoral care, and the other around the more macho image favoured by some of the Holmfield staff. More and more, references to individual children were negative, rather than affectionately critical. Standards slipped, and corporate spirit seemed impossible as individuals either sought security in one of the groups or decided to walk a lonely middle way.

The introduction of DFL, intended to bring about a consistent approach to discipline, further polarized the two factions. Some senior staff argued against it, seeing it as a very mechanistic way of dealing with misbehaviour, but after long arguments it was introduced. However, teachers who saw the policy as a panacea applied the checks too quickly, passing problems up the line, invariably ending up at the Headteacher's door. Other staff saw it as a fast track to exclusion and, as a result, a very high proportion of pupils were temporarily excluded. When they returned they started back on the cycle to another temporary exclusion. The use of rewards was almost completely forgotten, and students lost their fear of the sanctions. In fact, the situation got so out of hand that pupils would say, 'You can't give me a check if I stand on the table, 'cos it doesn't say standing on the table is wrong!' The developing anti-Karen clique then started rumbling their dissatisfaction with the way disciplinary problems were handled, undermining the pastoral system and Karen's standing as Head.

The crunch came in the summer of 1996, when the governors permanently excluded one of the pupils, Sarah Taylor, for violent behaviour. By then the DFL system had lost all credibility with the students and all but a handful of staff, who were clinging to it as their only weapon against disruptive behaviour. At this time Peter Bartle's professional assessment of the school was that the most likely cause for failure in the forthcoming Ofsted inspection was that both the head and the staff were convinced the school would fail. When the councillors ordered Sarah's reinstatement, her return to the school in the middle of a blaze of national publicity further undermined the fragile disciplinary structure. Sarah's second permanent exclusion at the start of the autumn term, and her reinstatement for the second time by the councillors, started the chain of events that led to Karen's resignation and Peter's phone call to me that Friday morning.

2

THE APPROACH

'It's really urgent,' Peter Bartle was saying. 'We need to get a new headteacher in place before the Ridings' Ofsted inspection in December. How do you feel about taking the job on?'

The feeling of *déjà vu* was very strong: I was reminded of the phone call I had received in 1984 from Ian Jennings – then the LEA's Secondary Schools Officer, now Director of Education – which initiated my move to Reins Wood 12 years before.

I agreed to meet Peter for a chat later that morning. Apart from anything else, I was desperate to find out what was going on; I was very put out that my antennae, normally so reliable in keeping me abreast of the minutiae of the LEA, had failed so dismally. In the meantime, there were two people to sound out: Paul Armitage, the Deputy Head with whom I had worked since Rastrick High School had opened, and Rastrick's Chairman of Governors, David Nortcliffe. Paul was supportive; David's first reaction was to advise caution. 'But,' he added, 'if that's what you decide, I'll back you.'

I found it difficult to concentrate that day. I kept asking myself why the authority was approaching me. I thought I was less than popular with many of the councillors: I remembered being described by one as a 'thorn in the authority's side'. It had not helped when Rastrick High School had been the first comprehensive to 'opt out' of the LEA and become grant maintained, drastically reducing the influence the Education Committee had over the management of the school.

I felt that there were two far more likely candidates – David Scott, Head of Calder High School, and Morton Roberts, at Brooksbank. David Scott had been a head only a couple of years less than me and, whilst the school he took over had never been bad, it had improved considerably since David's appointment. He ran an LEA school and was also someone who was prepared to 'have a go'. To my mind he must have been the odds-on favourite. Alternatively, if heads of grant-maintained schools were being considered, Morton was the obvious choice. He was seen by many as the father of the Calderdale heads – in fact, as he had been a headteacher in the authority for more than 20 years, he was probably better described as the grandfather. During that time, Morton was recognized as having rescued a very difficult secondary modern, Ryburn, which itself had been a *cause célèbre*, before moving on to Brooksbank. He was the most experienced head in the authority, well respected by many of those involved in the choice of Karen Stansfield's replacement.

I was convinced that these other two must have been in the frame. However, David had only just appointed two new deputy heads, and couldn't rush off and leave the reins in inexperienced hands, and coincidentally Morton had phoned earlier that very morning to say that he had announced to his governors that he would be retiring in the summer. He could hardly say to them, 'I'm not going to be here from September, and by the way I'm also off to save the Ridings.'

Peter Bartle arrived and, after some preliminary gossip, got down to business: would I consider taking over at the Ridings a week or so after the half-term break – just a week away? The idea was that I should be Acting Head, preparing the school for December's Ofsted inspection, then continuing until a new head could take over. I was very tempted. The Ridings would certainly be a challenge – and I enjoy challenges.

A series of questions began running through my head. I could see why the education officers had asked me: they probably felt I had a track record as someone who could get things done. But what about the councillors? Certainly I had successfully merged two Calderdale schools, but my decision to take the resulting new school into grant-maintained status and away from LEA control could hardly endear me to them. Calderdale had to be desperate to turn to me; the political embarrassment of the DfEE taking the school out of their control to be run by an independent education association would be too awful for them to bear – especially in an election year.

I also wanted to know if the kids at the school were really as bad as everyone had been saying. 'No, most are OK,' Peter said, 'but some are causing really difficult problems, especially outside classroom situations. They're running round the school corridors, disturbing the other classes, and there is a lot of bullying and some extortion. The irony of the situation is that the two groups of kids have come together reasonably well. It's the staff who can't get on!'

'It's a job for two people,' I told him in the end. 'If I did it, I'd need someone to watch my back inside the school. And I would need the *full* backing of the Education Committee, senior councillors and officers, especially on disciplinary issues.'

'You needn't worry on that score. It won't be a problem', he assured me. 'If you agree to think about it over half term, I'll give Ian the gist of our discussions and then the ball's in his court. If he wants to pursue it, he'll get in touch.' After he left, I could think of nothing but the possibilities of the situation. There was no denying that I was interested.

It was a fine, bright autumn afternoon, and I was due to start on the annual school sponsored walk. I plodded through the hilly countryside around Rastrick with Alan Flux, my Vice-Chairman of Governors. Alan had been headteacher of a secondary school in Halifax until his retirement, so he knew the local educational scene. I told him about the approach, and asked what he thought.

'I can easily see the attraction of taking on the challenge of "saving the Ridings", but what about the governors and the politicians?' he asked. 'Do you really want to take on that level of hassle? It won't be like running a grant-maintained school where you're relatively free of LEA control.' I had to agree, but I could not dismiss the idea from my mind.

'I've worked in the LEA since 1981, so I've a clear understanding of the personalities involved and I should know which buttons to press,' I told him optimistically. 'Anyway, a crisis like this is more likely to bring everyone together. After all, they're always talking about partnership; if the place actually *does* fall apart it will be a hell of a mess – and that'll be a big problem for us all.'

My thoughts were still full of the Ridings when I got home. Carol, my wife, listened with amazement. 'I cannot believe that you're daft enough to even think about taking the job on!' she declared. 'You've only just got to a stage where Rastrick High is running reasonably smoothly. How can you even think about taking on another school that needs turning around?' So everyone around me was advising caution. Although I could see the sense of what they said – of course, there was a strong chance that in me the Ridings would claim another scalp – it only made me more determined. I was willing Ian Jennings to get in touch.

However, now it was half term, time for gardening and relaxation. On Monday morning I was balancing high up in a tree lopping branches when Ian Jennings rang. I arranged a meeting later in the day from this incongruous position, with Carol relaying messages between us. As the day wore on my schedule slipped, and I arrived at Rastrick hot and dishevelled. Hardly the most auspicious way to turn out to discuss a job.

Ian had brought along Peter Flower, in his role as the local authority's Assistant Director of Policy and Planning, and despite my casual appearance, this was a much more formal approach than my chat with Peter Bartle. This was no hypothetical discussion: after the usual opening pleasantries they came straight to the point. 'What exactly would you want if you were to take on the Ridings?'

'At this stage there are really only two absolute requirements,' I replied. 'First, if I'm going to take on this job I need to know that the local authority, not just the officers but also the elected members of all parties, will support me *unconditionally*, at least for the important first few months.'

'That's not a problem,' Ian assured me unhesitatingly. 'Everyone's agreed. They all want you on board.'

'Second,' I went on, 'there is the question of someone to go in with me, someone to watch my back, someone I can trust to deal consistently with any problems to do with pupils, parents and staff. You know that some of the staff have worked against Karen. I don't want to prejudge them, but I do need an experienced deputy head to be seconded with me. If you chose an LEA deputy there would be the added advantage of making the whole exercise more palatable to members. Choose who you want, but the person has to be good. I don't want an Acting Deputy Head. I need a partner – an Associate Head – with equal powers and in everyone's minds clearly in charge if I'm not around.'

Ian agreed in principle, so I said I would go away and consider my position over the rest of half term. We agreed to meet again on the first Monday back, the 28 October, this time with the Chairman of the Education Committee, Councillor Michael Higgins.

A casual remark by Peter Flower during the meeting came back to me later: 'This is all going to be *News at Ten* stuff, you can forget the *Halifax Evening Courier*!'

3

'WE HAVE A PLAN'

Over half term, the Ridings' troubles continued to escalate. By Wednesday, a full-page feature appeared in the *Yorkshire Post*. Under the headline, 'TEACHERS AT THE END OF THE LINE', it described the violence and disruption that had occurred over the last month, and reported that the National Association of Schoolmasters and Union of Women Teachers (NASUWT) was balloting its members for strike action.

The teachers, desperate that something should happen, had given their version of what had gone wrong. Under a separate headline: 'PRESSURE KEPT BUILDING – AND THE LID HAS FINALLY BLOWN', Will Long, the union's teacher representative, was quoted as saying, 'We have 60 pupils who would be out of any other school by now.' For the first time a need to exclude 60 pupils was mentioned, an issue that would figure large in the crisis that followed over the next two weeks.

The national press picked up the story. An editorial in *The Times*, rather less sympathetic towards the teachers than the *Yorkshire Post*, thundered, 'When teachers have lost the ability to control their classes, their horizons shrink. They expect bad behaviour, and their expectations are seldom disappointed.' Not surprisingly, the local authority felt obliged to make a statement. The situation was getting steadily worse, and becoming politicized.

After *The Times* editorial, the media, alerted to the story at the school by the exclusion of Sarah Taylor in the summer, had returned in force during October. They had begun what amounted to a vigil outside the school in Nursery Lane, and besieged Karen at home. Martin Bashir from the BBC persuaded her that she would have the opportunity of getting her story across through a *Panorama* programme: this confidence proved to be misplaced. On Thursday, Ian Jennings went to give her the news that I had been approached, that it was mainly a matter of getting things sorted with the Rastrick governors, and that as soon as everything could be settled, she could go. If the half-term holiday could be extended, it might be possible for her not to go back at all. He would let her know at the weekend. Karen was apparently pleased at the news. She felt guilty, seeing her resignation as giving up on the pupils and her staff, although she still believed it was her only available course of action. However, she was unable to relax for long. That afternoon, Ian Jennings was back on the phone. The DfEE had refused to allow the school to be shut beyond the normal half-term holiday and were about to announce an emergency Ofsted inspection on the following Tuesday and Wednesday. Karen would have to go into school the next day to complete the Ofsted forms, and then continue as headteacher until further notice.

Carol and I were far away from it all, enjoying a trip to the New Forest. I had been following the story closely, but with a strange feeling of detachment. I heard Ian Jennings on the radio saying, 'We have a plan.' I turned to Carol and said, 'That's all right then,' and we got on with our holiday. When we arrived home on the Friday there was an urgent message on the answer machine to call Ian.

'I heard you on the radio,' I said. 'What's the plan?'

'Oh, you're the plan!' he said.

I laughed. 'God help us!'

Monday dawned and the Ridings School once again opened its doors to the pupils. Karen was desperately trying to complete the paperwork for the next day's inspection. Luckily, most of the required documentation had already been sent to the Bradford Inspection Group, which had originally been contracted to carry out the inspection planned for December 1996. When Karen had learnt that a team from her old authority was to undertake the Ofsted inspection, she had been relieved. She had been using the Bradford LEA's Advisory Service, rather than Peter Bartle's team, for some months. Not only did she feel comfortable working with them, but she had little alternative due to the shortage of advisers within her own LEA. Some years previously Calderdale had made redundant five key advisers – for Maths, English, Special Educational Needs (SEN), Design Technology and Modern Languages – and without these important specialists the Curriculum Support Team was of limited help to a school with the Ridings' problems. (Ironically, the effectiveness of the senior advisers was limited because, just when Karen needed their help, they were spending much of their time appointing replacement specialist advisers.)

But at the last minute another team was appointed to carry out the inspection instead, and Karen had to retrieve the documents to give to the new team of senior inspectors (officially called Her Majesty's Inspectors, or HMIs) who were to undertake the emergency inspection initiated by Mrs Shephard. Although Peter Bartle was again offering help, in Karen's disillusioned eyes it all seemed too little – and definitely too late.

The Chief Inspector dealing with failing schools was Elizabeth Passmore, who arrived that Monday to agree the ground rules with the LEA and the school. The teachers were subdued as she outlined the arrangements; they were anxious and some looked a little ashamed. Although Karen had agreed that there were at least 60 pupils who were causing intolerable pressure, the last thing the teachers had intended to bring on themselves was this emergency inspection. However, some were realistic enough to see that it could be a way forward. One of them later explained, 'No one else would listen to our cries for help. The governors, the LEA and the school's management had failed us. At least by taking some kind of action everything would be brought into the open – and perhaps the whole business would come to a head.'

The staff had by now become resigned to running the press gauntlet every day – some reporters had taken up regular positions outside the school gates – but were worried that the arrival of the inspectors would create more chaos outside the school. Elizabeth Passmore assured them that, 'After an initial statement from the Lead Inspector, within ten minutes the "rat pack" will disappear.' After everyone left, Karen worked long into the evening trying to get ready for the next day. When she finally went home, it was to field yet more calls from the press and apologize again to her neighbours for all the intrusions of the photographers.

Meanwhile at Rastrick High, I was trying to carry on much as normal. Ian had arranged a meeting at the authority's offices early on Monday evening, but in the meantime CASH (Calderdale Association of

Secondary Headteachers), which I chaired, was meeting that afternoon at David Scott's school. The local press had been abuzz with speculation about who had been 'headhunted' to take over the Ridings. The *Halifax Evening Courier* had decided David Scott was to have the honour of saving the school; over the next few days the nationals had backed the *Courier*, and David became a bit of a celebrity. As I walked in, I heard my colleagues quizzing him. Despite his persistent denials, they were insisting that he must be the man.

Then I was spotted and someone suddenly said, 'It's Peter. It's you, isn't it?' I was stopped in my tracks. I stalled, saying, 'You must be joking, they'll never ask me.' Then Morton Roberts changed the subject and the talk miraculously moved to other issues.

After the meeting I took Morton Roberts and Tony Thorne aside. Tony was Head of Ryburn Valley High and convenor of the local branch of the Secondary Heads Association (SHA) trade union. I described what had happened over the last few days, and told them, 'I've decided to take the job if the details are sorted out satisfactorily, but I need some help. If I go to this evening's meeting on my own I'll get enthusiastic and jump in with both feet. Will one of you come with me? You'll be less personally involved and provide a more objective view. You can advise me, and act as a witness later on if it's necessary.'

They both agreed that it was a prudent move, but Morton felt he was already too involved in the search for an acting head for the Ridings to be an independent supporter, so Tony volunteered. I felt more confident with a 'second': Tony was a good negotiator and could be counted on as a reliable witness.

As Tony and I headed off, we joked about what excuse we would give if anyone we knew were to ask us why we were there. However, it was clear from the knowing looks we got as we walked through the administrative section that everyone had guessed. Once in the room we met Ian Jennings, Peter Bartle and Councillor Michael Higgins, Chairman of Education. Some in the field of education had little time for him, possibly due to his appearance, which was characterized by an earring, shaved head and stubbly jaw, and a dress code most generously described as casual. However, I usually found him very approachable: there was no doubting his commitment to keep the school open. It felt a bit like an interview, but it was far from clear who was interviewing whom. We had an embarrassing start when no one seemed to know what to say, but things became easier as we got down to the serious issues.

I was determined that I would need to be given a free hand in applying reasonable discipline. It was clear to me that some children would have to be excluded in order to establish acceptable behaviour and sound a clear warning to those pupils who felt the normal standards did not apply to them. 'If I take on this job,' I stressed, 'some pupils will have to be excluded permanently, and the first pupil who decides to take me on will have to go instantly!' I looked around for reactions. Everyone nodded.

This was a crucial issue. There were too many precedents where the 'Star Chamber' had insisted on an excluded child returning to the school against the advice of the professionals involved. If I were the Managing Director of a commercial company I would not be expected to function if my decisions were continually undermined; similarly, if I was to improve behaviour, I needed the authority to act. I had to push this point hard until I was confident that everyone understood that some children would inevitably have to be excluded – and that suitable alternative provision would need to be found. I continued, 'You're expecting me to put myself in the firing line. If I'm to establish my credibility with students, staff and parents, I *must* know that you'll back me all the way. If I'm unable to carry through my actions, my position will be untenable, and I might as well not bother taking the job on in the first place.'

I got what I wanted: a clearly stated commitment. All three accepted absolutely that for me to do the job they were asking, some pupils would have to go. If I excluded a child, the authority would ensure the exclusion happened. The children would have places at other schools or, failing that, could be referred to either the local Pupil Referral Unit, Beaconsfield, or the Learning by Achievement project. I still had my doubts about whether these promises would be delivered, but Ian and Michael assured me that they and the councillors were clear that they would have to support my decisions on exclusions. I needed to know about every individual councillor: some worried me more than others. 'Don't worry,' Michael replied, 'they all understand the importance of backing you. We all have confidence in you to do it your way. After all, you have the power to walk away – and we all recognize the repercussions that would follow. Don't worry.'

My next concern was how the governors would react – for the Ridings governors still had no idea I was about to be foisted on them. I remembered being introduced to the Reins Wood governing body as their new Head. They had not interviewed me, but I am sure they had been more involved with that appointment than the Ridings governors were in this one. 'It's not a problem,' I was told. 'The governors understand that an acting head will take over and will accept our choice. If they don't, then we'll create other governors to give you the backing you need.'

'Who's going to pay for the changes necessary to improve teaching and the school's management systems?' was my next question. Ian replied, 'The school has reserves of nearly £100,000 and we'll make other funds available, within reason.' So money was not a problem. The LEA never moved away from this commitment, which was to prove essential. It also agreed to press ahead with the capital programme of promised building works, which had been delayed, and had been a cause of friction between the governors and the Council.

'Peter Bartle will work closely with you. He's spent a lot of time there and has a clear idea of what is needed,' Ian continued. 'We'll make all the authority's personnel available to you – Educational Welfare Officers (EWOs), advisers, peripatetic teachers, anything. Just get on and do what is necessary.' I couldn't help wondering what Karen's reaction would have been. This was all such a far cry from the LEA's policy towards the school when it first opened.

We discussed the quality of teaching. It was acknowledged that there were some good staff: in fact, Michael Higgins had attended Ovenden and was confident that some of his ex-teachers still 'had it in them'. However, there were others about whom the LEA's support staff had concerns. It was clear that part of my job was to improve the quality of teaching at the school, even if it meant that some staff had to leave. The LEA was unhappy about offering pension enhancement to those teachers old enough to retire, but promised to reconsider it.

I was also conscious of my own position. Was I prepared to take on the job for my current salary, or should I ask for more? In the end I decided that I should ask for some financial benefit, if only as another test of their commitment. This was, for me, the most difficult part of the whole discussion. In a rash moment Michael Higgins said, 'Name your price!' and we all laughed. I told them I didn't want a higher salary, but an enhanced pension, as I had a short contribution gap in my service. A few days later the LEA agreed.

We talked through the whole situation, including the emergency inspection. Not surprisingly, given their previous involvement, no one from the LEA expected the school to pass. The current plan was to get the inspection over with and then close the school at the end of the week. I would have the Monday and Tuesday of the next week with the staff, and then the school would re-open with me in charge on the Wednesday. Ian outlined the progress on identifying an associate head: he was trying to get hold of Anna White, Deputy Head of Todmorden High School. I was pleased at this. 'I've met her and she sounds exactly right,' I said, 'if she'll do it!'

The conversation became wider reaching. We discussed the attitude of the DfEE, the Secretary of State for Education, the local politicians, and the Ridings governors, parents and pupils. There came a point when it was clear to everyone that I had accepted the job, but there was no formal acceptance, no swearing-in ceremony. I never even actually said, 'I'll do it'.

I felt that the meeting had gone well: with Tony's support, I was being promised everything I wanted. On reflection, this was hardly surprising: Karen had resigned, the emergency inspectors were due the next day, and the NASUWT were still deciding whether to take strike action. There was obviously little teaching going on, so it was inevitable that the school would get a bad report and, at best, be put into 'special measures' as a failing school. At worst, it could even be closed. The authority knew only too well that there was no way that over the next few weeks everyone at the Ridings could quietly go about their business. Any story about failing schools was of high media interest, with the political parties in a battle to prove who would be best for Britain's education as they squared up for the coming general election. Just that week, the wife of Philip Lawrence – the headteacher killed outside his school – had made the front pages, calling for more emphasis on teaching citizenship in schools, whilst Gillian Shephard had argued for the return of corporal punishment. In the midst of this, the LEA faced a media firestorm about a school in chaos, uncontrollable kids, extortion rackets in the corridors, dreadful teachers and so on. No wonder I found little resistance to my demands: if I blew it, the authority could be forced to hand the Ridings over to the government, probably in the middle of a general election campaign.

I felt excited at the challenge – and confident that at least two out of the four others present would back my version of the meeting if there were future problems. I went home with the intention of keeping my head down for the next few days while the emergency inspection took place and the press speculation about the new head continued. After all, I had only the rest of that week and a couple of days the following week to get my governors to release me – and to work out what to do.

4

THE OFSTED INSPECTION AND ITS AFTERMATH

The morning of Tuesday 29 October, the first day of the emergency inspection, was bright and clear. The massed cameras of the media were once again camped by the Ridings entrance: the front steps were becoming a familiar backdrop to newspaper stories. The reporters were not bored during their vigil. Many had turned to page five of that morning's *Daily Mail* to read about 'THE GIRL LEARNING TO BE A MOTHER': Sarah Taylor, the girl twice excluded from the Ridings, was pictured with her newborn daughter Chloe. Below what was basically a 'human interest' story, they would have noticed the real news – 'HEAD HUNTED, A MAN TO END THE "ANARCHY"'. Ian Jennings had been forced to agree, when put on the spot by the *Mail*'s reporter the previous day, that a new head, 'someone who is highly regarded and has the skills and experience to offer clear, decisive leadership' was being drafted in. He had still declined to name me. The *Mail* reported that I had been approached the previous week by the Labour-run council, and made some political capital out of the fact that Rastrick had opted out and become grant maintained. The story finished on a positive note, reporting that Rastrick High pupils had received the best GCSE results of all Calderdale comprehensives in the previous year. The cat was out of the bag.

As the pupils began to arrive, Karen rushed around the school, encouraging and reminding before the arrival of the inspectors. There were five of them, male and grey-suited, clutching briefcases and box files, dropped outside the school by taxis. Ignoring the press, they entered the Ridings for day one of the inspection. Contrary to Elizabeth Passmore's optimistic assurances, the press presence was not only maintained, but increased with the arrival of the world's media in the shape of CNN (Cable Network News) from the United States. The anxiety around the school was almost tangible. There was the odd scuffle amongst the pupils and much jockeying to be caught on the now resident television cameras. Karen and the staff tried to carry on normally – or as normally as one could under such scrutiny. The situation must have been particularly difficult for Karen. She had, after all, already resigned, and been told that all she had to do was see out the week. She was simultaneously responsible and not responsible, and it must have been well-nigh impossible for her to maintain any feeling of commitment to the process.

The first day went reasonably well. The inspectors observed a number of lessons, mostly staying for about half a lesson. They talked to the heads of departments, the deputies, and the Chairman and Vice-Chairman of the governors. Small group meetings were organized so they could talk with pupils and both teaching and non-teaching staff. When the final bell of the day rang and the pupils and staff drifted away, the work went on: with such a short inspection period the inspectors were under great pressure to complete the required documentation.

The next morning started in similar fashion, although there were now rumours that the less scrupulous members of the press were paying pupils to misbehave for the cameras. The staff were appalled to see the *Panorama* crew with an enormous 'cherry-picker' hoist, the type used in outside sports broadcasts. The camera could now peer right into the classrooms and the previously hidden parts of the school site. The police were called, and the team moved on, but a local businessman, who was also a governor, allowed them to park it on his site. 'They said they only wanted some background shots,' he said later. The camera lenses focused in on staff and pupils through the windows, heightening the pressure on the already dispirited teaching force.

Karen was so nervous that she asked Peter Bartle to sit in on her assembly, but afterwards she felt it had gone well, and the inspectors told her there was little she had to do to comply with the rules on collective worship. The HMI responsible for evaluating Karen's report on the school, an ex-headteacher, told her he would circulate it to the other inspectors as he felt it would give them a better picture of what was going on, and one teacher, praised for teaching in small progressive steps, was told, 'Everyone in this school should be doing what you're doing.' While Karen felt grateful for any little bit of understanding and support, overall the 'vibes' remained ominous.

As the inspection continued, the pupils' behaviour gradually grew more out of control: it was all Karen and her staff could do to get them into classes and keep them there. Even the brightest, most well-behaved child could not help but be affected by the tension in the school that day. Ian Calvert, Head of English, was attempting to teach his own group whilst 'keeping an eye' on a teacher next door who had been having problems and who now had an inspector in his lesson. The class was not responding well, and the inspector realized that his presence was making the situation worse. As Ian left his class to help the teacher, the inspector was just leaving.

'I think I'm exacerbating the situation,' he said, as he moved towards the door.

'Are you going now?' asked one of the pupils.

'Yes.'

'Well f— off, then.'

The lunchtime bell went. The time-bomb of excitable pupils, who had been just about contained in their classrooms, exploded out of the building and into the gaze of the media. Karen, realizing that there would be trouble, particularly if the more enterprising pupils went seeking sponsorship from the press, was out patrolling the school field, so it was Maggie Binns, a senior member of staff, who was called to deal with 'some kids throwing stones at a man in the car park.' The rather drunken man often deliberately provoked pupils. She broke the disturbance up and returned inside, but a few minutes later the drunk was involved in another fracas at the front of the school. Some pupils were inevitably filmed attacking the old man, and Karen instructed that the police be called. The inspectors were aware that the staff were unhappy at dealing with the incident in front of the sensation-seeking press corps, and one of them, Mike Tomlinson, volunteered to go. Fortunately, the situation broke up and the police arrived. They reported that the drunk and the television cameras were more to blame than the students, but that was not the kind of statement to make headlines.

In the middle of the commotion, a Health and Safety official had arrived to look at the Ridings' gym, an appointment made before the inspection had been arranged. The ceiling was in such poor condition that a fine dust was continually falling, making the floor slippery, and an Adult Education student who had fallen had made a claim against the school. Instead of rearranging the appointment, Karen left the fraught situation at the front door and went to the gym. The inspector gave Karen a choice: shut the gym down, or have it mopped every hour as a temporary measure. Although her inclination was to shut the gym, she realized that rather than attempting to re-room all the PE classes, mopping was the better alternative in the circumstances.

In the light of all this, it was no surprise that when Mr Webb, the lead inspector, and Mike Tomlinson, Ofsted's Deputy Chief Inspector, asked to see her, they told her that they were about to inform the Chairman of Governors, the local authority and Ofsted in London that in their opinion the school was in danger of getting out of control. There was nothing much Karen could say. The inspectors were right: things *were* getting out of control. When she had tried earlier to reprimand one boy, he had asked, 'Why should I listen to you any more? You're not my headteacher now.' Somehow she had to calm the pupils down and reassert her authority, or it really would become 'Anarchy at the Ridings', as the papers had already called it. As the inspectors got busy on their mobile phones she decided to call an assembly to read the riot act.

'How will the world regard you when you look for a job?' she appealed to them – words repeated almost verbatim the next day by some of the pupils interviewed for the *Six o'Clock News*, so at least some of them must have been listening. But, as the hall was only big enough to house half the pupils at a time, she had to get them together in two groups. Rather than let the 'first house' out early, as some senior staff suggested, Karen decided to keep the pupils from the first session in school for the final quarter of an hour of the day. This proved to be an expensive mistake: some became 'demob happy' and they played it to the hilt, throwing books across the classroom in full view of the 'supportive' *Panorama* team, now filming from the windows of a pensioner's flat. The inexperienced teacher, in the first half term of her first job, was seen to lose control. An hour later, the inspectors were ready to present their initial findings.

Karen, the Reverend Stan Brown (Chairman of the Ridings governors), Peter Bartle, Peter Lloyd and Ian Jennings waited in the staff room. The five inspectors entered and Mr Webb proceeded to explain that the school had failed on all counts. There was no real discussion and Karen only spoke up when it was suggested that the school had massaged its GCSE results. Her hackles rose at other moments, but by now she realized it was pointless to argue. Her memory of the meeting is quite clear. She remembers Ian Jennings looking distraught and Stan Brown attempting to explain the pupils' problems, whilst Peter Bartle and Peter Lloyd looked as though they were distancing themselves from what was going on.

As Peter Bartle listened to the inspectors he must have felt a sense of vindication: the inspectors agreed with all he had seen emerging over the previous months, and his professional assessment of the previous summer had highlighted the same issues. In many ways the school was now in a much worse position, burdened with the national notoriety gained during the last week. With hindsight, however, the debacle of the inspection made it possible to take much tougher and more far-reaching action. Would the LEA's plans for quiet closure, followed by Anna and myself working with the staff toward an Ofsted inspection in December, have given as good a springboard for action?

The meeting ended and the inspectors went out to make a brief statement to the press. They said little except that they had finished, and the report would be published when it was ready. They got back into their taxis, clutching even more papers than they had arrived with, and left. The press stayed.

Karen walked to her car ignoring the turmoil around her; the sea of cameras now stretched in both directions as far as she could see. She drove straight home, but some of the press had beaten her to it. All that she could remember later were the *Mail on Sunday* and the *Sunday Times* offering large amounts of money for her story. The journalists left her with a general impression of polite, friendly, sympathetic people who all wanted to be her friend and help her. She went to bed after taking the phone off its hook.

Thursday was not to be a good day. As Karen drove into work, the skies were grey and the rain was pouring down. There were no inspectors to contend with, but the media rat pack, half-drowned and busy trying to keep the rain off their cameras, was still around the school gates. The pupils and teachers straggled in: as if everyone was shell-shocked, and because of this, lessons started quietly. Later that morning, Karen was called to a classroom to find a teacher distraught after one of his class had refused to accept his authority and thrown a chair across the room. A very conscientious man, the teacher had finally buckled under the constant pressure. Karen decided to drive him home to his anxious wife. Although he was clearly at the end of his tether, he insisted that he would be back in school the next day. Unable to persuade him or instruct him to stay home, Karen took the drastic step of formally suspending him. She took David Bond, who had driven the teacher's car home for him, back to the Ridings. Realizing she had little time before a meeting she had arranged with me for that afternoon, she did not go in, but dropped him off and sped off down Nursery Lane.

Meanwhile at Rastrick, we had been trying to clear my move to the Ridings with the governors. The Chairman, David Nortcliffe was in an unenviable position. He worked for Calderdale, and they had made it clear to him that they wanted his help in delivering the governors' approval. At the same time, he was trying to serve the interests of the governing body and the school, and to support me. A governors' meeting was called for Thursday 31 October, the day after the Ofsted inspection at the Ridings, the letter couched in the vaguest possible terms. David was under no illusion about how important it was to avoid unnecessary disputes and was keenly aware of the need to keep the story out of the papers before the governors met. He was also aware that the press, particularly the *Daily Mirror* and the *Yorkshire Post*, had been contacting individual governors. I was unsure about such a high level of secrecy, but I was desperate to avoid a disruptive press circus outside Rastrick High School.

All efforts to keep out of the limelight were doomed. The press speculation had become intense, and gradually David Scott from Calder High School was mentioned less and less. He joked to me, 'From now on we'll have codenames. I'm Stalking Horse, you're Dark Horse!' My phone rang constantly at work and at home. Carol and my grown-up children, David and Joanne, intercepted most of the calls. They tried hard to stay calm, polite and firm, but at times the journalists made it difficult for them.

The media spotlights had been turned on me. On Wednesday, a reporter from the *Yorkshire Post* told me all the details of the story and threatened to print it. (As I was to find out in future months, much confidential information about the Ridings was communicated directly to the *Yorkshire Post*. Many months later, I found out who had leaked this story, and I believe that they were trying to stop me taking up the position, or at least to make it more difficult.) In an attempt to keep it out of the paper until after the governors' meeting I – with hindsight naively – agreed to pose for a photograph if the reporter held over the story until Friday morning, after the governors' meeting.

However, given the rumours, I felt I had no option but to tell my colleagues what was going on. So during the morning break, I called a meeting in the staff room. The room was packed as people crowded in; virtually all the teaching staff were there, plus the classroom assistants, the clerical staff, lab technicians, caretakers and about a dozen student teachers. Nobody was going to miss a moment of this unfolding drama, and the tension in the room was tangible. I had to ease it somehow. It was my birthday that day, so I began 'I really appreciate you all coming together to wish me "Many Happy Returns!"' It worked: the tension dissolved in the laughter.

'I've been instructed not to say anything,' I went on, 'so this meeting isn't happening. I'm breaking a confidence because you're more important to me than anyone else. It's unfair to leave you relying on newspaper stories or local gossip-mongers.' I then outlined what was going on. There was no dramatic response – a few teachers came up to wish me luck and one said, 'I think you're mad, but you did the right thing in telling us.'

Peter Bartle rang shortly after. 'Anna White's interested, but she wants to meet up. There are a few points she wants to clear up, mainly on the definition of the term Associate Head. Can we come round?' Peter brought her over at lunchtime.

Anna is an excellent teacher. Her fierce focus on her job and determination to prove herself in all circumstances are complemented by a wardrobe of long jackets and short skirts. She can be downright mischievous, and has a terrific sense of humour – I can vouch for this as she is one of the few people who understands all my jokes. Anna was obviously keen, but wary: she was anxious not to be seen as a patsy or gofer, doing all the lousy jobs. I had to assure her that I would do everything possible not to leave her carrying the can, while leaving her under no illusion as to the possibility of us both being dropped in it. I explained my ideas about the role of the Associate Head. Anna was very keen that the status should be recognized outside the school as well as within it, and suggested that she should become a member of CASH in her own right to emphasize her position as my equal. As Chairman of CASH, I agreed instantly.

During our talk there were mysterious noises outside my office door, and eventually one of my deputies interrupted and dragged me outside to the dining room. The staff and students had planned a surprise 50th birthday celebration with a huge cake in the shape of a litter bin overflowing with cans, crisp packets, and so on (I'm always nagging about litter), all carefully made out of icing by one of the midday supervisors. As she left with Peter to see Ian, Anna looked at it all and said, 'You must be mad leaving all this.' I would miss Rastrick, but I had made my decision and could see the partnership with Anna working: if both our governing bodies could be persuaded to release us, we were definitely on our way.

By Thursday it was clear that my deal with the *Yorkshire Post* reporter was worthless: the paper contained my picture and a garbled story, which confused the issue and, not surprisingly, upset all the governors. In response to the report, the first television crew arrived outside Rastrick High School. Fortunately they only stayed briefly whilst the children were in class, but they were soon followed by another. Some might have said I was naïve to trust a reporter, but this broken promise was a rare occurrence in my dealings with the press. However, this episode taught me an important lesson: that for many journalists the story comes first. This particular reporter was last in the queue for stories over the coming months.

I set off to meet Karen for lunch. We came to that meeting from very different mornings: Karen was at the end of a long and bruising period in the press limelight, while I was just stepping into it. She had been waiting some time when I arrived and was writing notes on the staff and the children. She was holding up remarkably well, and still superficially, the bubbly, cheerful character I had known since she arrived in Calderdale. Underneath, though, the strain and disappointment were evident.

I was anxious to hear her personal views. We talked for a long time, and I found her insights very useful. Inevitably, of course, some of what she said was coloured by her disheartening and demoralizing experiences, and I decided not to refer to her notes until some months later, after I had made my own assessments of the people she described. Apart from the main players within the school, her biggest headache had been the media coverage. She was outraged at the intrusive nature of the press, especially the added pressure of *Panorama*'s cherry picker. It was a mark of how isolated she had become from those who should have been on her side that she was more angry with the governor, wondering how much he was paid, than she was with the *Panorama* crew, still feeling that she had a sympathetic listener in Martin Bashir.

Karen had obviously been distressed by the episode of the V-signs which had been widely publicized on television and in the newspapers. After asking the photographers to stay outside the school grounds, as she turned her back on the cameras to walk up the now-infamous steps a photographer shouted encouragingly to some of the pupils, 'Flick some Vs.' Two girls enthusiastically obliged, and the moment was recorded for posterity, the lowest of low points in the publicity saga. I later discovered that, although the picture had been set up by one of the photographers, it was pure bad luck that it had been recorded for television. Most of the cameras had been switched off, but one cameraman had been distracted and left his running. Those pictures made an enormous, and unfair, impact across the nation – and the world. They struck a chord with all those who like to see young people as nasty, violent and anti-authority, and epitomized the Ridings as the 'school from Hell'. What upset Karen most was that she had accompanied the two girls back to meet the press, and they had apologized tearfully and profusely in front of the cameras, but that interview had only been shown once – and at a time when few people were watching.

Karen outlined the instances of press bribery to either misbehave or report misbehaviour that had never taken place. Children were being encouraged to set off fireworks in the school grounds, and relatively minor incidents were reported in the most sensational terms. Many pupils were paid, or at least promised payment, for their stories, and some of those interviewed were in fact pupils of other schools. Stories claiming to come from the 'inside' may not have come from Ridings pupils at all: a popular girls' magazine headlined a story about the school with allegations of sex in the toilets – then going on to say much lower down that this rumour was in fact not true. Some of the stories were outright fictions, such as the reports of boys urinating in drinks cans and throwing them at teachers. Other interviews were with unsupportive parents, happy to criticize and undermine the school's efforts to discipline their children, and some families were taken to stay in quality hotels in London and actively encouraged to speak disparagingly about the school.

But Karen had co-operated fully with *Panorama* by giving two long interviews and was convinced that those she saw as responsible would be 'exposed' and held to account, a prospect that she understandably viewed with some relish. The background to the *Panorama* programme (as it had been outlined to her) was a fantastic tale of intrigue involving a number of local personalities: some of it rang very true, but I felt that it failed to hold together completely. I was surprised that they had gathered so much hard evidence to broadcast.

After a couple of hours we parted. Karen looked much better and seemed quite optimistic. She was confident that her story would be told, and the relief of leaving all the pain behind was palpable. I left to prepare for the Rastrick governors' emergency meeting whilst Karen returned home, expecting to count the days of the next week until it was all over: the plan was to close the Ridings on the Friday of the next week for a staff training day, then re-open under new management the following Monday. But unknown to either of us, there had been a dramatic turn of events at the Ridings.

The appearance of the cherry-picker had heightened the press activity at the school, resulting in deteriorating pupil behaviour and staff morale. As one teacher rather dramatically put it, 'The cycle of decline inexorably dragged us down into the vortex of despair.' In one lesson a boy made some sexually explicit remarks to one of the younger female teachers and touched her bottom. At a lunch-time union meeting it was decided that staff would not take their timetabled lessons, but only work with their own form groups. Children were roaming the corridors, fighting amongst the general shambles. Maggie Binns looked on it all in despair with Peter Bartle and Peter Lloyd. She turned to Bartle and said despairingly, 'This can't go on.' Bartle walked away. 'Don't worry,' Lloyd said, 'we are doing something.'

In fact, Peter Bartle had gone to phone Ian Jennings to advise him in the strongest terms to close the school. Ian met with senior councillors, party leaders, the Chief Executive Michael Ellison, and his deputy, Paul Sheehan. Everyone agreed: the children would be sent home with a letter to parents informing them that the school would be closed until further notice. Peter Bartle held three separate assemblies in the undersized school hall to inform the pupils. The staff watched with mixed feelings as he explained the circumstances very carefully and clearly. 'Unfortunately, it's the only option, but it's not a permanent closure. You'll be told the arrangements for re-opening very soon.' The children took it remarkably well. The older ones were concerned for their futures and GCSE courses, but when the younger ones were told there were many smirks. 'I understand why you're pleased,' Peter Bartle told them, 'but in time you'll look back on all this with regret.'

Many staff were very upset. Others saw the closure as a step forward; at least, they felt, something would now happen. Some also saw it as an opportunity to make sure that when the school re-opened it was on their terms – perhaps they would play a more significant role in its future management. So, Karen had spent her last day at the Ridings and, ironically, the final act that closed the school had occurred whilst she was absent.

After the children left the building the assistant caretaker locked all the doors of the main school. The staff whose teaching rooms were away from the main block had to run the gauntlet of cameras in order to fetch their belongings. They noticed some of the journalists writing a sign on a piece of card. Fittingly, the journalists, who had passed from merely recording the situation to being an intrinsic part of the problem, provided the final image: the television news programmes on that evening and the papers next morning showed a sign propped against the gates, reading 'SCHOOL CLOSED'.

5

A MEDIA BAPTISM

Shortly after I returned to Rastrick, Peter Bartle rang to give me an abbreviated account of the afternoon's happenings at the Ridings. Suddenly the crisis had escalated, and it was imperative that the Rastrick governors allow me to go: the plan now was to re-open the school the following week, on Wednesday 6 November. Some of them had political connections and were being lobbied by their parties at both local and national level. The Chief Executive of the Funding Agency for Schools (FAS, the body that oversees grant-maintained schools) had been asked to fax a letter to the governors requesting that they consent to the secondment, and it had been suggested that a letter of request might be sent by a government minister. I was overwhelmed, but sure that the governors would agree to second me.

Once the meeting with the governors began, my optimism flagged. The session lasted well over an hour, and a number of things were said which are better forgotten. David Nortcliffe was, very unfairly to my mind, the object of most of the bad temper. It was understandable that some of the governors would complain that we had not told them about the proposal to second me, but it had simply not been practical to do so: the situation had changed daily and had worsened considerably that very afternoon. I could see that they were worried about what would happen to the school if I was absent, but I felt that my work and commitment for over 12 years should have made their decision fairly straightforward. I was supported by a good team of deputies – Paul Armitage in charge of Curriculum, Helen Lennie responsible for Personnel and Primary Links, and Trish Sheard overseeing the Pastoral System and Special Education Needs – as well as other senior staff, who were more than able to run the school.

One or two governors also felt that they had no responsibility for, as they put it, 'bailing Calderdale out of the mire'. The turning point came when Stanley Firth, a long-standing governor and ex-chairman, intervened, 'Whatever we might feel about the LEA, the pupils at the Ridings are getting a raw deal. If we as a governing body can do something to help, we should!' The decision was eventually taken to release me until the Spring Bank Holiday.

The main worry of some of the governors was that the parents would be unhappy at my going. In an attempt to allay any fears, I explained my point of view in a forthcoming Rastrick weekly newsletter, saying, 'Sometimes life has a way of catching you by surprise. During half-term I was asked if I would consider taking temporary control of the Ridings School in Halifax. It was a difficult decision, but made easier by the knowledge that my colleagues, especially Mr Armitage, were more than capable to run the school during my six-month absence.' The school was part of the Investors in People scheme, which committed it to a high-quality training and development programme for staff. I put the question, 'What could be more developmental than this opportunity for me, and the greater involvement in the management of the school by those who will take on my duties?' and reassured parents that I would 'be "in and out" of school for the next two weeks and additional staff will be recruited quickly to reduce the timetable commitment of Mr Armitage, Mrs Lennie and Mrs Sheard. However, I am sure the work of the school will be scarcely affected by these arrangements.'

I left the meeting to phone the Chief Executive, Michael Ellison. He sounded relieved and asked me to pass on the authority's thanks. He said I had all-party support and was needed more than ever now the school had closed. I was reminded of Ian's confident assertion that 'We have a plan'. Everyone expected so much from me – and many of them hardly knew me. How much was it a belief in my abilities and how much was it clutching at a straw – Peter Clark?

By this time a television cameraman had arrived outside with some reporters from the *Halifax Evening Courier*, so we decided to write a brief statement for David to give. The other governors filed out of school under the camera's gaze, looking faintly embarrassed as David, Alan and I prepared to meet the press. After David had finished the statement, Liz Lord from the *Courier* asked me what my priorities were. 'To restore a kind of semblance of normality,' I replied. I didn't mean to say ' kind of', it just slipped out – subconsciously I must have been hedging my bets. I arrived home at about 8.30p.m. and was utterly amazed to see I was the top story on the BBC's *Nine o'Clock News*: a full-face shot staring out at me whilst I was eating my beans on toast – my main meal that day. Realization of the scale of things finally struck. What on earth had I let myself in for?

The following day, I had arranged with Tony Thorne and Morton Roberts to attend a meeting at the DfEE concerning the funding of Calderdale's grant-maintained schools for the next financial year. On the train to London we talked more about the Ridings than the Common Funding Formula that was the reason for our journey. I looked around the carriage and saw other passengers reading their newspapers. The account of my appointment was in them all, and my picture in most. I felt a bit like a fugitive, with that nagging feeling that everyone was looking at me. One of the quotes that caused most amusement was from a Calderdale councillor who, after a series of statements during the week extolling the qualities of David Scott, was now to wax lyrical about me: 'He's not one of your open-toe-sandalled, bushy-bearded, anorak-wearing, seventies-style teachers.' (Well, he was standing for Parliament!)

Ensconced in a windowless basement room in the DfEE headquarters at Sanctuary Buildings – most inappropriately named, as it turned out – we were interrupted by a clerk asking 'Is there a Peter Clark here?' Morton and Tony had volunteered to protect me from any journalists, even to the extent of joking that I should be anonymous, so they simultaneously said, 'No' – to the surprise of the officials who knew I was present. The clerk seemed disappointed, saying, 'Oh, we were told he was. There's a lot of interest in him. We're being besieged for requests for an interview.' So much for sanctuary. I admitted who I was and she went away to consult, returning to take me upstairs to the press office. This was a much bigger office, with windows. Apparently the press had thought I was meeting with Gillian Shephard to get my orders. I was introduced to a press officer.

'Look, we can try to hide you,' he said, 'but they'll catch up with you at home. Or we can try to manage it for you. If you like, I'll make you a few appointments and help you through them.' It was excellent advice, and I agreed. I had seen Karen and the Calderdale officers attempting to cope without any professional assistance, and I knew I was out of my depth. I returned to the meeting and, in the following half hour or so, I wrote down a series of points I would try to make when the time came. After a quick editing session with Morton and Tony I ended up with the following 'manifesto':

> My major concern is for the pupils. I know the majority will be a delight to meet and that I will get their, and their parents', support. We have recently seen the negative aspects of the Ridings School. However I am aware of the many good staff employed at the school and the good behaviour of the majority of the pupils. They must all be feeling insecure and concerned for their futures.
>
> We must all work together for success. I have been assured of the full support of the LEA and governors, but I need the support of the wider community – and the media. It is difficult to establish a normal routine with cameras on the streets.
>
> My basic aims are to:
> * Establish a proper school routine
> * Build up the morale of the whole school community
> * Implement the Inspectors' Action Plan
>
> And I will be successful if I can establish a firm foundation so that the school can attract a good headteacher to take it on to future success.

Over the next hour and a half, the press officer and my two colleagues helped me through a blur of ten television and radio interviews, including live appearances on the ITN, BBC and Sky television news programmes and Radio 4's *The World at One*. The previous evening, speaking at the governors' meeting in support of my secondment, vice-chairman Alan Flux had predicted that I would face a 'steep learning curve'. He was nearly right, but vertical would have been a better description.

We started with an interview on the steps of Sanctuary Buildings followed by a walk to the television studios at the Millbank Centre. My 'entourage' – Morton, Tony, the press officer, an ITN producer asking me questions on one side and a Press Association reporter on the other – strode purposefully on. Two cameramen walked alternately behind me, at my side and backwards in front of me, and I was vaguely aware of negotiations going on around me regarding which news organization got me when. I felt like a cross between a superstar and a major criminal. On arrival at the ITN studio I saw my first interview being broadcast as a trailer for the midday news. I was taken into what seemed to be a large cupboard painted entirely in black, which I soon realized from the presence of a fixed camera below a large television screen was a studio. 'Is it live?' I said to the DfEE man. 'Don't let me go in on my own!'

Unbeknown to me, my entire family was watching at home. I don't remember much of my first live television interview, apart from that it was with Dermot Murnaghan and the final question concerned Mrs Shephard's recent stand on corporal punishment. 'Would the ability to use the cane be an advantage to you in your new job?' he asked. According to Joanne, I smirked – it was in fact a nervous smile – and replied firmly, 'No!' When I saw it later, I was mesmerized by the back-projection, which had resulted in a crane growing out of my head. Morton assured me it had been alright and I had been, in the now more common parlance, 'on message'.

The Millbank Centre is a remarkable place. Each major television and radio organization has a studio, and I was taken from one to another. Then on to the famous College Green, with the Houses of Parliament as a background, where I was interviewed all over again for the evening news bulletins. Each interview was different, as the journalist questioning me seemed to develop my answers from the previous interview, and each time the DfEE press officer would advise me as to the tone of the next engagement. For instance, for the *Ruscoe on 5* interview I was told to refer to her as Sybil: she asked, 'Are you the Seventh Cavalry?' and I replied, 'I hope I'm not General Custer!' I was warned that *The World at One* would be a 'more intellectual approach', and sure enough I was given a thorough grilling by Nick Clarke. I was told I coped well with his antagonistic style when I said my bit about 'getting the cameras off the street to give us a chance', and had to rebut the implication that I was trying to ignore legitimate press interest. Although I passed the test according to my minders, I wish I had known more then about the pressures caused by the media, as I would have put the case much more strongly.

All the time I was conscious of the bartering going on for my services, and at one time I heard the PR man say, 'Well if you want him at all, you have to have him now!' The next minute I was led into another newsroom with a fairly frenetic atmosphere and I heard someone shout, 'Clark's here!' I was getting a bit brassed off with all this – or perhaps it was all going to my head: meaning it as a bit of a joke, I said *'Peter Clark's here,'* to one woman who seemed to be in charge. She was so contrite I felt very embarrassed, but as it turned out I was about to feel much more so. I was ushered towards a small studio as Ann Widdecombe, then Prisons Minister, was shown out. The background was changed and I did my stuff. It wasn't until I was leaving that I realized Ann Widdecombe was waiting to return to her seat. The implications of the bartering and excitement hit me: they had made a Minister of the Crown wait for me. 'I'm terribly sorry for all this,' I said apologetically. She smiled, 'Don't worry, it happens all the time.'

And so on to the BBC *One o'Clock News*, where I sat on the green settee with the newsroom behind me, nervously waiting for my turn through a seemingly endless item about Paul Gascoigne. At last the introduction came; it showed a group of pupils protesting that the school had been closed, denying them an education. 'THE INNOCENTS' and 'GOOD KIDS WIN' proclaimed their banners, and one boy said, 'My mate's got special needs, he needs teaching more than any of us.' This image of pupils protesting that they could no longer attend school made a big impact on the general public. For the first time, the other side of the story was highlighted, that of the 'good kids' who were being affected and the urgency of recognizing their needs. The real implications for the majority of failing to rescue the school were forcefully brought home to us all.

My last interrogation was the most bizarre of all. Not only was a supposedly live interview for the BBC's local evening news programme *Look North* recorded at lunch time, but for some mysterious reason it was to be recorded on the roof. I was led along corridors which I now recognize as locations for other interviews. (My family claim I'm a bit of a bore during news bulletins, regularly interjecting, 'I've been there,' to assorted groans.) We came out onto the roof, walking on duckboards between a parapet on one side looking down five floors to the traffic and a steeply rising slate roof on the other, around a turret straight off a

Disney castle. There was only room for me – balanced against the parapet – a large camera and an Australian technician who exuded confidence as she coaxed all the technology into operation. I relaxed just too soon after the last question, and when I watched myself later that day I could see all the tension of the previous day and the gruelling round of interviews visibly leave me. The interviewer wished me luck and I rejoined the others in time to hear Morton say, 'No, he's not doing *Breakfast with Frost*. He's had enough. We've finished now.' He was right. I was exhausted. We walked past the Houses of Parliament and went into the first pub we saw for fish and chips and a couple of pints of bitter.

On the platform at King's Cross on the way home, my secretary, Jo Sexton, called on my mobile phone. It had also been chaotic at Rastrick, with David Nortcliffe and Alan Flux spending all morning fielding press queries. Apparently the LEA had released a statement that I was staying at the Ridings until the summer, rather than the Spring Bank Holiday agreed by the Rastrick governors. I had argued against returning immediately after the Spring Bank Holiday at the governors' meeting, as I thought it would be less disruptive for both schools – Rastrick and the Ridings – if I worked to the end of the summer term. As Chairman of Governors, David Nortcliffe had been forced to tell the LEA in words of one syllable how this kind of thing did not help.

Although all I really wanted to do that Friday night was to relax, I was obliged to spend the evening placating Rastrick governors. No doubt the pressure of having to work through the problems when I was feeling shattered was good training for future months. If I had thought the press coverage after the announcement of my secondment was excessive, it was nothing to my appearance on every news bulletin that night and the deluge of publicity in the morning's press. Typical was the *Daily Telegraph*, in which the headline boasted, 'NEW HEAD IS DYNAMIC, FORTHRIGHT AND VERY POPULAR WITH HIS PUPILS'. I thought, *I bet that's news to a lot of people.*

The weekend brought no respite. On Saturday morning Nigel de Gruchy, General Secretary of the NASUWT, phoned. He wanted to know where I stood on his members' most important concern – restoring discipline. He had a pretty clear idea of the realities of the situation, as he had met with the staff on a number of occasions. I told him, 'I'm dead serious about restoring discipline, but I'm not going to be given a hit list of sixty names. I've been promised the full co-operation and backing of the LEA, and if I'm to succeed I need to make my own decisions and not be pushed into a corner by anyone.' He accepted my point of view and I got the impression that he would be helpful if I got into real difficulties. We agreed to meet the following week.

I tried to get away from it all with Carol on Saturday afternoon, walking along part of the Pennine Way, but returned to talk to Liz Lord from the *Halifax Evening Courier* in the evening. One of her questions concerned an article by the former Education Minister, Sir Rhodes Boyson MP. Supported by a picture of some of the Ridings pupils larking about on the school steps, it was in the form of an open letter to its new head. It was hard-hitting, and not a little patronizing, and extolled amongst other things the virtues of the cane. One piece of advice stood out: 'You must take the initiative. Tell the governors and the local education authority that after one month you will inform them which staff must be transferred to other schools because they do not have the skills, dedication or flair that your school now needs.' Now, taking the initiative was fine, and that was certainly my first priority, but how could you redeploy staff willy-nilly to schools throughout the education authority, and just where would you get replacements from? Each governing body is responsible for the employment of staff, and all of them would have to be persuaded to release their best teachers. With the time needed to negotiate all the necessary transfers, we would be lucky to re-open the school before the end of my secondment.

The world of education that Boyson's article seemed to describe was no longer the world in which we operated, and he had been an Education Minister in the government that had designed the new system. The final paragraph of the letter contained his prediction for my chances at the Ridings. 'I suspect that the rapid flight of teachers from the classroom and of pupils from your school is going to continue.' A little negative and obvious, I felt. I decided, on balance, to put Rhodes Boyson's advice on the back burner, and do the job my way.

6

FIRST ENCOUNTERS

Monday morning. I looked round the hall at the Ridings staff, sitting in a semicircle three or four rows deep. Teachers, classroom support assistants, secretaries, technicians and caretakers – everyone was there, silent, apprehensive, waiting for me to begin. This was the reality behind the false images of the television studio and the soundbite. They were looking to me to rescue them, and I knew I had to convince them that rescue was possible, if only they would work with me.

Many of the faces were familiar, and I knew the telephone lines had been busy between Ovenden and Rastrick, to get the 'low-down' on me. Opposite the assembled staff were a table and three chairs for Peter Bartle, his Deputy Peter Lloyd and myself. Peter Bartle introduced me, and I was on. I came to the front and sat on the table so I was part of the group, without the formality of the table between us. I talked for about a quarter of an hour.

I thought back to the advice given me way back in the 1970s by Len Moss, Head of Polesworth School where I worked: good teachers are those who have an inner self-confidence: they have an air of utter certainty, leaving no one in any doubt that they mean what they say. I have always tried to remember this when facing daunting situations, so that no matter what inner turmoil I feel, I try to look confident and speak with a certainty that I may not entirely feel; I imagine lion tamers must have to develop the same skill.

'You must be feeling awful,' I started. 'But between us we can do it. I know you've been put in an impossible situation, but we just have to put the past behind us and look forward with the common objective of turning the school round.' I explained, 'I know it will be difficult, but I will back you, and if you back me we will succeed.' Having been as positive as possible about what we might accomplish, I finished by saying, 'Don't play games with me. I need and expect your whole-hearted support.'

Then it was time to face their questions. Inevitably, one was at the top of everyone's list: 'What will you do if the LEA overturns your decision to exclude a pupil in the same way as they have with Karen?' I answered, 'I have been assured that the LEA will back me. Anyway, I'm in a unique position and I will resist any attempt to undermine our combined efforts to restore discipline – from any source. If I exclude a pupil permanently, he or she will stay excluded, or I will leave – or cause enough fuss to win.' It felt like a cinematic cliché of a First World War officer rallying his troops to go over the top.

Peter Lloyd then explained the timetable for the rest of the day: to look at the behavioural issues generally and, specifically, to consider individuals. The Peters seemed to think the meeting had gone well. After chatting for a few minutes with my new colleagues I left to meet Anna White at the Heath Training Centre, where we were to be interviewed by the BBC.

I met Anna in the car park and told her what I had been doing. She was upset that I had seen the staff without her. I was taken aback by her reaction, because I understood she had been unable to come to the school that morning. It was obvious that she thought I had gone back on my word to include her in everything. 'I'm sorry,' I said, 'but it wasn't my fault and we'll have to get used to things going off at half-cock. Let's get on with the interview and you can sort it out later.' Looking back though, whether by accident or design, meeting with the staff on my own was probably best as it focused their attitude directly on me and concentrated their minds on the most important issue: having to work together and be committed to improving the situation radically and quickly.

The interview for TV went smoothly and I met Liz Meech, the BBC's North Eastern Education Correspondent, for the first time. Anna and I answered a few questions; we were both projecting a lot of excitement and confidence that things would rapidly improve with hard work and co-operation. We also made our debut 'walk'. Being interviewed for news programmes is not just a matter of answering questions: there comes a point when the interviewer asks you to walk across a street, through a door or along a corridor for a shot to introduce or close the story. In this case we walked along the pavement, Anna looking very interested whilst I talked nineteen to the dozen and waved my hands about.

Anna left for the Ridings to meet the staff and help them with their deliberations, while I returned to Rastrick to finish tying up loose ends, including the date of my return to Rastrick after the secondment. Ian Jennings agreed that I would be released for up to 20 days during the period to deal with Rastrick business. Paul Armitage, who would be running Rastrick whilst I was away, supported this – we both understood that long-term stability was best served by us maintaining as close a working relationship as possible – and later the governors approved it as well. I also agreed with Ian the text of a letter to parents explaining the position and apologizing for the confusion, which smoothed a few ruffled feathers.

Then some shameless lifting of the Rastrick High School Behavioural Policy, replacing all references to Rastrick with 'the Ridings'. Copies were taken over to Peter Lloyd, so that the staff could consider the policy the next day at a session to prepare for the re-opening on the Wednesday. The session was to be held in a Todmorden hotel, set in hilly Pennine woodland, a far more constructive atmosphere than the school, still besieged by the press.

During the afternoon, a reporter from Sky had come up with the bright idea of filming me throughout the Wednesday, suggesting that he should follow me round for the day, seeing me deal with everything that arose. 'We could start filming you cleaning your teeth…' I was amazed. My detractors have accused me of being on an ego trip in my dealings with the press, but even I was not prepared to expose every detail of my life in this way. Over the next few months I received even more ridiculous suggestions.

I arrived at the hotel next morning to find that Peter Lloyd and Peter Bartle had just arrived from the school, where they had run the gauntlet of a posse of photographers and journalists.

'Peter!' one of the press pack shouted, and they both looked round.

'Which of you is Peter Clark?'

'Neither,' they chorused, and both laughed. Coming to Todmorden had obviously been a good idea.

Most of the talk was about the previous night's *Panorama*, the programme on which Karen had pinned so much faith to tell her side of the story. One of the researchers had pestered me to take part, but I had been very wary. I wanted to be seen as the newcomer, not tainted with the past, and I did not entirely trust what I was being told. However, I did agree to pose for them at the school, and early on the Monday morning I had slipped in quietly to be filmed entering my new office and sitting at my desk. My suspicions were immediately confirmed by the attitude of the cameraman. 'The LEA have been busy over the weekend,' he commented.

'Why?'

'The school's been painted, there's no graffiti! Take us round so we can get some good shots of the vandalized bits.'

It was pretty obvious that the school had not been painted recently. I unceremoniously escorted him off the premises. Needless to say, my 'important contribution' was not used, but neither was the programme the exposé Karen had been promised.

The tone was set by the ironic use of theatrical footage. Ovenden School staff were talented at writing and producing their own musicals, both to avoid the royalties and restrictions that commercial shows carry and to build links with parents and the community. At one point, the Ridings staff had decided to revive one of the shows, *The Ballad of Buzzard Creek*, written by music teacher Chris Binns and his wife Maggie. Excerpts from a home video of the production were shown throughout the *Panorama* programme. Ian Calvert had the surreal experience of channel-hopping from watching his football team, Blackburn, to seeing himself in the chorus. The clips repeatedly used were of a bravura performance of a song called 'Mighty Fine News', featuring the chorus, 'Good times comin', place'll be hummin', mighty fine news, mighty fine news!'

It was all predictable stuff: the teachers were at fault, the LEA officers and governors refused to help – superficial, and starkly lit to convey the tension under which the participants were operating. There was an implication that the school was falling down through a lack of resources, and the state of the gym ceiling was given major prominence, but there was no mention of the £120,000-plus reserves held by the school at the start of the financial year. Ian Jennings admitted that the LEA had made mistakes, but instead of giving him the credit for doing so, the producers tried to turn his admission into a scoop.

The buzz around the staff that morning was a mixture of gallows humour and intense sympathy and support for the young teacher who had been portrayed in charge of an unruly class, covertly filmed from a pensioner's flat for a few minutes in the fraught atmosphere after Karen's 'stiffening assembly' on the Wednesday of the Ofsted inspection. The programme implied that this was a typical classroom situation. Later in the week one of the boys admitted ruefully that he had been given 'a right belting by me Dad!' for his part in the fracas. The teacher concerned put on a brave face, but it was unforgivable that she should have been publicly characterized as 'the worst teacher in the worst school in Britain'. But then, the *Panorama* crew didn't have to pick up the pieces after their 'hard-hitting' effort filmed from behind the curtains.

There was much concern for the young teacher whose bottom had been pinched in the chaos of Thursday. She had been so upset that she had 'gone walkabout', and nobody knew where she was. Several staff had tried to contact her, but she was not at home and had left no message. She finally reappeared during the next week, but was still shaken by the experience. I felt outraged that those least to blame for the breakdown of discipline within the school should bear such a high proportion of the cost. It is particularly important that teachers starting their first job have a structured introduction to full-time teaching; although changes to teacher training mean that students now gain more on-the-job experience as part of their course, there still needs to be a carefully considered process to see them through their crucial first year. The Ridings had no support or induction programme for these newly qualified teachers in circumstances where even experienced staff were battling to keep above the chaos.

Post mortems of the media coverage aside, we got on with the business of the day. Discipline was the main point for discussion. The staff were eager to abandon the DFL policy of checks and sanctions, and indeed the senior staff were going through the discipline records with Peter Lloyd when I arrived. The NASUWT contingent arrived and spent some time consulting with their members. Eventually they said that their members would trust me to decide on all disciplinary issues. Then in the afternoon we finalized the list of which children should be excluded. After considerable discussion, I decided to exclude 12 pupils permanently and 21 for either two or the legal maximum of three school weeks.

In order to increase the staff's confidence, and impress upon the pupils that things had changed, Peter Bartle agreed to arrange for all the LEA's advisers and other relevant staff to report to the school on Wednesday until further notice. Where the Ridings teachers asked for help, or where we felt they required it, each class would have at least one, and sometimes two, people to assist the teacher. Because many of the disciplinary problems – especially the incidents of extortion and violence – occurred at breaks and lunchtime, and because some pupils ran around the corridors disturbing lessons, the whole team of EWOs would also attend. EWOs act as the liaison between school and home, and are mainly involved with attendance issues. They were to patrol the corridors and the site and try to get the truants back into school. This was an excellent idea: it was only a pity that these additional staff could not have been made available when the school first opened. However, given the circumstances at that time, it would probably have been seen as either unnecessary interference or another example of whingeing teachers. Nevertheless, it is an initiative that could be employed by LEAs in similar situations.

The majority of the classrooms were organized around a circular corridor, so Peter Bartle had organized the fitting of security locks to the corridor doors to curtail movement around the school. These locks were successful, although after the first few days we stopped programming them because some of the staff (mainly myself) could never remember the combinations. They slowed movement down considerably just by ensuring that children stopped to operate the handles. The days of charging along and slamming the doors were to end. Areas of the school were carpeted, both to cut down the noise and to demonstrate to the students that things had changed for the better. The Ridings School was now under new management.

'What about security guards?' I asked. 'They could keep the photographers out of the school grounds and give us some breathing space.' It was felt to be a good idea, as long as they were not wearing uniform (because of the press presence). And whereas previously nearly all the teachers had left the school each lunchtime, they all now volunteered to supervise the site and the areas newly designated as social bases for each year group.

As I travelled along the Calder Valley back to Rastrick, I felt a glimmer of confidence. I even looked forward to attending my first meeting with the Ridings governors, arranged for that evening at Halifax Town Hall where we were to receive the report from the Ofsted inspectors.

7

THE FIRST GOVERNORS' MEETING

Driving into Halifax for the governors' meeting that Tuesday evening, I was listening to the news on the car radio and was stunned when I heard 'Peter Clark, the trouble-shooting superhead brought in to sort out the Ridings School in Halifax, has excluded 12 pupils permanently and 21 temporarily.' How did they know, and so soon? But it was out, and I walked to Halifax Town Hall wondering how the news would be received. I should have been prepared for the massed television crews around the entrance. I nearly made it: head down against the wind and the drizzle, I walked quickly through the waiting media. By the time someone called 'It's Clark!' and the lights came on, only my rear view was recorded running up the steps and into the solid safety of the Victorian building.

Over the last few years, much effort has been put into restoring the splendid interior, perhaps in an attempt to recapture the pride felt by the burghers of Halifax during the Victorian age. We gathered in an upstairs committee room. Ian Jennings, Peter Bartle, and Paul Sheehan (the Deputy Chief Executive) were there, together with a newly recruited representative from a Leeds-based PR firm, called in to beef up the authority's response to the publicity. Michael Higgins welcomed me warmly, with a humorous reference to the 'media star', and said encouragingly 'Keep it up, you're doing really well.' We talked about the leaked news of the planned exclusions.

'I'll back you all the way in private,' he said, 'but I might have to say other things in public.'

'That's fine,' I replied. 'All we want is your political support to back us up.' I was not surprised by his warning: I had always known that the real issues were likely to be clouded by political and even personal relationships.

Each person who entered the room exclaimed about the television cordon. No one seemed to know who had leaked the story, but it was decided that I would have to make a statement. I went down and faced the mass of cameras and reporters in the pouring rain, briefly stating that I had excluded the students, that I was sure my actions would be supported, and that I was confident that the school would successfully re-open the next day.

Back in the committee room the meeting got underway. Stan Brown introduced Anna and me. I said, 'We're very keen to work with you as governors to turn the school around. I know we've been foisted on you, but we hope you'll trust us to get on with the job.' As I spoke, I got the impression the governors were not entirely convinced, and that some had very clear views of their own as to what was needed. I remembered how I had been assured, 'Don't worry about the governors, they'll be OK'. It seemed that it would not be quite that simple.

Anna and I sat at one end of the room, with the governors, the councillors and officers ranged along the table and the two inspectors, Mr Webb and Mike Tomlinson, facing us. The inspectors distributed printed copies of their report. This surprised me, as we were expecting the usual Ofsted procedure of reporting verbally to the governing body so that any matters of fact could be challenged, and perhaps changed in the final draft. However, Mr Webb said that the circumstances of the inspection were unique. We were told that this was the finished report and there were sufficient copies for staff and governors to read before its release to the press the next day, when Gillian Shephard was to give a press conference.

Mr Webb mentioned difficulties the team had found in establishing clear figures for attendance and exclusions. For the report, they had made a 'guesstimate' for exclusions, trawling through the pupil records to establish the published figure of 150. He was inclined to believe that the true figure was much higher – nearer 300 fixed-term exclusions during the last 12 months. I was shocked that so many pupils had been excluded. There are very few sanctions open to schools, but over-using one of them to such an extent dramatically reduces its effectiveness. It was no wonder that the pupils were not deterred from anti-social activities when they saw how ineffectively the school reacted, merely sending them home time and time again, especially when they realized that any attempt by the school to exclude them permanently would be vigorously resisted by local councillors.

All Ofsted reports include what are called 'Key Issues for Action', and schools have to draw up a plan to address such criticisms. Schools fail their inspection if they require drastic action to deal with poor examination results, management, levels of attendance, behaviour, and so on. Sometimes schools have a few months' grace to improve their efforts, followed by another short inspection. The situation at the Ridings was so serious that the inspectors had immediately identified it as a school requiring 'special measures'. The report identified eight Key Issues to be taken up by the staff, governors and LEA with urgency:

1. Take immediate action to re-establish good order and control, to ensure the physical safety of pupils, and to have systems in place which will make sure that the school knows the whereabouts of all pupils
2. Raise standards of pupils' achievement in all subjects
3. Improve the quality of teaching in order to tackle underachievement and in particular improve classroom management and discipline
4. Strengthen management and leadership at every level and ensure that communication is improved and policies are implemented
5. Improve the governing body's systems for decision-making, financial control and for monitoring the life and work of the school, and the quality of its educational provision
6. Raise levels of attendance and improve behaviour
7. Fully implement the sound policy for special educational needs
8. Collaborate to bring about a unity of purpose among the staff, including a collective and individual acceptance and consistent discharge of responsibilities, on behalf of the pupils in the school.

There was little discussion of the report, and the two inspectors left. There was a clear need to draft a statement to the press, and the PR man was anxious that it should be delivered in time to be broadcast on the main evening news bulletins. However, what followed was the most disorganized and incoherent meeting I have ever seen – and that's saying something.

One member, a political representative attending his first meeting, had apparently been primed by his outgoing colleague to ask a series of questions about the past operation of the governing body and the accuracy of the minutes. Given the current circumstances, this seemed completely irrelevant. Another reiterated his long-standing view that the schools should not have been amalgamated until all the building work had been completed – possibly a valid point 18 months ago, but utterly trivial compared with the problems we faced now. Others demanded to be more involved in the management of the school, and one had written on his agenda paper under Any Other Business, 'When will Andrew Bateman be appointed Headteacher?' – thankfully a question he had the common sense to leave unasked.

The only positive decision at this stage was to make Anna a full member of the governing body. At one point I said to Anna, 'Kick me if I'm undiplomatic!' Shortly after, she did and, as she can be as forthright as I can, kicking each other under the table became a regular feature of those early governors' meetings.

Suggestions for the content of the statement came thick and fast, interspersed with irrelevant observations and interventions on other agenda items. The meeting became increasingly unmanageable until finally, at the suggestion of the PR man, it was decided that a small group should leave to write the statement. I thought, 'Here's my chance,' but before I could move, Anna was up and away. Smiling, she pointed out, 'We can't both go,' as she escaped, leaving me on my own.

My memories of the rest of the meeting are vague. I remember some governors being irritated that the officers and Councillor Higgins were present, but it seemed to me reasonable that they should be. After all, the governors had hardly distinguished themselves in their management of the school, and it was the LEA that had had to close the school and was taking most of the flak from the press and Gillian Shephard.

Eventually the working group returned. They had hardly changed a word of the previous draft: the closeting had just been a tactic to get things moving and organize the press. As we descended the winding staircase, we saw that the television crews had been allowed inside because it was now raining even harder. This was obviously the influence of the PR man – make them comfortable, and they may look on you more favourably. The cameras rolled, and Stan read out the statement, which said that the report had been received and everyone was confident that things would improve.

When he had finished, we walked down to chat with the journalists. One of the BBC reporters took me to one side and told me that the *Today* programme would like to interview me in the morning before I left for school. My immediate reaction was that I wasn't sure I could cope with that, as I'd be too preoccupied with re-opening the school in front of the world's press.

'Do you want me to manage the Press side for you?' he offered.

'Can you do that?' I exclaimed.

'If you agree to participate in a BBC interview, I'll arrange with the other television companies to pool the footage, so you won't be pestered by each of the crews.' This was definitely an offer I couldn't refuse: I agreed instantly.

Back in the governors' meeting the business was finished quickly, if inconclusively, and we left the building to see the television crews packing away their equipment. Our performance had been shown live on the *Nine o'Clock News* and transmitted to the various studios for editing in all the other news programmes that night.

I drove home tired and hungry. It was Guy Fawkes night, and as I drove through Huddersfield the glow of the bonfires and the spectacular fireworks lighting up the night sky evoked the imagery of the First World War that had come to mind as I addressed the staff the previous day. Was this the bombardment before tomorrow's battle? Would tomorrow end with a victory celebration – or mired down in a shell hole?

8

REOPENING THE SCHOOL

On Wednesday 6 November I woke up feeling slightly apprehensive – but at least there was no Sky television crew in the bedroom filming my waking moments. I wanted to leave for the Ridings early to avoid the embarrassment of not being able to find the car park (although I had visited on many occasions I had always parked on the road). I did not want to be caught sailing past the entrance and have to turn round. After a circuitous but jam-free journey, I arrived at the school well within my timetable for beating the press.

I might as well not have bothered. I had heard all the staff's stories about the media encampment outside the school, but had suspected they had exaggerated. As I drove down the road to the school, a row of trucks and vans sprouting aerials and satellite dishes stood along the right-hand side. They bore the logos of all the national television companies, as well as a number of foreign ones.

Unknown to me, as I ran the gauntlet of these television cameras my progress was being monitored by my family at home. My daughter Joanne later teased me, saying that she knew I must be important when a camera homed in on me driving along the road. Fortunately I found the entrance to the car park first time. I skidded round the final turn, narrowly avoiding a cameraman. This is perhaps not the best way to establish good relations with the media, but no bad blood ensued: when I met him months later, he introduced himself with the words 'I'm the one you nearly sent flying'.

The parents had been informed that the school would re-open on a phased basis. As everyone agreed that the younger pupils were the biggest problem, they would be the last to return. We would start the first day with Years 10 and 11 and the Sixth Form, about 250 students altogether. Year 9 would be added on Thursday, and on Friday the remaining two years would be admitted. By coincidence, a group of Year 11 students was due to travel to Stratford that day to watch a production of *A Midsummer Night's Dream*. In the interests of normality the trip had to go ahead, and so the students and staff embarked on a coach in the glare of world publicity. Head of English, Ian Calvert, was interviewed on television (with the caption 'Headteacher') and the resulting publicity led to a lady from the theatre audience writing to me. 'I enjoyed the production immensely,' she wrote, 'and I could not believe that any children in the audience belonged to the "school from Hell".' In fact our staff returned slightly worried that the bubbly behaviour of one group from another school might have been blamed on our pupils.

Anna and I took the first assembly together. The students behaved impeccably. Attendance was around 75 per cent, so there were about 170 children in the hall. I introduced the two of us, making a joke of my 'celebrity status'. We operated as a double act.

'Things have now changed,' I explained as they listened – politely and attentively. 'We're here to ensure that there'll be no return to the shambles of the previous weeks. It's not in your interests – and it won't be allowed to happen. I have excluded some students who will return if they promise to behave, but some others will not return. We want to work with you to rebuild the school.' I read out sections of the Ofsted report that were positive about the teaching and the behaviour of pupils, telling them, 'It's not all bad – there are plenty of good things about the school that together we can build on.'

When they heard that we had abandoned the hated DFL there was an audible sigh of relief and smiles all round. We handed out new guidelines on our 'Positive Behaviour Policy', which emphasized taking responsibility for looking after oneself, each other and the environment of the school. I told them, 'This is the new deal. It's not all about punishment, rewards will be introduced to reinforce good behaviour. But there will be a range of sanctions, including tellings-off, detentions, and so on, not simply isolation and exclusion.'

Anna carried on to outline our other plans. 'We plan to set up a School Council to look, with your help, to amend the behaviour policy over time and suggest other improvements.' She also explained the purpose of the locks and extra staff. 'It's to make the school a better and safer place to attend,' she said. 'Other schools are carpeted, why shouldn't you have the best?' We ended by saying that we had every confidence that they would play their part and that we would all meet again at the end of the day to congratulate everyone on a job well done.

The students filed quietly out of the hall and went to their lessons. Anna and I took a deep breath. We had got the show on the road without any of the problems that we feared: unruly behaviour in the assembly, challenges to our authority and other nightmare scenarios. Our next priority was to sort out the press, so we could be left alone to get on with the real work of restoring a normal routine.

I had decided not to appear on the school's steps. They were a symbol of the old regime: they reminded people of the undisciplined behaviour and the V-signs. My idea was to set up a photo-opportunity in the library with some students. I outlined this to Anna who volunteered to arrange the event. 'I'll get Bruce to do it,' she said. It was one of Anna's strengths that she easily remembered names (one of my failings), and a measure of how quickly she had got to know the individual members of staff in the day and half she had been working with them. Bruce Thompson, the head of Year 9 and a history teacher, was keen to help, and within minutes we had assembled a small group of well-dressed and studious-looking Year 10 students with their history books. I met my BBC contact from the previous evening in the entrance hall, explained my plan and said I was prepared for the photographers to come first, as long as they promised to go away afterwards. He went off to negotiate. I stayed in the background, desperate to avoid being photographed on those steps.

Later one of the photographers told me how delighted they were. Cold, wet and bored, all they wanted was a photograph so they could go home. On reflection, the goodwill gained from being more open began a new phase in the school's relationship with the press. This favour would be repaid many times over during the next months, but at the time it was just a way of getting some peace and quiet.

The photo-opportunity was an extraordinary experience. Crowded into the library were about 30 photographers, plus a couple of television cameramen, all jostling round whilst Anna and I watched the students pretending to complete a worksheet on the rise of fascism in Germany.

'This way, sir.'

'Look over here, sir.'

'Give us a smile, love.' This was to Anna.

'I'm not your love!' she retorted, unamused.

Finally, after about ten minutes they went away with their pictures and we breathed again. Now for the television.

Cautious from my experience of the previous Friday, I asked Anna to watch my back in case I said something stupid. I was again interviewed by the BBC's Liz Meech, who had a good understanding of the story and asked sensible questions, making the exercise much easier. It seemed to go well, and true to their word, within an hour they had all left, with the exception of a single freelance photographer, who plagued us for the next few days. The staff thought I was wonderful. I had got the press, a major disincentive to good discipline, off the street.

When I saw that night's television coverage and the pictures in the next morning's papers it was brought home to me again how the camera distorts reality. All the public saw were two teachers leaning over, encouraging some pupils. They never saw the frenetic activity of the photographers, using roll after roll of film to get the best pictures. When I look at those pictures now, I still see the whole scene, not the image the rest of the world saw. I kept this in mind a number of times over the next months to explain to the students, staff and governors the importance of projecting the best image of the school. 'It doesn't matter how much we improve if the public still see us as the "school from Hell",' I urged them repeatedly.

I was later told that these pictures were broadcast across the world. The re-opening of the Ridings School, Halifax, was one of the three biggest stories world-wide: we were up there next to Boris Yeltsin's heart bypass and President Clinton's re-election. The next day I popped into Rastrick High School, and it was impossible not to see the photograph taken from the morning's *Guardian* of my picture with the students. Some wag had drawn a big bubble coming out of my mouth, saying, 'So this is what a pupil looks like?' I felt very homesick.

Lunchtime was the next crucial point. Denis Midwood, the Youth Tutor, had spent the morning shopping for radio-cassettes and games, and the Youth Club was opened for the Year 10 and 11 students to use. The Community Constable, PC Gordon Dickson, was fantastic. He watched out for intruders during the morning and chatted to the students at lunchtime. The message from everyone was one of encouragement, support, and a wish to get back to normality.

The only tricky moment was when the midday supervisors, who had not been at the Monday staff meeting, demanded to speak to me before they would work. They were still concerned that the pupils would be out of control. I explained what we were trying to achieve and that the school was 'under new management': they would be backed up and assisted in the first days by the EWOs. I also promised them new anoraks. Another potential crisis averted.

Finally, it was time to leave. A couple of the inevitable television crews turned up, but this time the students did us proud. Instead of the usual high-decibel stampede the students walked out of the school in an orderly manner, even commenting how much better it had been. The only real problem had occurred towards the end of the morning, when one boy had sworn at a teacher. Apparently it was the first time he had been in school for months. I gave him a choice: apologize and be excluded for two weeks, or don't and be excluded permanently. He chose to apologize and, after making his peace with the teacher, left the school and was never seen again.

The first day was behind us and we had already gained positive publicity for the Ridings students and staff. That evening I had arranged to attend a meeting at Longroyde, a local primary school, to talk to parents of children due to transfer to Rastrick at the end of the year. Fired up by the events of the day I probably talked more about the Ridings than Rastrick. I found the opportunity to chat with John Richardson, the school's Chairman of Governors, who held a senior position in the Halifax Building Society and also chaired a group of business and council representatives looking to improve the commercial environment of Halifax. 'Will you ask for support from the local business community?' I asked. 'The priority would be to beef up the administrative staff, perhaps through a secondment.'

When I drove down Nursery Lane the next morning, everything was quiet and peaceful. No press! I parked and walked into the building. The Year 9 students returned that day. Along the corridor two boys were larking about, jumping up to hit the lights and ceiling. I told them to stop.

'Are you the new Headteacher?'

'Yes. Calm down and go to your form room.'

'We've seen you on the telly.'

It became a routine conversation as more and more youngsters returned.

Once again we started the day with an assembly and explained the new routine. I began to realize how chaotic the administration of the school was. There were not enough office staff and, like the teaching staff, their relationships had not yet gelled. We had arranged for a clerical assistant to work on the Wednesday we reopened, and my personal assistant from Rastrick, Jo Sexton, came in on Thursday. By the end of the week, I had arranged long-term support from the Rastrick receptionist, Carole Blakey, and my ex-secretary, Jenny Fulcher. Their immediate tasks were to enter the new pupils on the school's database – this had not been started yet, although we were eight weeks into the school year – check which children were attending each day, and deal with the never-ending requests from the press. This pressure was so intense that Peter Lloyd was drafted in to answer the phones. One call he received was from a school in Bogota, Columbia, asking for advice on how to deal with poor discipline in schools. No one believed him when he told us this – until they rang again. My conversation with John Richardson the previous evening brought immediate help when the Halifax presented us with a cheque for £500 and the temporary secondment of a Halifax employee, Gill Hellewell. She seemed undaunted by the shambles and agreed to work as school administrator from January until Easter.

The school's Educational Psychologist, Mike Vigures, showed me the statistics relating to literacy. Over 40 per cent of the youngsters in Years 7, 8 and 9 had reading problems, and a third of them had a reading age more than three years below their real age. Mike ran the recently established Behavioural Support Team, together with Louise Preston, a support teacher, and Darrell Carney, an EWO. Working with the local primary schools had given Mike a keen insight into the educational problems of the area, and he gave me a valuable briefing on the limited educational background experienced by many of the students. For example, not only did a number receive little support at home, but some had been marginalized in their primary schools, experiencing little that was purposeful or challenging.

For the second day running, we met the students at the end of the day to congratulate them and remind them of their responsibilities. They left quietly – though of course now there were no reporters to record their well-behaved exit through the school gates. We braced ourselves for the next day when all the children would be in school, including Years 7 and 8 – by reputation the two worst-behaved years in the school.

The return of the younger pupils on Friday was much as we predicted. For the first time we had real problems in lessons as one or two youngsters continued to be disruptive, failing to appreciate the significance of the new regime by refusing to go to lessons, and when taken in by the patrolling EWOs, disturbing the work of the others. They may not have been many and involved only a few pupils, but were enough to show that the younger children had little idea of school routine or acceptable behaviour. In the afternoon assembly, I said that a few of them had let the others down, but I was confident that all would be well. A small group were talking to each other in front of a member of staff, so I stopped, expecting the staff at the side of the hall to have a quiet word. But everyone was looking at me. 'That's enough. Behave!' I called out firmly – and they did – but still not one teacher helped by standing by them or even glaring at them. At the end one of the staff said, 'You should have asked me to remove them.' I tried to explain that, if he had used his common sense and helped at the outset, I would not have had to stop and deal with it myself. This was my first personal experience of how some of the staff had lost the habit of meeting disciplinary problems simply and at an early stage.

The phones were still ringing incessantly, but our enhanced clerical team were doing sterling service filtering the calls and gradually bringing more order to the school's administration. At least we had got through our first week. Anna had bought a dozen bottles of pink champagne and we got all the staff together, including the cleaners, and I thanked everyone for their hard work and read out a selection of the many, many messages of goodwill we had received. I had been overwhelmed by the public's response both to the school and to me personally, and I had felt all through the week that the whole world was on my side. Every day, more and yet more letters poured in: from friends and ex-colleagues, from well-wishers in every corner of the country, as well as from a few eccentrics. The most heartening were from primary school children who were following the story through assemblies throughout the land. I meant to reply to them all, but somehow I just never had the time.

Anna and I didn't dare say it too loudly, but we both thought that we had made a good start. However, there was a long way to go.

9

THE PLAN OF CAMPAIGN

Anna and I had agreed that for the time being she would concentrate on overseeing the pastoral side of the school and work with the Learning Support staff to bring some order to the teaching of youngsters with Special Educational Needs (SEN). Children who have identifiable special needs – learning, emotional or behavioural problems, and physical disabilities – have 'statements' drawn up, agreed between the parents, school and LEA, outlining any special provision required, for which schools receive additional resources. The inspectors had acknowledged that the school had an excellent SEN policy but, as Mr Webb had wryly observed to the governors, 'There is no evidence that it is being implemented in any significant manner.' To deal with Key Issue 7, we needed to ensure that those pupils were having their statements fulfilled and, more importantly, to identify those who should have statements, or at least have special programmes to enhance their normal class provision.

The co-operation of the majority of pupils, coupled with Anna's high profile around the school and the concerted effort by the school and LEA staff, now virtually based in the building, ensured that it was much calmer. However, we did have our moments. Some of the pupils tended to fly off the handle at any minor perceived slight, or when they became frustrated at not being able to do the work that was expected – or simply if they did not get their own way. In most schools this might result in fights or swearing: at the Ridings it could well involve throwing a piece of furniture. At one point, after Anna had vigorously remonstrated with one pupil, she exploded, 'Is throwing furniture a subject on the curriculum of this school?' We looked back a while later and realized that no one had thrown anything for weeks – such were our rather unusual performance indicators.

There were hiccups with the new behaviour policy. Many of the staff still lacked the confidence to use the full range of sanctions available –

starting with a simple, 'Stop that!' As a result, too many children were being put in detention, and we discovered that an unofficial rule had been established that after three detentions a child would be automatically excluded. I explained to the staff that this was not the case.

'Remember the problems with DFL,' I urged. 'No behavioural system can work if you lock yourselves into a rigid application. You need to adjust your responses to the circumstances. That doesn't mean that you let pupils get away with bad behaviour, or that you're on your own: it means that you are responsible for managing behaviour in your classrooms, and when serious problems develop you can count on the back-up of other staff. To make this work we must all deal with problems consistently and fairly. Anna and I will help you, but you must do it our way – and you cannot determine that a child will be excluded.

'Sanctions are only effective if they are used fairly and sensibly. Pupils need to see that there is some discrimination between the trivial, the serious, and the very serious. We have to motivate the students, get them on our side, and isolate those who cause difficulties – then deal with them effectively. More important than any of that,' I went on to say, 'is that you should not only use the sanctions, but look for every opportunity to reward good behaviour and praise students when they do things right or make a real effort.'

The discovery of this detention/exclusion rule brought home to me how far we still had to go to give some of the teachers the confidence and skills to control their classes effectively. In conversation with Peter Bartle it also became clear that some of his staff were anxious to take a more active role in helping some of the teachers. So, at the end of the second full week I attended the weekly Friday afternoon meeting held by the LEA's Curriculum Support Team to discuss moving to what I termed Phase 2 support.

'I want you to develop your supportive role so that you start advising those teachers who require it how to use alternative approaches.' I told them. 'We must improve some of the teachers' skills in classroom management and curriculum delivery – and reawaken the skills some others have forgotten.' The meeting went pretty well until one senior support teacher expressed the view that it was a waste of time giving advice as it was always ignored. 'I find that surprising,' I replied. 'You and I have always worked well together in the past and by now you should realize that I am quite clear in what I ask you to do. If advice is ignored, I need to be told. All LEA officers have to understand that we are endeavouring to build up the skills and confidence of the staff – and you must support us. It's no good if you're also locked into the patterns of the past, because then nothing will change.' I wasn't sure I had convinced him, but the others seemed OK.

Key Issue 4 was the improvement of administration and management structures. We began to create Heads of Faculty to oversee the curriculum, taking this responsibility away from the Key Stage Co-ordinators, who were re-designated Heads of Upper and Lower School. Over the next months this exercise allowed us to address a number of the points of friction that still remained from the initial appointment process.

I was keen to find a new purpose for the corridor that had been used for isolation under the DFL policy, both to utilize the space and to make the point that the old regime was dead. It was also imperative that Anna and I had offices with telephones: Anna was using a mobile phone in a room near the front door and I was using a small room up a narrow flight of stairs, although at least it had a phone. All the school's pastoral staff shared an empty classroom next to the general office. We decided that the reorganized pastoral staff should move into their own offices, located in the newly partitioned isolation corridor, and that the classroom should be converted into offices for Anna and myself, plus additional space for the secretarial staff to use for more sensitive and confidential work. We also planned to extend the computer network and replace the antiquated telephone system.

As usual, all this was going on against a background of continual interviews with press and television, including *The Times Educational Supplement* – which called me 'genial' – and the *Financial Times* – which described me as 'grey'. However, my attempts to work with, rather than against, the media were resulting in a marked change in the way the school was portrayed. The coverage was much more positive: it began to concentrate more on the issues and how we hoped to tackle them and less on the sensationalist 'school from Hell' or 'Superhead' angles.

A group of older girls were interviewed on Radio 4, and I was asked to write a monthly diary for the *Daily Mirror*, a deal that never came off. Sky television gave us a free video camera, on condition that the students made an on-going documentary, which Sky would help them edit. Jenny Baker, the Head of Art, was enthused by the project and immediately collected together a group of talented volunteers, who worked hard over the next months. Some of their efforts were broadcast as part of the Sky news bulletins. As a record of day-to-day life, this certainly beat the idea of filming me brushing my teeth.

A researcher for an independent television programme was also intensively lobbying me. Her idea was to produce a documentary on the events of our first few months. It would require about ten full days' filming to track the progress of a selection of pupils: one of the excluded pupils, one with special needs, and so on, and a 'fly-on-the-wall' element to show how we coped with managing the school. Although I was unsure, Peter Bartle and I spent some time trying to negotiate a deal, as they were offering to pay. In the end it fell apart because, like many television organizations, they wanted too much – unlimited access, total editorial control and exclusive television rights, all for the magnificent sum of £1,000.

Some stories were still negative. The security guards became the subject of press speculation. Their contract had been extended after the LEA had had a series of arson threats; the insurers were keen to keep the guards on until the tension in the area died down and the planned security fence was built. By now they were part of the team, and one especially was very popular with the girls because he looked like Jean-Claude Van Damme. The press pestered us for details and in the end I agreed to be interviewed on Radio 5. It was all predictable stuff: security guards were having to patrol the 'school from Hell', and I had to explain that 'The guards are there to keep intruders – including the press – out. Not keep the students in!' Over the next few weeks, we gradually reduced the guards' hours until they left without anyone noticing.

The best publicity came from outside the school. In the midst of the disruption of the previous half term Richard Hobday, Head of Careers, had organized a fortnight's work experience placement in a local firm for every Year 11 student. By coincidence they were due to start on Monday 11 November – the start of our first full week. It was important that the arrangements went off without a hitch, both to improve our image and to relieve the pressure on the staff, who would have to cope with one year group less. It also enabled some of the teachers to get away from the school, visiting their students in the workplace. At the end of the fortnight, several employers contacted the *Courier* to report that it had been a pleasure to have the Ridings Year 11 students with them on work experience. The story made Saturday's front page: a huge picture with the headline 'THEY DID THE RIDINGS PROUD'. It was a real boost to our confidence at a time when we all needed it. I suspected that the firms had been nudged into action by the Principal Careers Officer, John Heraty. When I quizzed him later, he just smiled enigmatically.

On the same Monday that the pupils started their work experience, Kath Cross, the senior HMI responsible for overseeing our progress, made her first visit. After watching some lessons, we all sat down to discuss the Action Plan. Schools have 40 days after an Ofsted report to draw up an agreed plan addressing the points for action identified in the report. Normally schools undertake this on their own, but for schools under 'special measures' – the euphemism for a failing school – a member of the School Effectiveness Unit usually meets with the head and governors to explain the procedures and give general advice. The Chairman and Vice Chairman of Governors, Stan Brown and Paul Leach were there, together with Ian Jennings, Peter Lloyd, and Peter Bartle. As well as Kath Cross, there was her manager, Elizabeth Passmore, and a DfEE official, Simon James. I had talked with Elizabeth Passmore on the phone and she felt that, given the high-profile nature of the situation, it was better if she accompanied her colleagues to discuss drawing up the Action Plan.

'I have read the Rastrick High School Action Plan and it's a bit thin,' she had said. 'You do understand this plan will have to be much more substantial?'

'Rastrick's didn't need to be any thicker.' I replied, slightly stung by the apparent criticism. 'We'd had a very good report which highlighted no fundamental problems.' However, I took her point: the Ridings Action Plan would have to be much more detailed and carefully thought out, and putting it together would occupy a considerable amount of our time.

We were told that Gillian Shephard had decided that we should have only half the normal time: just 20 days in which to formulate our plans and targets. The clock should have started with the inspectors' report to the governors the previous week, but given the circumstances they would start counting from today, making the deadline Sunday 1

December. This was a real bombshell. To make the deadline tighter, the plan had to be agreed by the governors and seen by the Education Committee – and posted – by the last week of November, so we had only 14 days, including the weekends, to complete the whole thing. So much for a carefully thought-out plan involving staff, governors and the LEA. We were also informed that Kath Cross would visit every fortnight to assess our progress and report back to the DfEE.

A governors' meeting had been arranged for that evening. Old habits die hard, with one of the governors insistent that Mrs Shephard's deadlines should be challenged: an unproductive stance that prolonged the meeting and would have diverted us from our main business. There was just no time to indulge in long, wrangling meetings of this kind.

But the majority of governors had a much more positive attitude. Perhaps the tight timescale had concentrated everyone's minds. I knew the only hope we had of meeting the deadline was to ensure that as few people as possible were involved in writing the Action Plan – no management by committee. Of course, everyone wanted to be involved; after all, it was their plan and their lack of effective planning that had been criticized in the report.

In the end we agreed that Peter Bartle, Peter Lloyd, Anna and myself would comprise the writing team. We would meet the governors twice to discuss our draft plan: once to consider the first four Key Issues, and once again for the second four. A third date was fixed to approve the final effort. The timetable was tight, but we were all determined to meet the deadline. It was agreed that the LEA should re-assume the powers normally delegated to schools for finance and personnel. This was an obvious step, as the 'rebirth' would require additional finance, and the LEA was better placed to deal with any staffing problems that arose.

Although there were eight Key Issues identified in the Ofsted report, they were less than clear-cut: they tended to overlap, repeating and reinforcing certain areas of concern. It was more helpful to think in terms of five basic goals for radical improvement: behaviour, teaching and learning, attendance, the implementation of an effective SEN policy, and management and administration. I repeated this essential list at every opportunity to staff, parents and pupils, directly and via numerous press, television and radio interviews. I was sure that if we achieved these improvements we would automatically create a climate where staff accepted their responsibilities and undertook them in a consistent manner, thus demonstrating the 'unity of purpose' required.

Peter Bartle and I also discussed the politics of the plan. It was no use trying to fudge some of the issues, particularly that of teacher competence. The plan had to be convincing: it had to persuade Gillian Shephard and the DfEE that we were taking a professional and competent approach to re-establishing the school on a firm foundation for continuing improvement, whilst assuring councillors (whose long-term support was essential), that they were not being asked to throw good money after bad. It also had to convince the staff that we were serious and that fundamental changes were necessary – and were going to take place. Most importantly, it had to demonstrate to parents, and potential parents, that their children's education would be safeguarded.

The plan therefore needed to include a thorough appraisal of current teaching quality – a teaching audit – backed up by a comprehensive training programme. It was essential to set targets to improve the levels of literacy, especially amongst the younger pupils, in order to improve their performance in all subjects. As they recognized they were making progress, they would be motivated to achieve more. We needed to chart a course that would lead to a real – and quickly identifiable – improvement in the quality of education at the school.

However, the plan had to address the Key Issues as they were written, so Peter Lloyd drew together all the comments in the Ofsted report that related to each of the eight issues. We each took responsibility for suggesting objectives and targets for two issues, and met twice after school to share ideas. By the Friday of that first full week, we had a clear idea of the overall shape of the plan. I borrowed a laptop computer and spent the weekend collating everyone's work into something coherent, while Anna drew up a flow chart showing the type of staffing and communication structure for which we were aiming.

The teaching audit was a key element in the Action Plan: it needed to be credible, fair and simple to organize. We decided not to include staff who were definitely leaving, but every other teacher was to be observed teaching over three lessons and graded on a scale of 1 to 3. A grade 1 was be satisfactory, a grade 2 in need of improvement and a grade 3 unsatisfactory, resulting in the application of Competence Procedures. The LEA undertook to design a slimmed down 'fast-track' approach to apply to any teacher graded as unsatisfactory, as its usual policy on teaching competence was unwieldy and time-consuming, rarely resulting in dismissal.

Initially, each Head of Department would be assessed by an LEA adviser. If they were satisfactory, they would then assist the adviser in assessing the other staff in the department, thus reinforcing their expertise and management role. If the Head of Department was leaving, or had already left, the adviser would work alone. Complementing this approach would be a training programme designed to improve curriculum planning and classroom management.

I distributed my weekend's efforts to my three colleagues on the following Monday, and we each refined our sections. By Wednesday – ten of our days gone – we had a draft of the whole plan ready for our first meeting with the governors. Although it still lacked detail regarding the timing and performance criteria, it was a coherent statement of the steps needed to achieve our overall targets, and the governors accepted it after making some valuable suggestions. They also agreed to cancel the next meeting, giving us vital extra time to complete the task.

Some of the targets had already been achieved: to my mind, the hallmark of a good Action Plan! The new Headteacher had already been appointed, the behaviour policy rewritten, new arrangements put in place for lunchtime supervision, and so on. The priorities now were on the one hand to re-integrate the excluded pupils, improve attendance and institute sensible policies and procedures for the future, whilst on the other taking steps to assess the levels of pupil attainment in order to plan more appropriate provision. It was important to make an immediate impact, so Peter and I decided to include an electronic registration system to improve the recording and analysis of attendance and a computer-aided learning system aimed at improving the literacy and numeracy of the younger pupils.

We had to plan for the future. Specifically, we had to reconsider the building programme in the light of our new curriculum plans, estimate potential pupil numbers in order to make accurate budget predictions, and set targets for improving the work of the governing body and making better links with parents. Much of the important spadework and the underlying philosophy were contributed by Anna and Peter Lloyd, while the final performance indicators and timescales were mainly the result of my conversations with Peter Bartle in the frenetic last few days before the clock finished ticking.

Given the low base we were starting from, we were unsure what targets we should set for future examination success. Finally we decided to attempt to double the previous figure of 8 per cent A*–C grades at GCSE, on the basis that setting a high target might encourage greater effort from all concerned. However, we were more confident in setting targets to increase significantly the number of pupils entered for GCSE and those achieving grades throughout the whole A*–G range.

Although the shortage of time made it difficult, we attempted to involve the staff by pinning photocopies of each draft on the staff room noticeboard as they were completed. This led to an embarrassing clip of me pinning up a copy of the plan being shown repeatedly on local television. However, given the timescale and the complexity of the task, there was no way staff and governors could be party to all the discussions. Nevertheless, the final plan gained the support of all those involved: governors, staff, and senior members of the Education Committee. It satisfied parents and the DfEE, and it was completed within a tightly restricted period of time.

Legislation also requires the LEA itself to draw up its own plan, and Peter Bartle was determined that this should dovetail with the school's plan. So, as soon as ours was complete, he set to work on theirs. My approach in completing the school's plan was to write 'LEA responsibility' at every opportunity, especially where money was involved. It was therefore important to ensure that the LEA plan provided the necessary resources. Again the plan had to be written quickly – in a week rather than the normal fortnight – and agreed by councillors before it was sent to Mrs Shephard.

Whether or not this is a model for drawing up an Action Plan for a failing school I am not sure. It says much about the pressure we were under that posting the school's Action Plan on Thursday 28 November left us not so much satisfied at a job done well as simply relieved at another job done at all.

10

WINNING BACK THE DISAFFECTED

Whilst we were writing the Action Plan we were simultaneously seeking to reintegrate the pupils on fixed-term exclusions and find alternative provision for those permanently excluded. One of the visitors in those hectic three days of our first half week was Denise Faulconbridge, the LEA's Assistant Director responsible for exclusions and SEN. About half the pupils on fixed-term exclusions had been suspended for ten days and the others for fifteen, in order to enable us to phase their reintegration and plan more suitable provision where necessary. I had been promised additional places on the LBA scheme. It would make a lot of sense if we could move some of the older pupils onto this scheme, as they weren't getting much from the school and might benefit from a more vocationally based programme.

Anna and I began to interview those on fixed-term exclusions together with their parents. We took half each. I teamed up with Louise Preston and Anna with Darrell Carney, both from the Behaviour Support Team, who could ensure that those who needed additional support got it speedily. They also knew many of the families involved and had access to the limited range of support available within the LEA.

I drew up a contract, which included the following statement:

> I wish to be re-admitted to the Ridings School. I agree that the problems I have had in school are because of my behaviour and that if I wish to continue coming to the Ridings School I must: follow all instructions given to me by a member of staff – without argument; be well mannered and polite to other pupils and staff; never threaten or touch other pupils and staff; never use foul or obscene language or gestures; conform to the school's behaviour code, and code of school dress.

These are my basic ground rules for any pupil. It is also important to bring home to the child and parents that the past record of misbehaviour will be taken into account if there is future disruption, so this was also covered in the contract. Of course there are responsibilities on both sides in any contract, so there was also a section committing the school staff to dealing with the youngster in a fair manner, developing appropriate programmes to take account of any special circumstances and laying down clear procedures in case things went wrong. Parents were encouraged to talk to us at an early stage, and students were clearly told the importance of asking for help in situations where they felt they were being treated unfairly, or were likely to misbehave. For three or four children, simply in order to ensure that they returned to school, we agreed to withdraw the clause that explicitly stated that future lack of discipline would result in a more severe penalty because of the previous record of serious misbehaviour, although we made plain the consequences of any further disruption. Getting the children back into school was more important than sticking rigidly to every point.

As well as the contract, we had a couple of other options open to us. Firstly, there were those extra places on the LBA scheme, and secondly, there was the Beaconsfield Centre, which had recently been designated a Pupil Referral Unit. This was designed to take younger secondary pupils for one or two terms in order to modify their behaviour sufficiently to allow them to be reintegrated into mainstream schooling.

Most of the interviews went according to plan. Pupils and parents alike expressed a positive commitment about future behaviour and regret for past misdeeds, and we were confident that they would be reintegrated successfully. It also became clear that a number of children had not always been given the help they required, and that their misbehaviour was in part a consequence of poorly designed and delivered programmes of study. In these cases, Louise or Darrell noted what specific action was required and undertook to liaise with those best placed to improve the situation.

However, some interviews were not as productive. My most difficult case concerned a pupil with a history of disruption and violent behaviour that had culminated in an attack on younger pupils in the school changing rooms. Both child and parents claimed that this was caused by the desire to exact retribution on the children, who he claimed had bullied one of his relatives. He also claimed the teaching staff who had broken up the fight had assaulted him. We ended in an impasse, as he refused to return to school unless a certain teacher was suspended. I refused, saying, 'We all know that if he returns without accepting he's in the wrong, he will think he's got away with it and get into further trouble. Whatever the rights and wrongs of the situation, he's admitted thumping these younger pupils and he must be punished for it. If I discover any grounds for saying that the teacher provoked the situation, then I'll deal with that separately.' I felt the obvious solution was for the youngster to join the LBA scheme. Apart from anything else it was his preferred option, keeping him in education, but away from the inevitable difficulties that would occur with a full-time return to school. But the parents were adamant: no LBA, the teacher punished, no acceptance of blame on their part. I called a 'time out'. Eventually, after a series of further meetings, solicitor's letters and help from the EWOs, the pupil was placed on the scheme, with an option to return to the school full-time from Easter; this option was not taken up.

There were other problems. Some parents still refused to take responsibility for the behaviour of their children, or believed that we would back down if they threatened us with the press. The mother of one Year 7 boy, whose history of school attendance was appalling, refused to sign the contract or make any undertakings that her son would either attend or behave. She threatened to go to the papers; I told her that the contract had to be signed. The story appeared some days later. In summary it said that in her opinion I was very unfair to expect her child to attend school under the conditions of the contract. Given that the conditions covered such matters as behaving courteously, obeying instructions and attending regularly, this was excellent publicity showing us in a very reasonable light. The boy's father made considerable efforts to ensure that his son attended and was keen to sign the contract, but he did not have custody. After an appearance on national television, in which the unfortunate boy was shown in his pyjamas trying unsuccessfully to hide under his mother's duvet (an incident he took a long time to live down), the contract was signed and he returned. As she brought him in, his mother said, 'I agree with everything you're doing. Those journalists just make it all up. I never said any of that stuff written in the papers!' Unfortunately, within hours the boy had run away from school. Later he joined a special programme we set up to help the younger, badly behaved pupils develop their social skills to the point where they could integrate.

Anna was faced with two cases where the families had recruited the services of a vocal ex-councillor. It was agreed that both boys should join LBA, the scheme operated for older disaffected pupils, and their first session was fixed for Friday 22 November. However, when the two youngsters arrived they were turned away. They returned to the school and asked me what to do. I imagined that it was just a mix-up and told them to go home while I sorted it out. I then found that, without any consultation, one officer had decided that the group was too expensive to run. I was furious: after all the promises that I had been given of full co-operation and extra places, something like this could still happen. Predictably, as it was a Friday afternoon, I had to wait until Monday to remonstrate with the officer who had unilaterally decided to cancel the programme. The encounter ran something along the lines of 'We needed time to see if we could afford it.' 'Well, you'll have to afford it.' It was agreed that the group would start in the very near future.

The next day started badly when Anna received the news that her father had suddenly been taken to hospital seriously ill. After lunch the ex-councillor, exuding confidence and prominently displaying a Houses of Parliament brooch, arrived with the parents of the two boys. She was definite: she knew her way around the LEA and would not let us ride roughshod over the rights of her friends. After refusing to speak to Anna, the three waited in the reception area for me. I was dealing with another case, so they had to wait – which did not go down well. We were meeting the primary heads that afternoon, and I arrived to find myself trapped between the three protagonists blocking the entrance lobby and the primary heads unable to enter. I apologized for the mess, and explained that the scheme would go ahead although I did not have a definite date yet. I had some sympathy with their situation: they believed we had let them down. But I knew I had been let down, yet was having to excuse those who had dropped me in it. My emollient approach was getting nowhere. They were in the mood for a row. The ex-councillor informed me that she knew *exactly* what I was allowed to do under Council policy and would *personally* see to it that these people got their rights. I'd had enough. I decided to go on the offensive, and responded that I was now in charge of the school and she could complain all she liked but things were going to be done my way regardless of her understanding of Council policy.

'You can't behave like this,' she bridled.

'Oh, yes, I can', I replied.

I wasn't sure I had handled the situation correctly, but my colleagues seemed to think so. On reflection, I feel that the row sent the message into the local community that we were not going to put up with disruption from pupils or parents, and that we would try our best to deal with problems fairly, given the opportunity. Although we still had problems to solve and often had to manage 'difficult' parents, the disputes were usually resolved in a civilized and courteous manner. By Easter, another of our unofficial performance indicators was achieved: the number of parents coming into school without appointments and attempting to get what they wanted by intimidating us had fallen to zero.

We still had disciplinary problems with some of the Year 7 pupils. I met most of them the Friday of the second full week, after being called by a teacher to help to control a pupil in a Design Technology class. I was with Anna when the message came. She smiled and told me, 'You'll never get *him* out of the room.' She had spent much more time sorting out classroom problems than I had, so I had not really met any of the younger children. She was right. The class was made up of the dozen or so Year 7 pupils classified as being of the lowest ability, with very short attention spans, in other words just about unteachable. The teacher was doing a sterling job, engaging the majority of the youngsters, but one in particular was refusing to co-operate, punctuating the lesson with shouts for attention and bickering with other pupils whilst wandering around the class. The work involved the use of scissors and, although as Anna had accurately predicted, he refused point blank to leave the classroom, I managed to sit him down and work with him and a couple of others so that they were no longer disturbing the rest and were mainly 'on task' until the end of the lesson. The next week, I found five or six of the same pupils truanting from lessons and running maniacally round the car park, cheerfully throwing stones and insults at each other; my only success in dealing with them was that they ran away.

These incidents brought home to me full consequences of the school's streaming policy. Journalists and politicians can get agitated about mixed-ability teaching, and often talk as if it is the source of all problems in schools, especially comprehensives. In reality, things are much more complicated: every class is to some extent mixed ability. Also, although teaching GCSE maths to a group of thirty students who are roughly of the same ability is obviously an easier prospect than if they range from the gifted to the innumerate, it is another matter whether the same can be said as definitely for a class of half a dozen pupils. In deciding how to group pupils within the curriculum. I have usually found that the most important factor is the attitude of the staff. Teachers who are committed to making a mixed-ability class work will be successful, but where they perceive difficulties, it is usually better to look for alternative ways of grouping pupils, especially where examination classes are concerned.

Most comprehensive schools use some mixed-ability and some 'setted' classes, where students are allocated to sets according to their ability in a particular subject. Some subjects actually benefit from being taught in groups with a wider range of ability, and in most schools art, music and drama will be taught in mixed-ability form groups. After all, one advantage of comprehensive education is that individuals learn to work with others from different backgrounds, and with a wide range of abilities and aspirations. Generally speaking, students are more likely to be setted when they are following examination courses.

Another approach taken by some schools is to 'band' children into broad categories of ability across all subjects and then group them randomly within the bands for each subject. I was continually confronted with the disadvantage of this system as a curriculum deputy, when I had to resolve disputes between, for example, the Maths and English departments as to which students should be in which band: clearly some were much better in one subject than the other, and as they had to be taught both subjects in the same band they had to be placed in an inappropriate set for one subject.

Yet another policy is to 'stream' pupils: grade them into ability categories and then put them in the same teaching group for all subjects. This produces the same problems as banding across the board, as many children are much better at some subjects than others, but also has the disadvantage of creating a 'bottom stream', which can be highly demoralizing to the pupils involved. D streams in grammar schools were considered failures and left school early; nowadays those same children would, in comprehensive schools, continue in education and often progress to university – just one example of the improvement in opportunity available from today's educational system.

The Ridings pupils were streamed, which meant that the worst-behaved and lowest-attaining pupils were grouped together for most subjects. It was an acceptance of low expectations, and at best reinforced their poor behaviour and low attainment; at worst it created the almost impossible working conditions for teachers that I now saw at first hand. We had to make changes in order to allow teachers to teach effectively, rather than merely contain those children who had few social skills and who were experts in egging each other on to misbehave. Their limited social skills were emphasized when they had to sit still and concentrate on one particular task, conduct a conversation without shouting others down, or sit to eat a meal using a knife and fork.

I became convinced that we had to re-timetable the school so that teaching could be more productive, and find a way of containing these few youngsters who had shown no improvement under our regime. We were constrained by the fact that there was little provision in the LEA for this type of behaviour apart from the Beaconsfield Centre, which we were already using. A panel met to allocate the scarce places on a regular basis, and parents had to make a commitment to support the programme. Overall the Centre had a good success rate, but LEA cuts and restructuring had reduced the flexibility of the support available. Beaconsfield LBA aside, there was only a limited level of home tuition or specialist education outside Calderdale, a very expensive option which could often cost over £20,000 per year for each child.

We needed to create a halfway house between the Centre and full-time school that was affordable and provided a high level of liaison with school staff. I suggested a separate unit co-ordinated by the Behaviour Support Team, perhaps based in a local youth club. This would be staffed with some of our Learning Support assistants, and run by one of the LEA's support teachers. The most difficult youngsters could be 'socialized' in such an environment and then reintegrated, before we could identify another group to work with. Anna agreed, and Denise Faulconbridge, the principal EWO, was enthusiastic. Success would require the support of the parents of the children involved, and Anna set about obtaining their agreement to let their children attend the unit and keep them at home until we could set it up.

As well as trying to bring the younger, disruptive pupils into line, we were seeking to improve the level of attainment of students who would be taking their GCSEs in the summer. These youngsters had had a pretty raw deal: they had started their GCSE courses with one teacher, been re-organized when the schools amalgamated, and then suffered the disruption which led to the school closing. It was vital that we make every effort to help them surmount these disadvantages.

Whatever the arrangements for grouping pupils, effective teachers are those who are very clear about the ability and potential of each child, continually gearing the work to a level that challenges and motivates their pupils to succeed. This is a pretty tall order, especially if you only see the class for around an hour a week, so the more data a school can collect on students, the easier it is to identify and set specific targets to improve performance. Anna, working within a system that had less than the usual amount of such information, had nearly finished setting up a mechanism to identify the potential of the Year 11 students so we could monitor their progress and improve their performance at GCSE.

Any system we set up would rely on good teaching to carry it through. Good teaching comes from motivated teachers who have wide subject knowledge and can enthuse and generate respect from their students, so it was a good start to our third full week on Monday 25 November to have the news that the Education Committee had agreed to offer a year's enhancement to any of the Ridings teachers over 50 wishing to take early retirement. This was one of the requests I had made at the initial meeting when I had agreed to take on the job, and the agreement was a major step forward. We could now bring in some new blood to fill the vacancies left by those wishing to accept the offer. Other staff were also leaving. Deputy Head Andrew Bateman was keen to gain wider experience by working in a large comprehensive school, and the LEA had agreed to his secondment to Calder High to replace someone on long-term sick leave. Some months previously it had been agreed that David Bond, the other deputy, could retire at Christmas: I tried to persuade him to stay until Easter, but his plans were too far advanced, and he was anxious to leave. However, Jeanette Wallace, Head of Sixth Form and formerly Deputy Head at Ovenden, was available to fill the vacancy.

Things were moving on, and I felt our efforts to get the children back into school and back on track would progress well. What I had not foreseen was the shambles that would follow over the children I had excluded permanently.

11

CONFRONTATION WITH THE COUNCIL

In theory, the 12 pupils I had permanently excluded when the school re-opened should have been relatively simple to manage. Normally, if the governors upheld the head's decision, and the parents did not appeal, no further action would be required. The pupil would only be reinstated if the Exclusions Sub-Committee, a sub-committee of the Education Committee, upheld any appeal. Calderdale required this body to review all permanent exclusions as a matter of policy, whether the parents appealed or not, and the sub-committee was a formally constituted body with a minute clerk and all the panoply of council regulations. This is a very unusual situation, and was the source of much discontent from schools.

Although I had been assured of full backing for my decisions on exclusions, it seemed to me that, given the track record of this 'Star Chamber', the fewer cases that came before it, the less political pressure would be exerted on Michael Higgins. Denise Faulconbridge was also rightly concerned at the prospect of 12 appeal hearings, and was looking for ways of managing the situation effectively.

Although I believed it was right to exclude the pupils, it was also important to minimize the disruption to their education. Denise proposed contacting the parents of the excluded pupils with suggestions of alternative schools. I told her that, as each child was placed, I would withdraw the permanent exclusion, so there would be no need for an appeal. She was confident that some could be found places at the Pupil Referral Unit in Beaconsfield, in other schools or the local college of further education, Calderdale College. I also agreed to approach some of my colleagues at other schools to see if there were any vacancies in their relevant year groups.

Denise and her team did a splendid job in those first two weeks after the closure; of the permanent exclusions, the parents of ten were happy and the pupils were getting ready for their new schools. Unfortunately, the LEA procedures stated that the Exclusions Sub-Committee had to receive papers and meet within three weeks of any exclusion, so they would hear the two cases remaining – only one of which was a parental appeal, already rejected by the governors – at the end of November. With most of the groundwork done, Denise left for a couple of days to attend a course. In her absence, an assistant wrote to the parents of the ten youngsters placed, stating that I had withdrawn the exclusions – as we had agreed I would do for administrative purposes. He was totally oblivious of the problems he had caused. As a result of his letters, some parents now asked for their children to be readmitted, and we needed the help of the EWOs in explaining that they could not come back to the school. Once again I felt let down. Unnecessary difficulties were being created by bureaucracy, by administrators who seemed to have little understanding of the consequences of their actions, and by the LEA that should have been supporting us reneging on previous undertakings, undermining our already precarious position.

I was grumbling about these problems to Carol that weekend as we took a walk in the crisp, autumnal countryside. The other thing that was preying on my mind was an interview the following weekend on *Breakfast with Frost*. The BBC had been trying to arrange this since the announcement of my appointment, and Peter Bartle was keen for me to appear, so I had finally agreed. I was apprehensive: short, live interviews or slightly longer recorded ones were one thing, but a ten-minute live interview on a high-profile programme was quite another.

'Oh well,' I joked, 'it won't be as bad as the councillors reinstating the two exclusions next week.' I was struck with an awful thought: *No, they couldn't. Could they?*

On Wednesday 27 November, halfway through our third full week and with the Action Plan deadline almost upon us, I attended the disciplinary meeting for the first of the two remaining permanent exclusions with a mixture of confidence and trepidation. As Rastrick was a grant-maintained school, I had not attended a meeting of the 'Star Chamber', although I was more than familiar with its notorious reputation for returning excluded pupils to their schools, in some cases even if both school and parents believed it was the wrong move.

Around the table were five councillors representing all three political parties, including Councillors Higgins and Rivron (respectively

Chairman and Vice-chairman of Education). Officers more directly involved were Denise Faulconbridge; the Principal Education Welfare Officer; an Educational Psychologist; and the Head of Learning Support. I was accompanied by Gordon Buckley, the governor who chaired the school's Disciplinary Committee. The pupil's mother and another woman acting as her 'friend', or second, came, but not the child herself. I was surprised that she did not attend to put her point of view directly, although I understood she had been invited.

I outlined what I thought was a strong case, given the child's history of misbehaviour and the serious nature of the final offence. Indeed, her actions had significantly influenced the decision of the authority to close the school. In response, the mother made a number of allegations about the honesty of the school's staff. The councillors had been sent a copy of the DFL policy and a couple of them expressed concern that the full range of the sanctions available under the policy had not been carried out in this case: if it was written in the policy that a pupil could not be excluded until a specific procedure was implemented, then the pupil should not have been excluded. They would not accept my argument that this was irrelevant because, as everyone round the table knew, we had dropped this policy because of its ineffectiveness, and had done so *before* the pupil was excluded.

Gordon was pessimistic as we left the councillors to decide the outcome. I told him not to worry, saying, 'I'm sure they won't decide to reinstate.' I was certain the promised political backing would be delivered, especially as Denise's colleagues and I had a place lined up for the child in a good school, which would have been offered some days before if the Council's protocols had not insisted on this meeting taking place.

Michael Higgins was due to visit the school that afternoon, and I knew things had gone wrong when he failed to arrive. Denise came with Peter Bartle to give me the bad news near the close of the school day. It was inevitable, I suppose: given the history of decision-making since the inception of the Ridings, I should have expected nothing else but a decision to reinstate the pupil. I had been very clear in my discussion with Michael Higgins and Ian Jennings, which I had repeated to the Ridings staff. I would not accept my stance on discipline being undermined. Michael had said, 'All you have to do is walk away if we don't back you.' They had called my hand.

Peter and Denise were distraught. Peter felt all his hard work towards the regeneration of the school was being destroyed. I think Denise felt that she had let me down, although I knew she had done all she could. I later heard from some of the officers and councillors present that she had been forceful and clear, but that the politicians had chosen to reject her advice and vote unanimously in favour of reinstatement, utterly failing to appreciate the consequences. We agreed not to broadcast the decision immediately, and the officers left to give Ian my response: I would not take the child back. I hadn't decided whether to resign or just refuse to accept the decision. *Let them sack me!* I thought

Anna said at once that if I went she would leave too. I was convinced that the committee would think again if we spelled out the consequences of their decision. I rang John Sutton, the General Secretary of the Secondary Heads Association (SHA), who was incredulous. He told me to stand my ground, and said he would try to exert some influence by speaking with national politicians. I also contacted Nigel de Gruchy to warn him that the situation might blow up again, and to repeat that I was not going to desert my staff without a fight. Anna and I went into the weekly staff meeting that afternoon seemingly without a care in the world, determined to conceal what had happened. We briefed the staff on the final draft of the Action Plan, and explained the teaching audit and the changed focus of classroom support I had agreed with the advisers. We also discussed how we would monitor the progress of the 29 children Anna had identified as candidates for improving their GCSE grades, and explained our ideas for re-timetabling lessons and changing the timing of school day.

The governors met that evening to discuss the final draft of the Action Plan. The only mention of exclusions was Stan Brown's declaration that, in his opinion, our handling of the 12 cases had been exemplary because we had found acceptable alternative placements without delay. Anna, Ian Jennings, Peter Bartle, Peter Lloyd and I said nothing. After the governors had passed the final draft of the Action Plan, Ian and the two Peters went to see Michael Higgins.

Thursday came, and Peter Bartle met me early. They had tackled Michael in the incongruous surroundings of a pub darts match, and, after an animated discussion, had convinced him that I would not back down. Tactically, they had all agreed that I would not attend the second Disciplinary Hearing arranged for that morning. I asked my deputy, David Bond, to attend the Town Hall meeting and present the case with Gordon Buckley in my absence. He was obviously intrigued by my request, but I felt I had to keep him and Gordon in the dark as to the exact circumstances. However, given Calderdale's pre-ordained procedures, it was not clear whether we could change things in the case already decided. I phoned both Ian and Chief Executive Michael Ellison, stating my position and demanding a meeting with them and the Leader of the Council, Pam Warhurst, later that day. I told them they had until 3.00p.m. to respond, and then rang Morton Roberts at Brooksbank to explain what was going on. He agreed to meet Anna and myself that afternoon to try to work out the best plan of action for the meeting.

It was to be a very busy afternoon, as the BBC had also arranged a visit to cover our completion of the Action Plan, in itself a major news story. While messages flew back and forth, Anna, Morton and I held our hastily called council of war while waiting for two BBC correspondents, our old contact Liz Meech from the regional news programme and Sue Littlemore, a national correspondent. For about ten seconds I was strongly tempted to give the two journalists a scoop and tell them I was about to resign because the Council had reneged on its promise to back me. But I felt rather more confident at the news that the second exclusion case had been unanimously upheld. I tried to answer the questions positively and express confidence about the future. I enthused about our plan and concentrated on my five basic points, reiterating, 'We need to improve behaviour, teaching and learning, attendance, the teaching of children with special educational needs, and management and administration.'

We walked into classrooms, so that the journalists could ask staff and pupils about the changes that had already taken place. Without any rehearsal, my colleagues rose to the challenge and answered the questions articulately and positively; they were all superbly 'on message'. The interviews were shown on the BBC local and national bulletins and, as each programme feeds off its competitors, this inevitably led to requests from television, local radio and the *Today* programme to interview me next morning.

I was now in a bizarre situation: I was desperately trying to save the school – and the LEA's face – and with some success. Yet those very people who had begged me to take on the job were making it almost impossible. I was being bombarded with requests for interviews, and I knew that with one slip of the tongue, or deliberate press briefing, I could blow up everything into an even bigger and more controversial story, potentially with highly damaging repercussions for the LEA. For them to make problems for me at this time was putting themselves dangerously in my power. I could have understood if it was the result of one party scoring points off another, but it was an all-party decision. This had to be more cock-up than conspiracy, surely?

As Morton, Anna and I entered the small room in the Town Hall I was confused, frustrated and extremely angry. It was a high-powered delegation that greeted us: the Leader of the Council, the Chairman of Education, the Director of Education and the Chief Executive. The traditional description of the ensuing meeting would be that there was a 'full and frank exchange of views'. In fact, it was a far from equal exchange, as I was just not interested in the problems they had caused for themselves, and told them so. I had an ultimatum to deliver: 'If you undermine us on this, how can we trust you not to undermine us on other difficult issues? You have to back us or decide to close the school.' When we left, I felt they could be in no doubt where I stood.

I was due to attend a Community Education meeting that evening, but I'd had enough. I sent my apologies and went home. Nigel de Gruchy phoned to say that he had contacted some national politicians who had promised to help and asked to be kept informed. I felt more confident as I fielded the journalists that evening. The telephone was red-hot, partly due to the exclusion issue, but also because the completion of the Action Plan was attracting such attention. My apprehension about my impending appearance on *Breakfast with Frost* increased after a discussion with their researcher, as she seemed more interested in drawing parallels with national politics than discussing the school. Then someone from BBC television's *Breakfast News* called asking to interview me the next morning about our efforts so far. As the woman from the *Frost* programme had stressed that I should not appear on television before Sunday, I explained that I could only agree if he got her permission and that I had an early-morning interview for the *Today* programme. He told me that would be no problem, saying 'Their office is just down the corridor, I'll go and fix it.' He rang back about an hour later. 'It's OK. I've sorted it all out and there'll be no problems from the *Frost* side. I've organized a car to take you to Leeds. It'll pick you up after you've been interviewed for *Today*.'

By now it seemed this round of interviews had become part of my normal working life. It was not what I had expected when I agreed to take on the job, but having decided to use the media to help restore the school's image and self-esteem, I had to take advantage of the opportunities as they arose. Fortunately most of them occurred before or after school, so they could be fitted in by simply extending my working day. Looking back, time spent dealing with the political difficulties took me away from working with the school staff more than the media did. And every day I was thankful for having asked for an Associate Head who could concentrate without distractions on the management of the school when I was otherwise engaged.

That Friday I sat in the morning darkness in the *Today* radio car with an enormous aerial extended 30 or so feet into the sky, watched by my neighbours, peering through their bedroom windows in their dressing gowns. I listened to the interviews recorded at the school the day before and admired the ease with which the teachers and pupils had spontaneously answered the questions posed to them. A new sense of purpose was beginning to show through, in stark contrast to the dispirited morale of less than a month before. I knew that, between us, we could make a success of the school, as long as the Council allowed us to continue.

I was interviewed for *Today* by John Humphrys, whose questions concerning the school's problems and our future plans seemed fair and, thankfully, relatively predictable. Then he said in what seemed a deceptively low-key way, 'It seems all the problems at the school were caused by the incompetence of the LEA.' I was irresistibly reminded of the catchphrase used by Francis Urquhart, the scheming politician who becomes Prime Minister in *House of Cards*: 'You might think that – I couldn't possibly comment', but I used my version, replying with a laugh, 'Those are your words, not mine.' I was dreading his next question, but instead, I gratefully heard the words: 'Thank you Peter Clark ...'

I climbed out of the radio car and into the waiting taxi to head off to my *Breakfast News* interview. Just over half an hour later I was sitting in the BBC's Leeds studio being asked questions by someone who seemed fairly clueless about the education system in general and the Ridings in particular. One unforgettable question was, 'The Ofsted report criticizes the governing body. Which governors are you going to sack?' I tried to explain that there were limits to even a 'Superhead's' power. Over the next few months I wistfully recalled this question when I failed to convince one or two individuals of the desirability of my actions or philosophy.

The media requests continued into the working day, with *The World at One* phoning mid-morning for an interview. Assuming it was about the Action Plan, I agreed. Later I found out that they wanted to discuss the contract we had asked the excluded pupils to sign, and that I would be asked for my reaction to some comments made by the ex-councillor who had accompanied the parents of the children let down over the LBA places. I now felt more confident in dealing with the media, and I was getting pretty cheesed off with interfering know-it-alls. I told the journalist vehemently that as far as I was concerned the pupils were being satisfactorily reintegrated, and re-opening the subject was completely unnecessary. I heard her talking to someone else, then she came back to say, 'Oh, you're going down the order anyway, there's a story from Northern Ireland.' She paused. 'And now there's a story about a pig. Sorry to bother you, we've not got room for the item. Goodbye.' There's nothing like being dropped because of a pig to bring you back down to earth.

Shortly after the phone rang again; this time it was *Breakfast with Frost*. I opened the conversation cheerfully with, 'I've just been dropped by the *World at One*. Are you dropping me too?' 'Yes,' said the caller. Apparently the *Frost* programme's producer had not in fact sanctioned my appearance on *Breakfast News* and was upset. I apologized, 'I was very clearly assured that I had your permission.' I got the impression that they did not believe me, but deep down I was relieved. I would not get to meet King Hussein of Jordan, who was also to be a guest, but I had a new line: 'I've been dropped from *Breakfast with Frost*, through over-exposure.'

The trouble with the exclusions rumbled on. I learnt that the LEA had now consulted a barrister to advise them on how they could unscramble the committee's decision. The child's mother was meeting with the headteacher of the school that had agreed to take the pupil, to see if it was a suitable alternative to the Ridings. The LEA were looking to reconvene the meeting; unfortunately, one councillor who had been most hostile at the hearing was extremely upset to learn about the outcome of our meeting with the politicians and officers in the Town Hall – 'went ballistic' is how it was gleefully reported to me by a senior officer – and was being highly uncooperative.

Things got worse over the weekend, and we entered December on the brink of disaster again. Someone leaked information to the mother of the child at the centre of the disputed exclusion. We had our suspicions as to who, but we had no proof. However, the leak had what must have been the desired effect, as the hearing could now not be reconvened. Another meeting was arranged at the Town Hall to discuss the options. Anna could not be there: as well as working all hours on the problems of the school, she had to fit in regular visits to her father in Manchester, who was still very ill. However, we met with Morton to discuss tactics. There was no way we could change our stand. 'I told them right from the start that if this situation arose I would not accept it,' I stated. 'Whatever they're now saying, they gave me their word I would have their total support.' I felt passionately about the school and was determined to bring about the success I felt we could achieve. This was threatening to become another case like that of Sarah Taylor, the girl twice excluded by Karen and twice returned by the LEA. I was not prepared to allow it to destroy all the credibility we had built up with parents, staff and pupils.

When we met again with the senior councillors and officers, I was determined to put my case objectively. I failed and argued very passionately for what was to me the only possible course of action. 'Why should the rest of the school behave if we're seen to be powerless to deal with those who exhibit poor behaviour? If we can always be overruled, the disruptive element and their parents can ignore us. Supportive parents are likely to withdraw their children, Mrs Shephard will probably reject the Action Plan, and inevitably the school will close, bringing chaos to the LEA. It's madness!' At one point one of the officers asked me, 'What do you want? Write a list on a sheet of paper.' I told them 'I only want one thing: the full support I was promised at the start.' After an hour and a quarter we seemed to be nowhere near an agreement and, when one councillor insisted that 'elected members have the right to the final say in all matters concerning exclusions and finance,' Morton called a halt. 'You know where we stand,' he said. 'It's up to you to decide where you stand.' And we left.

The next morning Morton called. Our strategic withdrawal had finally convinced everyone that I would not back down. He had been given a face-saving draft letter which stated that the appeal had been upheld, but suggested that a change of school would be better for the child than a return to the Ridings. He had been asked by a senior officer if this would be acceptable. I told him, 'As long as there's no possible way it can be seen as a criticism of my judgement, and the child will not return, I don't really care what it says.' It felt like an anti-climax, not a victory, but it was a crucial moment. Certain councillors resented having to accede to my demands, and my future relationships with them were strained as a result, but as far as the outside world was concerned bad behaviour had been seen to be punished. As an HMI said to me some months later, 'You drew a line in the sand – and no one overstepped it.'

The situation also served to highlight the conflicting issues that are present in the current debate concerning the rights and wrongs of school exclusions. Headteachers have to balance the rights of the individual against the rights of the majority in order to maintain effective discipline, and in a social climate where everyone expects to be given their rights and fewer and fewer accept they have responsibilities.

With this major hurdle behind us we could now turn our attention to fundamental priorities: appointing new staff to replace those leaving at Christmas, setting up the unit for difficult children, re-timetabling the school and preparing to implement the Action Plan – and all before the end of term. We had just under three weeks to do it.

12

OVERHAULING THE SYSTEM

Although the Action Plan had not yet been accepted by Gillian Shephard we had to assume it would be: with just three weeks of the term left, it was important to maintain the momentum of improvement, especially with the fortnightly inspections. We had to obtain quotes for the equipment and resources necessary to fulfil the targets, and at the same time move quickly on priority areas, such as truancy.

Non-attendance is often a symptom of serious social problems. Meeting Ofsted's attendance threshold (a minimum of 90 per cent) can be almost impossible in schools serving communities where there are significant numbers of inadequate families. Where truancy problems persist, staff usually phone or write to parents or ask the EWO to visit. Most parents are very concerned when contacted, and are happy to co-operate to ensure regular attendance. However, some parents are not supportive and condone the truancy, either by rationalizing it – claiming bullying on flimsy evidence – or by actively encouraging it because they use the child as a babysitter, or for company, or because they just do not care. Parents who arrange holidays in school time to take advantage of lower prices also condone truancy, although most would no doubt be horrified to think of themselves in this light. However, the most serious problems occur when the family supports all the attempts to make their child attend school, but the child still refuses. The Ridings faced all varieties of the problem.

Schools are unlikely to succeed if they lack effective relationships with the parents of their pupils. For children to reach their full potential, there has to be mutual trust and understanding: a three-way partnership between teachers, students and parents. Although most of the parents of children at the Ridings were keen for their children to succeed, there were groups of inadequate families, totally unable to provide a caring family structure. In these families, children are not brought up – they just grow older. Although this is the case in many schools, the Ridings had a higher than average proportion of children belonging to such families, characterized by poverty, unemployment, low expectations of life and low self-esteem. (One stark indicator of the social deprivation in the area was that at first I guessed almost every child's age wrong: these children were physically about a year behind the pupils at Rastrick.) A significant number of pupils were long-term truants from families with a history of truancy across generations. We cannot hope to transform these people overnight into responsible parents solely by, for example, introducing home-school contracts or reducing benefits. Such measures are more likely to influence better-off, socially mobile families, who have far less excuse for failing to take proper responsibility for their children and often expect society's institutions to fill the gap.

We were already making significant progress on attendance: up from the barely 70 per cent recorded when the school closed to nearly 80 per cent. How much of this improvement was due to students feeling safer, how much to more purposeful lessons, and how much to the introduction of more effective recording systems might be open to debate, but we'd clearly met our target, as the report had highlighted all three as factors for improvement.

I was surprised to find that systems for monitoring attendance at the Ridings were almost non-existent. Pupils who decide not to come to school on a particular day or part of a day should be quickly identified and punished, usually with detentions and extra work to catch up on what they have missed. Our short-term priority was improving the registration and monitoring systems, as pupils had fallen into the habit of choosing which lessons they attended. Before the inspection, many pupils only participated in lessons where they felt safe and learned something: they chose to be absent from those which were ineffective or where other kids misbehaved. Effective monitoring would reduce this opportunistic truancy, so that the more serious problems could be tackled individually by the two EWOs allocated to the school. We hoped to reinforce this strategy by engaging disaffected pupils through a curriculum that would challenge and enthuse them.

Paper-based records at the school had been haphazard, so I felt we needed to adopt one of the electronic systems available. One option was a swipecard system, where pupils 'clock in' at each lesson by swiping their personal card through units fitted into each room; its weakness was that problems could arise from cards being lost or stolen. After considerable discussion Peter Bartle and I eventually chose Bromcom's Electronic Attendance Registration System, or *ears*. As well as taking morning and afternoon registrations, each teacher would record attendance at the start of every lesson on an electronic pad, which then transmitted the information to a central computer. The system could be upgraded to send messages or be used as a mark book.

Getting long-term truants into school is only the beginning. One Year 9 girl was finally persuaded through the classroom door after nearly a year's absence. Whether as a deliberate strategy to get out again, or just to gain attention, she started telling all sorts of unbelievable stories about her imaginary pregnancy. Within days, when other girls expressed disbelief and ridicule, she claimed she was being bullied and phoned home. Her sister and mother arrived, full of righteous indignation, threatening to take her out of school and complain to the press about her treatment and our ineffectiveness. Following the now-familiar pattern of a lot of talking and a refusal on our part to back down, the girl remained in school, but with two years of compulsory education ahead of her, how many other excuses would she and her mother find?

The Ridings also had a handful of 'phantom' pupils, who had never attended at all. Pupils excluded from other schools, or with very serious learning and behavioural problems, had been added to the Ridings roll by the LEA for administrative reasons: Karen had been overruled in her objections. They had been 'parked' at the school because they had to be on a school roll in order to count towards the funds for education allocated to the LEA from central government. Many might be attending alternative provision such as Beaconsfield or LBA, or receiving home tuition, but these placements were not taken into account for funding. Officers and politicians pointed out that these pupils resulted in additional funds coming into the school budget. However, as they were included in the statistics for the league tables used by parents and Ofsted to compare schools, they merely served to make the Ridings' performance appear even poorer. I finally managed to have these phantom students taken off the roll in early January.

As well as dealing with the immediate problem of truancy, we were modifying policies, organization and staffing, aiming to increase pupils' attainment and so change the image of the school. If we could improve achievement in extra-curricular provision so much the better, but improvement of academic performance was the key. All parents I met voiced their dissatisfaction with the quality of education in the area at primary and secondary levels. They had known their children were underachieving from a very young age and felt let down by their local schools. Time and time again, conversations would include the phrase, 'We were promised extra help, but...'

Their frustration was compounded because, although there were many other schools within easy travelling distance, some were selective and others were church schools – so real choice was severely limited if children did not pass the 11+ or the parents did not have a record of regular church attendance, or if they could not afford the significant cost of bus fares.

There was a potential intake of over 250 children a year in the immediate area, and the Ridings was attracting fewer than 100 of them when they moved to secondary school. To compete, we would need a clear and positive identity and a reputation for commitment to individual needs and ground-breaking educational practices: the Ridings must be a school of the future. We had to start building the foundations for this from the emergency resources available from the LEA and the unspent capital programme to which the Council was now committed. If we made good progress, we could even seek to become a Technology College as part of the government's specialist schools programme. Although that would have brought many of the benefits Rastrick High School now enjoyed, £100 000 worth of sponsorship was required. That, I was confident, would come later. Right now, we had to convince parents that we cared about the individual needs of their children and could educate them to achieve their potential, so that those living within the catchment area would choose the Ridings instead of its competitors.

Our first step was to tackle poor attainment in literacy and numeracy, and under-achievement generally: these points were important to several Key Issues. We needed to restructure the whole SEN provision, firstly through identifying those pupils with the worst reading problems and then establishing the widely-used programmes such as corrective reading (an intensive system of daily tuition within a tight framework) and paired reading (teaming a poor reader with an adult so that each child can be encouraged and monitored on a daily basis). In other words, we should start to implement the school's SEN policy.

However, a high proportion of children had difficulties with basic literacy and numeracy. As we wished to make an immediate impact, Peter Bartle and I decided to investigate computer-assisted learning systems. A number of products were being tested by a national organization to see if they resulted in any lasting improvements in students' attainment, especially in the acquisition of basic skills.

We rejected the first system we considered because it seemed to work without significant involvement from the teaching staff. Although the inadequacies of some of the teachers had been laid bare by the inspectors' report, it was crucial not to sideline the staff but to work with them in order to improve their confidence, performance, and range of skills. We found another, the Global system, which linked more directly to the National Curriculum and required significant involvement from the class teacher to set and monitor each pupil's work; I felt this would help to improve both pupils' and teachers' confidence. Although through urgency many decisions were being taken without any real consultation with staff, this issue was so important to rebuilding the confidence and skills of teachers that I was determined they should play a major part in choosing the system. The obvious lead teacher for the project was Maggie Binns who was already involved in developing strategies to improve literacy.

There was also the pressing issue of the timetable. As a Deputy Head I had been responsible for timetabling a large comprehensive school, and I had compiled the first timetable at Rastrick, but that was many years before. Drawing up a new timetable would enable us to make fundamental changes to the organization of the school. My priorities were to remove the streaming arrangements responsible for establishing those 'unteachable' groups, reallocate staff previously deployed supervising the unlamented isolation corridor, and improve the SEN provision.

Some aspects of the school organization had to remain: the programmes for those following GCSE programmes needed to be protected from further disruption. One major shift in the timetable related to the teaching of French. A combination of long-term sickness and a shortage of qualified staff had resulted in a general lack of attainment in this subject, and I proposed to use the curriculum time allocated to French to promote reading skills. As such a high proportion of the younger pupils were so far behind in basic reading, this was more important than fulfilling the National Curriculum requirements for French. I discussed the proposal with Kath Cross, the HMI who visited us every fortnight, and the DfEE agreed.

Once all these issues were settled, I had less than a week to complete the new timetable: a process that would normally be undertaken over a number of months. By the first week in December I was able to give staff an outline of the proposed changes and pass my efforts to David Bond to enter into the computer system and check for the inevitable errors. He worked really hard and found gratifyingly few errors, which he solved.

In the meantime, Anna had made real strides in organizing the special provision for the five Year 7 students we had selected to attend our small behavioural unit. She had obtained the agreement of the children's parents, and the Behaviour Support Unit had designed a programme aimed at modifying their behaviour. The group was to be based at the Furness Youth Centre; we asked the pupils to meet at school to be taken there as a group on the first morning. We also invited parents to meet at the youth club later in the day to answer any questions they might have about the arrangements. However, attendance was initially disappointing – only two children turned up.

We were also trying to restructure the building programme at the school to provide a more coherent strategy for developing the site. I had outlined my ideas for a new science block and for creating an expressive arts area for art, drama and music to the governors' Premises Committee, who backed the plan; and Susan Julian from the LEA and the architect agreed to work along these lines. Long-term, we would relocate all technology teaching to one part of the school, instead of the three areas previously proposed.

The school had now been open again for a month, and we felt were ready to show parents something concrete. Our first newsletter outlined the changes we had made to the organization of the pastoral system and invited parents to meet us at an Open Evening on Wednesday 4 December. Chris Binns organized a choir, and the staff and students produced displays of work, so that when parents arrived to hear our aims and plans they would also see evidence of a purposeful start to real improvements in the school.

With the excitement surrounding the completion of the Action Plan and the timing of Mrs Shephard's decision whether to accept it, the media were very keen to be present. In my experience, there usually comes a point in tackling challenging situations where you have to take a bit of a chance. Conscious of the tremendous efforts being made by the staff and pupils to prepare materials for the event, I was confident that we could take that chance. The publicity to be gained from the successful event being broadcast on local television was too good an opportunity to miss. The BBC also decided to set up a live outside broadcast as parents were coming in: Liz Meech arrived with a team of four or five and created a 'studio' inside the hall; she held an extended interview with me, with Anna in the background showing bemused parents to their seats, like a cinema usherette.

The evening went well, and the journalists reported the parents' very positive comments about our work so far. Much of the credit goes to Anna, who supervised the arrangements whilst I was busy completing the new timetable. We were both overwhelmed by the appreciation of some parents who attended. However, one spoke, I am sure, for many when she said, 'The last Headteacher promised everything would be wonderful. Things are better, but I want to see a lot more before I agree everything's sorted out.'

On her second visit the following day, Kath Cross observed one extremely poor lesson, but also some good work, and she seemed impressed by the standard of behaviour exhibited during lunch time. She reported at the end of the day that she believed we were working along the right lines. We needed this encouragement.

13

PERSONALITIES AND POLITICS

Several of the Key Issues in the Ofsted report related to management, communication, and morale amongst the staff. One of the major elements of a successful school is the strength of middle management. Over the last decade this role has changed considerably. Formerly, Heads of Department were regarded simply as the senior teaching staff, undertaking little extra responsibility; today, they lead and manage other teachers, organizing teaching programmes and resources. Without any real preparation to train them for the changed role, the majority of the staff responded splendidly to the challenge. However, one or two Heads of Department still found difficulty in making decisions about the management of their curriculum areas, and tempers frayed as they were pressurized for timetable information.

Some tensions born out of the amalgamation still remained. In one department, a demotion and a clash of personalities had resulted in a strained relationship between two staff members. I found this incredibly frustrating because both were essentially very good teachers who I was convinced could work very effectively together. The cracks were papered over by re-jigging their respective responsibilities, so that one took on an academic role and the other a pastoral one. Sadly, the problem was ultimately only resolved with the retirement of one – a great pity.

Some staff had trouble understanding that good discipline and control in schools result from clear, shared expectations and pitching their responses to incidents at an appropriate level. They had lost their sense of perspective, so that often it was all or nothing: a trait shared by – possibly even communicated to – some of the pupils. Many of the children found it almost impossible to control their tempers, resulting in often spectacular tantrums. On a typical occasion, a member of staff broke up a fight between two Year 8 boys and one of the youths claimed to have been assaulted by the teacher in the process. He was almost uncontrollable; it took Ian Calvert well over half an hour to calm him down.

There were also problems in communication between members of staff. One Friday after school, I was comparing notes with the head of another 'failing school'. The door opened and one of the more senior members of staff came in, followed more circumspectly by another, wanting to question an aspect of the timetable. Although it was obvious that I was busy, he launched into a long tirade about how his subject should be timetabled. He was so wound up that he failed to take the hint when my visitor said, 'Well, you're obviously busy, so I'll leave.' Even when I stopped him in mid-flow, telling him 'I understand your problem and I'm planning to look at it at the weekend. I'll talk to you on Monday', he wanted to continue his argument. Thankfully, his colleague intervened and led him out of the room.

In a way I could understand how he felt: head of a large department, he felt that he worked in isolation from the rest of the school and that no one else appreciated his problems. After the weekend, I outlined my proposals, and the poor man looked bewildered: he expected to have to fight in order to get the result he wanted.

The newly qualified teachers at the Ridings had little support, so I arranged for two of them to meet others at Rastrick High School. Afterwards one of my Deputies at Rastrick, Helen Lennie, rang. She was concerned at the emotional state of one of the young teachers, who had been very withdrawn and unable to contribute to the discussion. Fortunately, we had some help at hand: Peter Bartle commissioned Jackie Bould, a counsellor, to assist those who found it difficult to cope or were interested in alternative careers. She encouraged them to support each other, and her help made a crucial difference to four or five staff.

As the Christmas holidays approached, some pupils, especially those in Year 7, were beginning to lose concentration, and Anna asked me to restate the ground rules in assembly one Monday morning. I explained the importance of keeping up high standards of behaviour and telling someone immediately if they were being bullied. While the message seemed to get through to the pupils, I felt it went over the head of at least one of the teachers, whose attitude to the pupils was at best laid-back and out of step with the new ethos. He did not appear to support our efforts, and as a result was undermining them in front of the students. I was unsure whether or not this was deliberate, so I gently reinforced the message to him. As I was to discover later, it was ignored.

Given the stresses and strains of the last few months – indeed, the last few years – it was not surprising that some staff were finding it difficult to change the bad, but familiar, old habits. I was constantly hearing a phrase that had been familiar at Reins Wood: 'Our type of child...' inevitably followed by '...can't, won't, doesn't', or some other negative statement. I explained to the staff how unhelpful I found this attitude, and (jokingly) said I would sack anyone I heard using it. Nonetheless, I was optimistic: lessons were much more purposeful and staff were tackling problems that previously they would have ignored, not only inside their classrooms, but during lesson changes, breaks and lunch times. The majority had recognized that things must change if the school – and their jobs – were to survive.

Almost every week another classroom support assistant found a job elsewhere, reducing the help available to pupils with learning difficulties, but we found it relatively easy to recruit replacements. More serious was the need to recruit more teachers. One member of staff was teaching full-time, although taken on as a trainee only; I decided he should lose his teaching commitment and work in other areas. And with two deputies leaving, one teacher reducing from full-time to part-time and the Head of RE leaving for another post, we were desperate to recruit at least one teacher, preferably able to teach RE. I wanted to ensure that the students who were to take their GCSE exam that summer had some hope of overcoming the disruption to their studies, but recruiting teaching staff was far from easy. It was also difficult to find supply teachers to cover for temporary absences. Supply staff preferred to work in other schools, so we had to use commercial agencies, which were more expensive. I decided to approach teachers who had retired and might be interested in part-time work, and I asked for recommendations. In this way we made our first small step forward: Hilary Heggarty, a recently retired teacher, came to work at the Ridings for two days a week teaching drama. Although this subject was dropped from the curriculum, there was a group of Year 11 students studying it for GCSE, and finding them a teacher was a major step forward.

Denise Faulconbridge identified Joan Williams, who worked at a local primary school, as someone prepared to consider a secondment to run the Furness Project, our behavioural unit. Joan impressed me. As a very experienced teacher, committed to bringing the best out of her pupils and with a good knowledge of the area, she well understood the role she was being asked to play. After visiting the group she agreed to join the school on a full-time basis after Christmas.

Despite these positive signs within the school, I was worried about the attitude of the councillors and governors. How genuine was their support? I was determined that we should avoid another exclusions debacle. 'We must find a mechanism for managing potential problems before they develop into crises involving councillors or governors,' I told Peter Bartle. Our solution was a liaison group made up of two of the governors, Denise Faulconbridge, Peter, Anna and myself. It was included in the Education Committee's plan for the school, and later expanded to include Peter Flower and Clem Rushworth, Denise's fellow Assistant Directors.

The law relating to failing schools meant that the LEA could nominate additional governors to strengthen the governing body. They put forward three names, two of them linked to local politics and one from the business community. One, who had seemed ideal, eventually withdrew his name, so only two were nominated: Jill Wilson and David Helliwell. Jill, a past Chair of the Calderdale and Kirklees Training Enterprise Council (TEC) and Chair of the Regional Further Education Funding Council, also ran a local building firm and an independent primary school. She was well-known as a supporter of Project Challenge, a charitable organization that helps young offenders to redirect their lives successfully. David Helliwell had been a prominent and sometimes controversial Labour Councillor, chairing the Education Committee and acting as Leader of the Council. He had also been a member of the West Yorkshire County Council and a long-serving member of the West Yorkshire Police Authority. He had gained national prominence when the Council had been closely involved with Halifax Town Football Club ('Football on the Rates' were the headlines) and was currently running his own business selling aromatherapy oils.

The governors' meeting the week after our Open Evening for parents produced a setback. One of the criticisms made about the governors was their inability to resolve anything: minutes of meetings were voluminous, and decisions taken by one group would be rehashed by another, deferred by the governing body to be discussed by a sub-committee, and so on. I felt it was vital that we break this cycle and conduct matters more effectively and professionally. I suggested that we needed to reorganize the committees since the LEA had taken back some of the powers normally delegated to governing bodies, and they agreed I should write a paper on a new committee structure.

We had arranged a Personnel Committee meeting to outline the position on early retirements and the other staffing issues, including the secondment of Andrew Bateman to Calder High as Deputy Head with Jeanette Wallace temporarily assuming his administrative responsibilities. We agreed that it was important to avoid rehashing the issues and therefore to present a short report on our resolutions to the Governors' Meeting. Needless to say, we ended up discussing all the detail once more – old habits definitely die hard.

The stickiest moment came towards the end of the meeting, when one of the governors made a fuss about the Open Evening, asking, 'Why weren't we sent proper invitations? We're being steamrollered.' The governors had received the newsletter containing the advertisement for the evening and he, as a parent, had been invited. It seemed petty, but I certainly should have invited them formally, and I felt defensive. I apologized, but added, 'You have to understand that these are very special circumstances. We are working under considerable pressure. Sometimes decisions have to be made quickly, sometimes the courtesies get forgotten.' I was annoyed with myself for forgetting, but more annoyed with him for 'nit-picking'. Perhaps our consistent reinforcing of the positive message worked against us, preventing them from appreciating how much there was still to do. I felt we were treading water: relatively calm above the surface, and frenetic activity going on below.

After one governors' meeting in December, I was asked if I wanted to continue as Head of the Ridings permanently. I declined. 'I've promised to return to Rastrick and I know from first-hand experience how much work is necessary over the next four or five years. This job needs someone younger, with energy and enthusiasm, at the start of their career.'

The LEA had arranged a meeting between parents and councillors in the middle of November, to which I had refused to go. It had been well attended and on the whole fairly optimistic, although I had heard there were some difficult questions. The parents had been promised monthly meetings to keep them informed. This week it was time for the second meeting, which I did attend, together with Ian Jennings and all three party spokesmen – Michael Higgins (Labour), Peter Coles (Liberal Democrat) and John Ford (Conservative) – plus two other elected members and a reporter from Radio Leeds. Peter Coles had visited the school that afternoon to photograph two younger pupils holding a candle, to use on his Christmas card, and with the successful Open Evening behind me I was hoping everything would go smoothly.

There were about 20 parents and pupils present, and, after an introduction by Ian, we answered their questions. One parent started to complain about my absence from the first meeting. 'Don't blame them,' I interrupted, pointing to the rest of the panel. 'It was my decision not to attend. I didn't want cramp your style if you wanted to have a go at the councillors.' I got a laugh, and I stressed how supportive the LEA was being, financing the additional costs and making a clear commitment to keep the school open. Two other parents were critical. One complained that some of the pupils on the LBA programme were being rewarded for bad behaviour: they were going ice-skating and not having to come to school. This issue recurs quite often, and has to be tackled head on, so I put her on the spot. 'Would you prefer for your daughter to attend LBA or be taught effectively in school?' There can only be one answer. Schemes like LBA are easily criticized by the tabloids as 'rewarding bad behaviour', but the best examples of them succeed in putting disaffected youngsters, who find the normal school routine too demanding, into situations where they have to take responsibility for their actions and actively seek to improve their education. Inevitably, the same critics are the first to complain if schools and LEAs take no action to change the attitudes of the disaffected. The other mother wanted to go over the old ground of how the school had let parents down. However, given the evidence of the changes that we were making, she agreed that we were trying to overcome the problems and ended up being thoroughly supportive.

The politicians were anxious to show they were united in their desire to improve the school. John Ford and Peter Coles both paid tribute to Michael Higgins for his role in ensuring all-party support. Afterwards I understand Michael Higgins said that he had been 'impressed by my rapport' with the parents. Although always happy to be praised, I felt it had been an easy meeting. I reflected on how politicians who oversee education policy often have a very limited grasp of the day-to-day realities of managing a school and the skills headteachers have to employ as a matter of course.

14

DECISION TIME

The rumour mill was predicting that Gillian Shephard would announce her decision on our Action Plan on the inauspicious date of Friday 13 December. As I had agreed to be interviewed for the *Newsnight Review of 1996* that morning, I prepared a press release on the Thursday based on the assumption that the Action Plan would be accepted.

When I got home on Thursday evening from a meeting of the Almondbury Junior School Governing Body – where my fellow governors embarrassed me by treating me as a bit of a celebrity and I embarrassed myself by falling asleep – I had a call from Sky News requesting a so-called 'live' interview early next morning, prior to Mrs Shephard's expected announcement. I explained I would be at the Brooksbank School meeting Morton, who was accompanying me to my interview with Kirsty Wark from *Newsnight*. I rang Morton, who agreed that the television crew could meet us there as well, although I felt guilty at imposing on everyone.

Next morning the Brooksbank staff and students were rather surprised to see the control van with its satellite dish parked outside the school as they arrived. The equipment was set up, but just before we started I was irritated to learn that they had also sent a camera crew to the Ridings. I told the director that I would not be interviewed until the crew were removed, and rang Anna to make sure they had gone: the whole point of agreeing to all the requests from the media was to keep them away from the school, or invite them in only on our terms. The problem was resolved, and I said my usual bit: we'd done little that was innovative, just encouraging good basic teaching, we'd written a well-thought-out plan which, if accepted, would tackle the major problems identified in the report, and I hoped it would be accepted so that we could get on and implement it. When I watched later I was amused to hear Rhodes Boyson comment, 'That man has got the right idea.' I don't know whether he realized I ignored the advice he had given in his open letter.

Later that morning Liz Lord from the *Halifax Evening Courier* rang the school. When Anna told her I was not there, she objected, 'He must be, I've just seen him on Sky!' My piece, recorded earlier at the Brooksbank School, Elland, and including an interview recorded in Rastrick, was broadcast as 'Live from the Ridings School, Halifax'. This sort of thing has altered forever the way I react to media reports. The camera never lies, indeed.

The *Newsnight* interview was conducted in a hotel near Leeds Airport: Kirsty Wark commutes weekly from Scotland to London, and could break the journey there. The researcher had asked if I could suggest a venue with a real fire, because the programme would be transmitted so close to Christmas. The hotel looked like a collection of log cabins, but in the event there was no fire. However, a few Christmas decorations and cards were scattered around, and candles lit. After the usual great length of time setting up, we started. Hedging their bets, they asked two versions of the central question: how did I feel now that Mrs Shephard had accepted the plan, and how did I feel now she hadn't? My second answer, I feel in retrospect, was not very convincing.

On the way back, we met the Sky van coming in the opposite direction. Apparently they had swapped operators by flying one up from London and the other back, as they wanted to interview me again at the school later that afternoon. The money they were prepared to spend was unbelievable in comparison with my own endless struggles for funding. To organize my involvement for the day must have cost several thousand pounds – enough to pay for a couple of months' salary for a teacher. However, if there was ever a temptation to let these interviews go to my head, the reality was always sobering: out of the half hour or so recorded for *Newsnight*, the eventual interview lasted about eight minutes and was screened after 11.00p.m. one night during Christmas week.

The Sky crew came back after school. Shortly before they turned up, Jeanette Wallace and I were interrupted by some students who reported that one of the permanently excluded youngsters had turned up high on drugs and armed with a knife, looking for another pupil. By the time I had rung the police Jeanette was out in the pitch darkness searching the school grounds, but it seemed, thankfully, that the boy had gone. I left Jeanette giving details to the police whilst I went to be interviewed; fortunately the television crew were too busy to pick up on this particular crisis. There had still been no announcement on the Action

Plan from Mrs Shephard: apparently it had been delayed in an attempt to maximize its impact. The television people told me that it would definitely be made at a press conference she had arranged for Monday morning. I packed up and went home.

The combination of long hours and missed meals was getting to me: I felt absolutely dreadful and went through all the symptoms of a cold in less than 24 hours flat. I semi-recovered in time to attend a carol concert at Halifax Parish Church, in which Rastrick High School Concert Band was appearing. The conductor was the retired Chief Adviser to Calderdale LEA, Donald Maxwell-Timmins. The church was packed with over 700 people, and after the Rastrick musicians had played – beautifully – Donald turned to the audience. 'They played like that, and they haven't got a Headteacher! Is Peter here?' he said. He made me stand up and I was overwhelmed by the warmth of the response I received from the audience, their applause communicating the support of everyone present for me and the school. Although it was a bit unfair on Paul Armitage, who was doing valuable work at Rastrick, and sitting next to me, it was a great boost.

Monday morning was chaotic. It seemed that every newspaper and radio or television programme was ringing up – typically, on the day that new phones were being installed – not about the Action Plan, but because Tony Blair, as opposition leader, had said that successful headteachers should be seconded to failing schools. It was an interesting idea, although it failed to take into account the difficulties involved in getting the governors of all schools to agree: another example of the tension between delegating power and responsibility to schools and the desire for central control to organize support when things go wrong.

At the same time we were meeting with the architects. Anna was expressing concern that we should ensure the school had enough classrooms. 'The priority is to ensure there is sufficient specialist accommodation. If more basic classrooms are needed later it'll be easier to get them because they're cheaper,' I said. The phone rang yet again. This time it was Simon James, the DfEE official linked to the school. 'The press conference is over,' he told me. 'The plan has been accepted, but be prepared. The Secretary of State's statement is a bit hard-edged.' He promised to fax me a copy.

The press started ringing all over again about this news: they reached me before Simon's fax did, so I had to operate in the dark at first. Gillian

Shephard had not ruled out the possibility that the school might be taken over by an Education Association, and was initiating monthly inspections to keep the situation under review. ITN arrived to interview me live for the midday news whilst I was recording an interview with Nick Clarke for *The World at One* – an interview that ended very quickly when he realized I was not prepared to criticize the LEA. For ITN, Dermot Murnaghan asked if I felt monthly inspections meant that we had failed so far. I replied, 'Not at all. As we're currently being inspected every fortnight, once a month seems like a vote of confidence to me!' I heard cheering from the staff watching in the room next door. At least Gillian Shephard was unwittingly helping to create team spirit.

The fax arrived, accompanied by the 'hard-edged' press statement, saying that Gillian Shephard had approved the plan but thought we were not doing enough, and a contrastingly complimentary letter from her thanking Anna and me for all our hard work. The letter included suggestions for minor amendments to the plan, but essentially it was a green light. Mrs Shephard rejected the LEA Action Plan as being too superficial, and followed up with the unprecedented announcement that Ofsted should inspect the LEA, if Calderdale agreed. Of all the political posturing I experienced during my time at the school, this upset me the most. If Mrs Shephard wanted to take a sideswipe at the Labour-run Calderdale LEA, fine, but I resented her using me and my school to do it.

Anna was quite upset; she had gone to Todmorden to deliver Christmas cards and had been quizzed repeatedly about our 'failure'. 'It'll backfire on Shephard,' I told her. 'If she imagines it'll lead to her political advantage, she's wrong.' Although most of the newspapers slavishly followed her lead the next morning, we gained considerable sympathy in the longer term, both locally and nationally. Typical was the reaction of one of the worst-behaved boys in the school, who came up to me after the Christmas holidays and said, 'My mum says that Mrs Shephard was right unfair to you and Mrs White. You've worked dead hard!'

Armed with the congratulatory letter and the knowledge that we were not being taken over, I approached the media that afternoon with more confidence. After Radio 5, Radio Leeds, Sky television, the *Daily Telegraph*, the *Daily Express* and the local papers it was time to appear on *Calendar*, Yorkshire Television's local news programme. This was my first time in make-up. They played an interview with Councillor

Higgins, who looked even worse than I felt. One of the presenters said to me, 'He looks like a man under a lot of pressure.' I followed with my well-rehearsed routine that the plan had been accepted; we knew where we were going and the whole school community was determined to achieve our aims.

We later received a letter from Ofsted to say that the school was now regarded as only requiring 'basic' special measures, although it was still being treated very differently from all other special measures schools because we were having the regular inspections. We took heart from the situation: it was better than being labelled 'the worst school in Britain'. I also found out later that Mrs Shephard was so constrained by the law that her only alternative if she rejected our Action Plan was to take the school out of the control of the governors and the LEA and set up an Education Association. This had only been done once before, at Hackney Downs, and it had not been a conspicuous success, as the school closed in fairly controversial circumstances. From talking to DfEE officials I knew the last thing they wanted was to repeat that situation.

As we entered the final run-up to the Christmas holiday, everyone was increasingly tired. The standard of behaviour dropped, but this was exacerbated by the way the Christmas parties had been organized. One year group party had been planned for each afternoon, so the party atmosphere permeated the whole school and affected the morning sessions all week. Each day the pupils from one entire year group would arrive with only the afternoon's festivities on their mind. The morning's lessons were almost a write-off, and at lunch-time, when they changed into their party clothes, they became even more excitable. Each afternoon the music from the parties distracted other pupils from their lessons and, as form tutors wanted to join their tutor groups, their lessons needed covering, further disrupting the school routine.

This situation could easily have been avoided by having all the parties on only one or two afternoons. Anna and I had failed to anticipate the problem, so however much we disliked the situation, we had to put up with it. More importantly, it confirmed my suspicions about the lack of structure in the pastoral organization of the Year 7 pupils, and I decided to make this a priority in the New Year.

The term ended with a farewell party for the staff who were leaving, which included the presentation by Stan Brown of long-service awards – a total of nearly 300 years' service – to ten members of staff. David Bond's farewell included the shredding of an immense pile of papers relating to the children put into 'isolation' as part of the DFL policy. It was the first time I had seen him publicly criticize the previous regime. The party lasted two and a half hours, and everyone had their say. I went home exhausted.

I was still suffering from the after-effects of my cold, but I find I am often ill during holidays: once you relax the germs and the viruses take hold. Not that the 'holiday' was all relaxation: I still had to ensure that the new technology included in the Action Plan was in place as soon as possible. The Education Committee agreed to all our requests for equipment – about £70,000 worth – and I finalized the purchase of the computer-aided learning package: as it was an 'Open Integrated Learning System' it became known as OILS.

The media interest continued throughout the Christmas holidays, and I spent a fair amount of time responding to phone calls from journalists. I had agreed to appear on the *Calendar Review of 1996*, a round-up of the year, and on the foggy morning of Wednesday 18 December, my daughter Joanne accompanied me to the studios. I am amazed how much time it takes to record the relatively short segments that make up the final broadcast – in this case two hours to produce five minutes. During lengthy 'time outs' I chatted with the presenters about the way the media had reacted to the story and had become part of the trouble. They were dubious of the staff's tactic in going public. 'They didn't have a clue what would happen when the "rat-pack" got involved,' one presenter said. She was right.

The Monday of Christmas week was our 25th wedding anniversary – reaching 50 years of age and 25 years of marriage within such a short time made me really feel my age. But our children, David and Joanne, presented us with a three-day break in Keswick after Christmas. The anniversary and Christmas celebrations, followed by three days in the Lake District walking around Cat Bells and Derwent Water, were exactly the right relaxing and restorative antidote to the stresses and strains of the previous two months.

15

THE NEW YEAR

The new term began on Monday 6 January, and got off to a mixed start. Both Anna and I now had relatives in hospital: my aunt Joan had been taken seriously ill at the weekend and had been admitted to the intensive care unit at Withington Hospital in Manchester, where Anna's father was still under observation.

The staff took longer than I expected to hand out the new timetable to the students, while the class lists for teachers were not distributed, so there was some confusion about which children should be in which classes. Taking half an hour extra to explain the timetable to students was not really a problem, but the frustration felt by staff in not knowing exactly who was in their classes was unnecessary – especially as the only reason the class lists were delayed was to save paper in case there were future changes.

To complicate matters, the weather during the first week in January was terrible. It snowed and, instead of melting quickly, the snow stayed around for days. Snow has a marked effect on children's discipline. Teachers realize early in their careers that there is a direct correlation between their pupils' behaviour and wind and, to a lesser extent, rain. The windier it gets, the more unsettled children become. But snow not only results in hyperactive children – it also affects parents. As the first flakes fall from the sky, the phones begin ringing as parents demand that their children are sent home immediately. Added to all this there is the danger that you might not get home yourself.

One of the difficulties of controlling behaviour at the school was that many of the children were unable to recognize the point where good-natured high spirits stop and stupidity begins. By the middle of the first school week we were getting complaints from the firm building the sports hall about our pupils throwing snowballs. Unfortunately, some of the workers on site would occasionally start some banter or throw a snowball back and then be unable to control the situation as things

113

started to get out of hand. By Friday, the contractors erecting a fence along one edge of the school site were threatening to stop work, and we were at our wits' end; fortunately the thaw came over the weekend.

As a result of Mrs Shephard's decision, we were now facing monthly HMI inspections as a 'reward' for our success in coping with the fortnightly visits. Anna and I discussed basic survival techniques at our weekly staff meetings. 'Lessons have to be properly planned, attention given to assessing pupils' work appropriately and, most importantly, you have to take IEPs seriously,' we exhorted. Teachers have to devise Individual Education Plans, or IEPs, for SEN pupils to demonstrate how their needs are being met. Although the SEN code of conduct was a recent innovation, and imperfectly introduced into many schools, with such a high proportion of children requiring additional help we had more reason than most to make the system work – aside from a monthly inspection. The Ridings staff, in common with many other teachers, saw the initiative cynically as just another imposition, with more forms to fill in, leaving less time for teaching. We needed them to see the plans as an essential tool in teaching children with learning and behavioural problems. If the targets in the plans were specific and achievable in the short-term, they would help to motivate pupils as well as improving their basic skills. This was a key reason for choosing the Global software: teachers had to set up a work plan for each child, which was a constant reminder of the importance of the plans.

I decided to broaden the curriculum for some of the Year 10 students who were finding the traditional courses difficult. I wanted to introduce a link with the local College of Further Education to develop vocationally based work with relevant qualifications. I met with the college staff in the first week of term and agreed the outline of the basic course, then explained it to the students, who were worried they would be labelled 'thick'. I explained that there would be a core of English, maths and information technology (IT) plus three options in catering, building and hairdressing and explained that arrangements had been made for them to visit the college at the end of the first week. However, we hit problems. For some reason the visit took college staff by surprise, and I was horrified when told the price was nearly £40,000 – considerably higher than I expected. Even after spirited re-negotiation the cost was, at £24,000, more than twice what we had in the budget and far more than I was prepared to pay. We were now near the end of January; the youngsters had missed several weeks and their enthusiasm was waning. With considerable help from the TEC, we agreed to put on a similar course for building and hairdressing at another college in Huddersfield. Although the cost was considerably reduced, it meant a longer journey resulting in more expensive transport and shorter lessons. Nevertheless, by the summer term the students on the building course had won a national award for their work. After the February half term, I was able to recruit a highly skilled teacher, Jill Thewlis, to teach a catering session each Friday afternoon, finally fulfilling my original promise to the students, but problems continued up until the summer. We learned from this experience and during the summer term planned the continuation of the programme so that appropriately trained staff could provide similar courses at the school.

However, the outside world would not go away. The Ridings School possessed a swimming pool – one of only two secondary schools in Calderdale to do so – and although the school was responsible for its day-to-day maintenance, we hardly ever had the use of it because priority was given to local primary schools. Whilst I had been at Rastrick on Friday afternoon, there was a minor incident with some primary school children visiting the pool – a group of our pupils ran through a door and barged into the primary school children lining up outside the pool entrance. Their Headteacher had complained to Anna that his pupils had been 'terrified' by the behaviour of our children, and his staff were upset. He said he had had an agreement with the Ridings to provide additional staff when his children attended, but they were no longer on duty. This was hardly surprising, as neither Anna nor I knew anything about such an arrangement.

Stories to do with the Ridings tended to gain something in the telling, and by the time a reporter from the *Halifax Evening Courier* rang me it was to ask for my comments on a sensational story involving children being attacked with knives. The story published in the *Courier* ignored my factual account of what was a relatively trivial incident caused by a few youngsters chasing about at lunchtime – and, unfortunately, answering back when reprimanded by the primary school's staff – and read as though violent knife-wielding students were roaming about terrifying primary school children. When I contacted the Headteacher to ask him why he had contacted the press, he denied all involvement, but nevertheless recounted a tale very similar to that in the paper – a long history of problems going back over the years, including his pupils being threatened by thugs with knives. He stated that his secretary had been so concerned at what she had witnessed when she accompanied the children that she and her husband had written to the paper. He could not control what she did: it was out of his hands. He said that the least his governors would expect him to do was to write a letter of complaint to the Director of Education about our lack of control, and he made the incident more public by sending copies to the education spokesmen for each political party. This obviously had the effect of increasing the pressure on me and I couldn't help the cynical thought that it might be related to his desire to be allocated time at a better pool. This strategy backfired somewhat, as a number of primary heads and politicians deplored his apparent acquiescence in involving the press. I wrote to all the schools using the pool, including the complaining Headteacher, assuring them of our continued support. I decided against sending copies to all and sundry. As I refused to agree to provide additional supervision for any one school, that school decided not to use the pool again.

Another incident in this half term concerned a local shopkeeper and three Year 11 boys. He rang to say they were abusing him and affecting his trade. I sent for them and they arrived in my office, truculent and resentful, convinced they would be blamed. Their version of events was different from his. According to them, one of them had worked for the shop, but left after a disagreement over pay. Since then, they said, the shopkeeper had regularly shouted at them as they passed, accusing them of harassing his customers (who as far as I could gather were mainly their friends and neighbours). They were convinced the shopkeeper would be believed rather than them, but I felt their story had the ring of truth and that they had probably been more sinned against than sinning. 'Walk away from confrontations,' I told them, 'and I'll put in a good word for you with the police.' I talked to PC Dickson the next day and found he had reached the same conclusion and given them the same advice. They kept out of trouble for the rest of the year, and I think they were impressed by the way that both Gordon Dickson and I had dealt with them. There were no more complaints from the shopkeeper.

It was two steps forward and one step back. After a week of good behaviour, someone set fire to the toilet paper in the girls' toilets while I was at a meeting at Rastrick. The plastic holders caused the most atrocious smell and thick smoke. By the time I returned Anna had called the fire brigade, who had extinguished the minor blaze. Anna led assemblies for all the year groups. Rather than berating them, she emphasized how very disappointed we were. Although a number of the staff clearly expected us to scream and shout, the 'I'm unbelievably hurt that you've let me down' routine was obviously the one to use. Anna knew it and so did I, but some staff still found it hard to vary their reactions.

By now we had agreed the broad outline of the capital investment programme. I had had a love-hate relationship with the LEA's architects since a sports hall planned for Rastrick had been replaced by a gym in order to save £20,000 and the cost of a car park. Ultimately the gym, without a car park, had cost considerably more than the estimate for the sports hall. This led me to emphasize that the specification should be designed to provide value for money and not include 'Rolls Royce' elements that pushed up the price (and the commission earned by the architects' department) leading to more important elements being cut to save money. However, since my previous experience things seemed to have changed: much more effort was made to involve the school in decisions concerning building work, and Susan Julian, the Education Department officer involved, was keen to ensure that any savings should be re-allocated to improve the overall school facilities. Together we established a constructive relationship with the architect, to whom we explained our priorities.

One of the constant irritants between the school and its neighbours was the way pupils took short-cuts through the gardens bordering the school site. A number of elderly people lived in some of the houses and most of the complaints came from them; schoolchildren and old people rarely mix comfortably. On one of my first days at the school early in November, Peter Bartle and I had walked around the boundary of the site to gauge the extent of the problem. One side was virtually unfenced, and where there was fencing, it was broken or easy to climb over. We were challenged by one of the school's neighbours, who lobbied us at length about the problems he and the other nearby residents suffered.

When we told him we were planning to build a fence, he replied that unless we could promise to have it erected within a week he would go to the newspapers. 'I know some people are expecting me to achieve miracles,' I replied, 'but there's absolutely no way a new fence will be completed before the end of January.' He went off muttering that nothing would change.

Susan persuaded the architects to pull out all the stops and finish the fence before the end of January. With its construction, many of the niggling problems with the neighbours disappeared. It also provided improved security, especially after we extended it to provide a barrier the full length of one side of the school site. However, the fence did not provide total security, and each weekend we had broken windows and attempted break-ins. Although the cost of repairing windows had to be met from the school budget, all the repairs had to be undertaken by the LEA contractors, who were not exactly prompt – until eventually I threatened to bring in private contractors, and things speeded up. Apart from looking unsightly, the damage was a constant reminder to the anti-social elements in the community that breaking windows was fun.

Meanwhile the initiative of introducing the Global learning system (the OILS initiative) was well under way. The staff involved were enthusiastic. Maggie Binns, the teacher in charge of the project, was worried that the less able were using the software at the same time as the more able pupils would be studying French. This meant the original scope of the initiative would be restricted, as not all the pupils would be able to participate equally as we had originally planned. Eventually we chose to encourage the use of the French modules with the more able classes but held to our central strategy of putting the initial effort into literacy for pupils in Years 7–9. We also sought to enhance maths: Peter Root, the Head of Maths, who was keen to learn more, visited a school in the Midlands which had pioneered ways of using the system, especially with GCSE students. As a result, he later introduced it to Year 11 students as part of an intensive revision programme.

Anna organized a staff meeting on SEN, presented by the staff involved. I was extremely pleased that individual members of staff were confident enough to demonstrate their particular skills, and all the issues were discussed in a positive manner. I sat next to Mike Vigures, the Educational Psychologist in charge of the Behaviour Support Team.

We looked through the names on the SEN register: it was clear that some pupils were not in the most appropriate categories, and we needed to reconsider the whole list very carefully. 'What's delaying the start of the Corrective Reading programme?' I asked a member of the LEA support staff. His defensive attitude gave me the impression that unnecessary difficulties were being allowed to hinder the start of the work. His team appeared reluctant to support the school in the development of the programmes, and consequently the required materials had not been obtained. I was unsure who was responsible for the delay – school or LEA – but it seemed that everyone was waiting for someone else. 'This is ridiculous,' I said. 'Forget the LEA, let's do it ourselves.' So we set up three groups: two for the poorest readers in Year 7 and one for those in Year 8. The materials were quickly acquired, and the groups started shortly afterwards, leaving us once again wondering why we had to rely on our own devices when additional support should have helped us improve the situation earlier.

With the OILS hardware and software to be installed shortly, it became obvious that we needed extra supervision and support for other teachers taking classes into the room. Although staff wanted to achieve the aims and anticipated benefits, not all were totally confident taking their classes into a computer room, and time constraints meant that formal training had to be restricted to those using the system the most. I approached Lynne Sharp, who was a science technician as well as a parent governor and a strong supporter of the school. She was keen to develop her role in the school and take on greater responsibility. I asked her if she would be prepared to change roles completely by assuming responsibility for the OILS room. Jo Clark, Head of Science, was understandably unhappy to lose Lynne. However, we reached a compromise which ensured sufficient hours of laboratory support, and Lynne changed roles. The OILS staff training went well, and we planned to put the first classes through the new programme after February half term.

Whilst all this was going on we had our first monthly inspection of the term. I wanted to use these regular inspections to our advantage and had asked Kath Cross to focus on Humanities, the curriculum area that I felt to be the weakest, and which had been severely criticized in the Ofsted report. She arranged to bring a colleague who was a humanities specialist, and I hoped this would concentrate the minds of the staff.

After the visit, the inspectors' feedback to Peter Bartle, Stan Brown, Anna and me was very positive. Although only 50 per cent of lessons seen were satisfactory, not on the face of it an improvement on the Ofsted report that 'less than 3/5 were satisfactory', the majority of the sub-standard lessons were in the targeted subject area. The criticisms of poor planning, classroom management, pace and challenge were fair and predictable – and the strategy of our Action Plan was to address these deficiencies – but the inspectors were impressed with the improvements to the overall level of school discipline. They considered that we had made sufficient progress to 'tick off' Key Issue 1, the restoration of discipline, and recommended that we should concentrate on other issues – especially the variable quality of classroom management and improvements in children's learning. We were on our way: one Key Issue down, seven to go.

16

CRITICAL FRIENDS

The media seem to feature a 'political theme of the week'. In the second week of term, the theme was the importance of setting homework, as I discovered after being interviewed, with Professor Michael Barber, by James Naughtie on Monday's *Today* programme. Apparently, schools that set homework had a better work ethic and set higher expectations for their pupils than those that didn't – a revelation! This theme, as far as Calderdale secondary headteachers were concerned, was reflected in the questionnaire issued by Ofsted as part of the inspection Gillian Shephard had 'persuaded' the LEA to accept. Listening to my colleagues at the CASH meeting that afternoon, I discovered that Ofsted, as well as looking at the LEA's procedures and policies, had decided that they should run 'mini-inspections' of a selection of schools (which did not include the Ridings). Some Heads felt they were being put through an inspection for purely political reasons; others thought that the LEA had deliberately over-emphasized the importance of the individual school inspections in an effort to shift the focus away from themselves, hoping that the schools would turn their resentment on Ofsted and not voice their many criticisms of the authority. Whilst the argument continued, my interest turned to the statistics prepared for the inspectors by the LEA, which seemed to identify Rastrick as the best school in the area. (Mind you, I was biased.) I looked at Paul Armitage, the Acting Head of Rastrick, sitting across the room and I am ashamed to say we exchanged satisfied smiles.

When Ofsted reviewed the LEA, they found no fewer than 14 sub-committees and nearly as many working parties. This multiplicity had arisen because Calderdale councillors were always keen to be involved in decisions as much as possible, rather than delegating management to professional officers or schools; they justified this by saying that they were accountable to the electors and the democratic process. The result was that, over the years, they had formed sub-committees and working parties, which met every six weeks (often, it seemed, merely to defer decisions until they met again), all requiring a high level of support from professional officers, who were taken away from more productive duties. This reluctance to delegate meant decisions were made very slowly – when they were made at all.

It was no surprise, therefore, that when finance and personnel at the school were put into LEA control under special measures, a special Ridings sub-committee was formed to oversee these functions and to decide at which point the powers could be delegated back to the governors. Fortunately, Ian Jennings managed to get the majority of powers given up by the governors handed over to him (although the councillors retained the power to appoint the new Headteacher, and later the new Deputy Head). This meant we could react faster to filling vacancies and making spending decisions. As the officers knew their judgements would not be arbitrarily overturned, the Liaison Group, (two governors, two officers, Anna and myself, as Peter Bartle and I had suggested for inclusion in the LEA Action Plan) was able to act as a 'filter' between the Education Committee and the Ridings governors.

Later that week we had a visit from Graham Lane, Chairman of the Association of Metropolitan Authorities Education Committee. I was impressed by his perceptive questions and observations. Peter Flower and Ian Jennings also came, together with Michael Higgins and Helen Rivron as Chairman and Deputy Chair of Education. Graham Lane's comments seemed to put the Calderdale politicians slightly on the defensive, and when he mentioned the exclusions incident, he gave the impression that he was critical of the way the LEA had handled the situation. I was pleased by the visit: I had mentioned to Michael several times that it would be useful if he visited during the day to see our progress. He told me he had found the atmosphere threatening on his previous visits, but now it felt very much better.

The Calderdale politicians were most interested in how David Helliwell had conducted himself at the governors' meeting the previous evening. I told them that I had been fascinated by his attitude. 'He made a point of contributing to every item on the agenda, complaining that he had not been given sufficient appropriate information about the governors or the school, making extremely disparaging comments about the acumen of councillors, and pointing out the obvious, like there was "an urgent need to recruit more kids",' I observed. 'He seemed to be trying to convey the impression that, as he was so knowledgeable and experienced, with him around everything would now be OK. It reminded me of an animal marking out its territory.' They advised me to 'channel his energies and use his strengths', which was all very well, but they had few suggestions on how this could be easily and constructively achieved.

We discussed the pressure from the media and their potential future interest. The councillors felt that two crucial events would be the publication of the Ofsted report on the LEA and the appointment of a permanent Headteacher. They were concerned that journalists might send for application packs and attempt to use the information for candidates as part of the continuing news story. I felt this was a bit far-fetched but, as it turned out, the publicity surrounding the appointment of the new head was handled very badly.

In an interesting aside, Graham Lane told me that Gillian Shephard was concerned for us to know that the 'hard-edged' press conference had not been her idea. He felt she had been told what to say by Conservative Central Office, and I was almost sure he was passing on a genuine message. One of the most important insights I have gained into politics over the years has been that politicians are franker with their political opponents than with members of their own party. I once sat next to a pair of local Labour and Conservative leaders on a train and heard them tear strips off their political allies and promise each other favours to keep their parties in line. I was sure their relationship was very different in the Council Chamber. At one point, noticing that I was listening, one asked me, 'You're not one of our voters, are you?' and when I said no, they said, 'That's all right, then,' and carried on.

Our visitors went off to discuss the wider political problems facing Calderdale Council and its Ofsted inspection, but I wasn't surprised when Ian rang the next day to inquire whether Anna would accept the headship on a one-year temporary basis. 'I'm not sure,' I replied. 'You need to talk to her. But why not offer her the job without strings?' I agreed to discuss it with her and he arranged to see her later that day. Anna spent a lot of time thinking it through. As Acting Head she would provide continuity and be in a strong position to get the job when it was eventually advertised, but she was concerned that a temporary position might not give the solid footing necessary to deal with the difficult issues – both inside and outside the school. In the end the offer was withdrawn because no agreement could be reached with her employer, the governing body of Todmorden High School, but the proposal concentrated Anna's thinking. I knew she would go for the job when the time came.

That week, the Liaison Group had its first meeting. We agreed to a new staffing structure, based on some ideas that Anna had worked out to form a number of faculties and reward the staff working in the pastoral system. Although it created additional responsibility posts, it reduced the cost to Calderdale of protecting the salary levels of staff in their previous schools and provided a far more coherent structure for the school. I agreed to cost it, including predictions of future numbers. In order to convince potential parents that the school was an acceptable option, we had to assure them that their children would not be faced with a restricted curriculum taught by non-specialist teachers. The main advantage of the LEA removing financial management from the governors was that the Council was no longer funding the school solely according to a formula based on pupil numbers. They could therefore subsidize the school so that it could offer the minimum curriculum that would attract parents; my job was to calculate the size of subsidy necessary.

But not everything was progressing: the governors were still not functioning as an effective unit, and this first Liaison Group meeting took place without any governors as it was as yet unclear which would attend. The Key Issue on which we had made least progress was the efficiency of the governing body, but it was difficult to see how to make any real improvement without their agreement that a problem actually existed. Stan Brown had agreed with my basic ideas for organizing the committee structure into three groups – one for curriculum, a second for pastoral and community and a third for finance and personnel matters – but, as he was likely to be moved to another parish, he intended to resign in the summer. Stan, a very fair man who tried to balance the conflicting forces present within the governors, had taken over at short notice when the previous chairman had resigned just before the crisis broke. 'It's very important,' I said, 'that his successor is someone who is neutral and has the confidence of the majority of the governors to work for the good of the school. Then we can isolate the mavericks and make swifter progress.'

Although many aspects of school management are the responsibility of the governing body, the headteacher is directly accountable for many others and, in practice, the governors have to rely on the head and senior staff to oversee much of their remit. To be effective, therefore, headteachers and governors need to develop relationships based on mutual trust. To use the phrase from the training manual, governors should act as 'critical friends'. The Ridings governors at this time could be divided into two groups: those who were critical and those who were friends. The majority were very keen to support the school and our work, but were often unsure of how to make a helpful contribution, especially as the governing body had operated without a clear framework within which to develop their skills and give their full experience and expertise. Jill Wilson, one of the two new LEA governors, could be characterized as a friend: she was very enthusiastic about her role and volunteered for her building firm to construct and fit the furniture in our new OILS room free. I learned that she had also been lobbying on our behalf for additional resources and expertise from the Training Enterprise Council.

Those who were critical, on the other hand, were typified by the other LEA governor, David Helliwell. He had been involved with many of the decisions taken by the Education Committee in previous years. When he visited, we spent two hours touring the school as he held forth on his educational philosophy, which was critical of teachers and the fact that schools were no longer so tightly controlled by local authorities. He was not impressed when a teacher who brought a pupil out into the corridor to be told off moderated his tone as we approached. 'See, we stopped that poor boy being unjustly treated by that teacher,' was his attitude, rather than acknowledging that disciplinary issues were being dealt with when they arose. As we went round the school, he saw the relative calm as evidence that nothing had really needed to be done – although he reminded me that he had, of course, always said that the amalgamation of the two schools would cause problems.

He was violently opposed to my initial exclusion of the pupils and asserted that my actions had infringed their right to be educated. He told me that he had made a group working for the rights of children 'aware of all the circumstances', in the hope that they could persuade the parents involved to re-open the cases. I tried to explain that all children had the right to be educated and with the previous levels of disruption that was impossible. When he described me as 'just a Benthamite' (following the Victorian economist's philosophy of the 'greatest good to the greatest number'), I had to disappoint him by taking it as a compliment.

He also gave me the full benefit of his views on the limitations of governors in general, and ours specifically. For example, he was against members of the police or the clergy being governors – being authority figures made them unsuitable: it would be better to seek representation from NHS Trusts and Health Authorities, whom he regarded as more representative of the community. He deeply regretted the changes which had resulted in the loss of power to the LEA, but was scathing about the current policies of the LEA and the role played by those councillors who were governors. 'Local management has resulted in far more effective schools,' I responded, 'especially if governors and headteachers base their relationships on common sense. After all, it's unrealistic for governors to manage at a day-to-day level.' He took this as an indication that I wanted the governors to be puppets. His view was that it was good to argue issues out, 'but most adults are afraid of argument, so consensus is the easy way out.' As he left, I felt my attempts to 'channel his energies' had not been entirely successful.

The governors' meeting on Wednesday 12 February was a shambles. We presented an anti-bullying policy in an attempt to encourage staff to take seriously any problems reported to them and to deal with them in ways that helped build up the confidence of the pupils in difficulties. We wanted to reinforce our positive behaviour policy, emphasizing the importance of respect for others and encouraging children to look after their friends by reporting problems rather than taking the law into their own hands. Neither Anna nor I even considered that such a view might be controversial. It was one of our standard 'off-the-peg' policies which reflected current best practice. Yet two governors decided to pick it to pieces, one because it was not 'legalistic' enough, another because it failed to identify teachers as the group within schools most likely to be bullies.

In his desire to promote argument as a spur to good decision-making, David Helliwell continually repeated his point of view and scorned those with the temerity to disagree, with the unfortunate result that he monopolized the debate. At one point someone said to him: 'But you're acting like a bully!' and we all held our breath. The moment passed without any reaction. Another governor, who had spent a great deal of time telling me what a wonderful job I was doing, whispered to him, 'He thinks he's still in a grant-maintained school.'

It got worse. He repeated everything said in the previous meeting, making considerable capital out of the minutes, when we all knew the way meetings were structured and minuted needed to be improved. He also complained that, as a new governor, he had had insufficient information about school policies – this was in fact true for all of us, as we were still writing them. A group of other governors reacted by proposing motions and amendments, and I could see looks of bemusement on the faces of the newly elected parent governors as the meeting lost all sense of direction and purpose. I asked six times during the meeting who was to write the Annual Governors' Report for Parents, but I got no answer. At one point I said exasperatedly, 'You're the only group in danger of missing your Action Plan objectives. Everyone else is busting their guts to fulfil their targets, and you should be leading them.'

By the time we came to deciding which three governors would participate in the appointment of the Head and Deputy Head, I was totally brassed off and determined that the panel was going to be focused on finding the best candidates, and nothing else. Initially only three governors volunteered, including Stan as Chairman. I mouthed to Jill Wilson to volunteer as well. Anne McAuley, a parent governor, asked, 'Can parents be part of the panel?' 'Of course,' I said. We therefore had to have a vote and when Jill, Anne and Stan were elected by a large majority I knew the attitude of the minority had backfired on them. The next morning Jill Wilson arrived with a massive box of Thornton's chocolates for Anna and me. 'That was awful,' she said. 'You deserve a treat.'

Later in the week came the second inspection of the term. We were constantly reinforcing the importance of getting the nitty-gritty right and had agreed with the staff a consistent approach to basic classroom rules across the whole school. The visit went well. The inspectors were impressed by the changes and, as the staff had responded positively to the past criticisms, about 80 per cent of the lessons were satisfactory or better, compared with the figure of less than 50 per cent a month previously. All our objectives were on target. This achievement, coupled with the fact that the first two reports from the teaching audit were both grade 1s – the highest grade – provided a fillip after the depression induced by the governors' meeting.

However, improving the effectiveness of the governing body was a Key Issue. At the feedback session I described the last governors' meeting to the inspectors, sparing nothing in telling them what a negative effect the confrontational nature of the debate had had on the majority of the governors, who felt excluded from making a contribution. Kath Cross asked Stan for corroboration, and he agreed it had been one of the worst governors' meetings he had ever attended. As a result, the inspection report included a very clear comment that the governors should work to support the school. Quite what else they might think they should be doing was beyond me.

17

CHANGING ATTITUDES INSIDE AND OUT

Staffing problems became more pressing this term. Although the new timetable had reduced the number of staff needed, we still required teachers for RE and English. There had been little interest in our advertisements, and the one or two possible candidates had not relished the trial day – or, in one case, hour – of supply work I had offered them in December, so I offered the job to someone who had just retired. This was not a resounding success.

I had clearly explained the difficulties before she started, but perhaps the reality was more daunting and there seemed to be something to complain about almost daily. Admittedly, she had a point in many of her criticisms: there was a lack of modern RE text books, the children could be difficult, and she was unsure who was in her classes. But all the classes had been re-scheduled, and we just had to make allowances for the fact that no one left at the school knew exactly where all the RE resources were or had been responsible for keeping them up-to-date. She did not seem to appreciate the help of other teachers in sorting out her disciplinary problems. The final straw came when she tore a strip off a support assistant who was helping control some of the children in her class. We agreed it would be best if she left.

So I still had the problem of ensuring that the GCSE group was taught by an RE specialist who knew the syllabus. My attempt to buy in the services of a departing RE teacher from his new school broke down when his timetable was changed at the last minute. We tried a number of supply staff, but they tended to cause more problems than they solved because they were unable to control their classes effectively. Peter Colyer, the Deputy Head at Brooksbank, came to the rescue, volunteering to oversee pupils' work and teach half the lessons, whilst Jeanette persuaded other staff to take over the other classes temporarily. Things eventually calmed down in February when Beryl Pickvance, the wife of a previous Chief Education Officer and a retired deputy head, was persuaded to take the classes for a time. A larger-than-life character and an excellent teacher, she coped magnificently. Fortunately, after she left Jeanette found a suitable teacher through an agency.

Not all the staffing was problematic. Hilary Heggarty threw herself enthusiastically into supporting the drama groups and teaching English. Some of the children were difficult, but most responded well to the many staff who showed they were interested in them as individuals. Strong and positive relationships were being built between some pupils and staff, even though – or perhaps because – all of us felt pretty insecure at times; pupils continually asked new staff, 'Are *you* staying?'

Those staff who failed to recognize and participate in the growing corporate spirit, gradually became more and more isolated. They were still locked into the attitudes that had characterized the battles with Karen, or lacked the common sense to appreciate the realities of the situation. Some were simply resistant to change, however positive. Shortly after the start of term, Brian Garvey, the regional NASUWT representative, arrived to voice the concerns of some of his members: 'Discipline is getting worse. We'll soon be back to the old days. We need to exclude more pupils.' However, when he met with his members, the complainers were outweighed by the majority of the staff. By now everyone had had the opportunity to decide whether to be part of the solution or part of the problem, and I knew which staff were supportive and which needed to be encouraged to leave.

One who continued to play the old game was the teacher I had had to nudge gently – to no effect – before Christmas. He referred every problem either to me or more usually to Anna, because I think he saw her as soft touch – after all, she was a woman! He discovered his mistake there very quickly and this lesson was reinforced when two of his female colleagues informed him that some of his year group were misbehaving in a lesson. He refused to move from the staff room to deal with the problem, saying 'Someone else can sort it out,' – meaning Anna or me. They told him what they thought of him and went to deal with the pupils themselves. When I heard this, I knew we had broken out of the characteristic failing school philosophy of: 'Walk away, it's not your problem.'

It was time to tackle this teacher about his attitude. I feel it is important to give people a chance to respond to the velvet glove treatment. 'You've got to fulfil your responsibilities properly – and not refer them to others until you've really tried to sort them out. Then you can follow the procedure and refer children to the Head of School,' I told him. He responded by identifying one particular pupil whose behaviour was very difficult to handle. 'I'm not suggesting you can never pass issues on. Obviously sometimes you'll run out of options, but you must have a go, in order to be seen as credible in the eyes of your colleagues and the students.'

The following week he sent an abrupt memo to Anna and me concerning a fairly trivial issue involving the child we had discussed, and which he should have dealt with himself or, at most, referred to the Head of Lower School. It got to Anna first, and she summoned him and told him exactly what was what. He continued to refer issues like this, but on each occasion we pushed back the problems he wanted to evade, to make him work within the system. Eventually, faced with a combination of this pressure, his increasingly isolated position and the dwindling numbers belonging to the 'anti-Karen clique', as well as the impending teaching audit, he went on long-term sick leave and decided to leave teaching. I was pleased that my strategy was working: support all those who were prepared to commit themselves to the future of the school and work to overcome their difficulties, and isolate those who continued to give second best.

I closed the school early on the afternoon of Friday 31 January, because many of the staff and older students wished to attend the funeral of Sue Buxton. Sue had been Head of Modern Languages, but had been fighting cancer for some time and had retired due to ill-health the previous year. I never heard anyone say a bad word about her: she was an extremely effective and caring teacher who had excellent relationships with pupils and colleagues, and her illness and untimely death were a severe loss to the school. The packed church contained many familiar faces, including Pauline Nicel, the former Head of Ovenden, and Karen Stansfield. Both of them spoke appreciatively of our efforts for the students and staff. I found Karen surprisingly unaffected by the turmoil of her experience, talking optimistically about the future.

Then the Head of Design Technology resigned unexpectedly to take a job as a car retailer and commit more time to his business interests. He asked to leave before the normal resignation date and I agreed. As a temporary measure Karen Dean, the very capable teacher in charge of textiles, agreed to act as Head of Department. This meant we now had another vacancy to add to the four jobs we needed to fill urgently: Co-ordinator for Special Educational Needs, Head of Modern Languages, plus two people to lead a combination of Humanities/History or Religious Studies, and now Head of Design Technology.

In normal circumstances we would have proceeded with advertising the posts as a matter of course, but the LEA had control of personnel matters. Ian Jennings agreed in principle to my staffing analysis, but he was worried about the cost. I was exasperated: we had to advertise the jobs urgently to get replacements who could start after Easter, or we would be stuck with temporary staff until September. 'Why can't we proceed?' I demanded. 'All these jobs are covered by resignations and the cost is included in the basic staffing budget. Whether or not we get a subsidy these are key staff, essential to any school. If at every stage difficulties are put in our way, we've got to question the commitment of the LEA to keep the school open as a viable institution. Unless they recognize the urgency of the situation and the need to put more money in, they should announce its immediate closure and stop wasting everyone's time.' The advertisements were cleared the next day.

Ian and Clem Rushworth (Assistant Director for Finance) arrived on Friday 7 February to discuss money and, after fairly amicable negotiation, agreed which payments should be the responsibility of the LEA and which should come out of the school budget. According to my figures from the staffing/curriculum analysis I estimated the maximum subsidy for the 1996/7 financial year to be about £200,000 and another £250,000 the following year. Ian and Clem agreed to ask the Education Committee for the initial amount as well as for a longer-term commitment to support the school until pupil numbers rose far enough for the formula-funded income to cover the expenditure.

About this time I won another battle with the LEA. The law gives parents the right to choose a school for their children, but in practice this is limited to a choice between those schools with vacancies. Many children change schools for sensible reasons, but sometimes the decision to move can be linked to behavioural problems: it may be the result of an exclusion or a disagreement over how the school has dealt with a problem, or because the child has been put into care. Karen had had no alternative but to take a number of such cases to fill vacant places, but I did not want to be forced into a similar situation. In fact, I feel very strongly that schools under special measures should be 'ring-fenced' so they can concentrate on raising the standards for the children already at the school and those who transfer from primary schools. 'It's unfair that we should have to add to our problems by taking so many pupils who have been excluded from other schools. Let us get our own problems sorted out before giving us other schools' failures,' I complained bitterly. 'Children with learning and behavioural problems should be diverted to other schools – or better still, it's about time you provided properly for them in the LEA.' The LEA agreed, but this issue was to cause constant friction, because very little provision existed within Calderdale for older, more disaffected students.

We reported the findings of our first monthly inspection – that we could tick off Key Issue 1 – to the Heads of Department who formed the newly established Curriculum Planning Group, and repeated them to the weekly staff meeting held the next day after school. It was a boost to everyone to realize that all the hard work had been rewarded with a marked improvement in the percentage of satisfactory lessons. Previously Anna and I had dominated the staff meetings, explaining, exhorting, enthusing; in contrast, this meeting generated genuine discussion, which I was pleased to witness – it was clear that the majority of the staff felt actively involved. When one member of staff queried the commitment and competence of some of the staff, implying that a few were carrying the rest, others disagreed, saying, 'Of course we're supporting each other, that's why it's better than before,' and 'It's nonsense to think that any one person has all the answers to every situation.' Anna and I encouraged the debate and, faced with this reaction, he began to back off and changed tack, becoming more supportive. He later told me that he had raised the issue to assist us by highlighting the problem of inadequate teachers. But as well as the truly inadequate, he was including those *he felt* were inadequate – not necessarily the same thing, and dangerously close to restarting the old rivalries. The reaction of the staff was another indication of the growing corporate spirit and improving morale: we were also achieving Key Issue 8.

External publicity was also important to the self-image of both staff and pupils. Towards the end of January, Joan Williams, who was running the project for difficult younger pupils based in the Furness Youth Centre, had attended the pantomime at the Bradford Alhambra, *Aladdin*, starring Frank Bruno. Each performance had a reference to the Ridings: 'You're thick – you must go to the Ridings!' or 'He's not very well-behaved. Where does he go to school? The Ridings.' Other parents and teachers who saw the show grinned and bore it; Joan, who had thrown herself into the project enthusiastically, with that mixture of dedicated care and cynicism which is so often the hallmark of truly effective teachers working with difficult children, did not. She sought out Frank's manager and spoke her mind. As a result, Frank Bruno offered to visit the kids at the Furness project.

The Furness Youth Centre is a dismal, steel-shuttered building, about a mile from the school site, covered in graffiti, in the middle of a patchy grassed area on a windswept council estate. Joan wanted the maximum publicity for her charges, so together we wrote a press release and sent it to the local television companies and newspapers. On the day, Joan and her staff managed the massed media beautifully, keeping them from being too intrusive. Frank was very good with the youngsters, friendly and encouraging: he told them, 'I wasted my time at school and I regret it now. You do as your teachers tell you – education is important'. He was the larger-than-life character he always seems when interviewed on television, greeting me with, 'I've seen you on telly.' 'But I've seen *you* on the telly,' I replied. Before he got involved with the press, he made sure he gave his attention to the kids, who were overwhelmed by his presence. By the time we left the centre to visit the school we were running late, and Frank's manager was worried that he would be delayed for his next appointment. But I couldn't go back on my assurance to Anna that I would get him to visit the school. We left the Youth Centre in a taxi, followed by the press pack, and after a couple of hundred yards were 'ambushed' by a group of obviously excited blokes. Although friendly and at ease with the kids, he became a bit uncomfortable with this level of attention at such close quarters. 'Oh man!' he exclaimed, 'Stop. Give me the photos.' The car stopped and Frank hastily thrust a wodge of pre-signed publicity photographs out of the window and, with their good wishes ringing in our ears, we resumed our short journey to the school.

Unfortunately we arrived at the beginning of break: to reduce the potential for chaos, the plan had been to give Frank a quick tour of the school whilst the pupils were in lessons. Now the lobby was packed with press and children, all wanting pictures or autographs. Jenny Baker, Head of Art, was anxious for her Sixth Formers to interview him with the Sky video camera, but it was impossible in the middle of the scrum that developed. I told her to go into the hall and then manoeuvred Frank out of the lobby and into the hall, where they interviewed him with professional aplomb.

After the school interviews, we went out onto the steps. Anna had learned a lesson some weeks previously, when the *News of the World* had taken a picture of the two of us with a Year 11 boy who had signed to play rugby for Wigan and, much to her chagrin, she had been cropped out. This time, as we posed one each side of Frank, she made sure he had his arms on her shoulders as well as mine. Dozens of photographs and a couple of television interviews later, Frank and his entourage left and the school went about its business. 'Do as your teachers tell you, get the most out of school' was the message Frank gave to our students. It made the headlines later that evening and in the next morning's papers. The youngsters, whose need for attention so often resulted in negative, anti-social behaviour, had been rewarded for their efforts. Frank followed up the visit with complimentary tickets to the panto for the Furness Centre pupils. The kids who attended were overawed: they had never seen anything like it before and sat transfixed, their eyes popping out on stalks. They visited his dressing room afterwards and he gave them a ride around Bradford city centre in his Rolls Royce, which utterly thrilled them.

In the midst of all this positive action, I had some personal sadness. Carol and I had been regularly visiting my aunt Joan, in hospital in Manchester, Carol driving while I worked on a laptop. Joan had been a nursery nurse for many years and was quite excited by all the publicity concerning me and my fame at the Ridings. She was so ill that I missed school on Friday morning to visit her; it was the last time that she recognized me, and she died on the Sunday.

We needed publicity, not only to improve morale, but to change the school's image. The Ridings was the first preference for the parents of just 33 children starting in September 1997. Such a low number would be educationally and financially catastrophic, requiring a much bigger subsidy than I had predicted. The future looked bleak: not only would low numbers restrict the curriculum to unacceptable levels and not generate sufficient revenue to make the school financially viable, but such a small intake would send all the wrong signals to local parents, leading them to lose faith that the school had a future. Without an intake of around 90 we would be in very serious trouble. Positive publicity would help persuade parents to trust us with their children, but the only current media interest was from Radio Humberside (because their LEA had four failing schools) and Radio Essex, because I had attended Essex University, whereas we had to generate coverage which would be seen in Calderdale.

Right on cue, GMTV contacted us, keen to feature the school in an extensive news item. I decided to use it as an opportunity to 'sell' the school. At the same time a daytime Channel 4 programme was eager to do a report on how the school had progressed in the few months since the crisis. Both crews arrived on Monday 3 February. Channel 4 went on to Calderdale College to film one of the excluded pupils who was successfully following a building course: I found out when Garry Bate, the Principal, rang me to check if it was all right. I was slightly surprised that the exclusions topic was still newsworthy, but I felt on balance the school would be seen in a good light: the boy was enjoying the course, so they would not get him to say anything particularly controversial, however hard they tried. After filming most of Monday, GMTV arranged to return the next morning. They wanted to produce a live programme from the school: would I be available from 6.30a.m.? I groaned. I hate getting up early.

It was dark and raining when I arrived next morning. Barbara and George, the assistant caretakers, had volunteered to get up even earlier than usual to open up for the crew. I was to be interviewed soon after the start of the programme, followed by a longer discussion with two members of staff and a parent and a child. I had asked Jenny Baker as Head of Art, Dave Robinson as Head of Year 10, and Lynne Sharp and her daughter, Amy – a very articulate Year 10 student – to take part. By now I had every confidence that my colleagues would cope well with any media situation.

There were about half a dozen in the crew, including two cameramen and the reporter, Duncan Woods. He was eager to make the item interesting. 'Reporter involvement, that's what they want,' he told me with a grin, throwing himself into the whole affair with considerable enthusiasm. My live interview was fairly straightforward, and led into a studio discussion with Nigel de Gruchy. With the 'trail' out of the way, we moved on to the main phase. Duncan planned to start on the steps to introduce the item, cut to some of the film and interviews obtained the previous day, and then interview Jenny walking down the corridor to the library, where Dave, Lynne and Amy were waiting. To round it off, I would again be interviewed by someone from the studio.

By now I had got quite used to the sound coming to me in an ear-piece, and I knew that in these situations one talks straight to the camera; when interviewed by journalists standing next to the camera, one looks at them. But it's still nerve-wracking. 'Who cares?' I thought. 'At this time in the morning, who's watching?' (The major trick is not to ask this question out loud, as the answer is usually 'millions'.) Unfortunately Jenny, who was not used to this rigmarole, had chosen her wardrobe with no regard to the problem of the radio microphone and had to disappear to fit it in privacy. On top of this, it was still pouring with rain and, as the cameras were all connected by heavy cables, there was a problem moving quickly from one location to another.

Despite the hiccups and the lack of rehearsal, it was a resounding success. What stays with me is the sound of the cables being pulled down the corridor, the cameramen bursting through the library door and catching me unawares, and the brilliance of my team. They spoke fluently and with conviction, answering the questions in an extremely positive manner. The piece lasted about 20 minutes in peak viewing time and it was seen, judging by the number of comments I received over the next few days, by the entire population of Calderdale.

The next day, a reporter from *Ruscoe on Five* spent hours in the school trying to find a chink in the united front. He seemed to have little experience of state schools, and was clearly expecting the 'school from Hell'. I took him round and introduced him to people whom he interviewed. He had just about admitted defeat when by chance I took him to the Art room at lunch time and we found some of the older students who had set up a fund-raising event, selling freshly baked scones with jam – complete with Vivaldi in the background: I took pity on him and let him go round on his own. Previously anyone with a microphone or a camera unaccompanied by a staff member would have been immediately surrounded by the worst-behaved children, but not now. He said to me later, 'Have you got them all brainwashed?'

Liz Meech from *Look North* had calculated that Thursday 13 February would mark our first 100 days, and came to record our progress. While we waited for her to arrive we heard that 108 new children had been allocated to the school for the coming academic year. Although two thirds had not put us as first preference, or even second, at least they were on our books and we had to do everything possible to persuade them to accept the places. After Liz had interviewed Anna and me in our new OILS base, she asked if she could question some of the pupils who were working on the machines in the background. I protested, 'But they don't know anything about it.' As the equipment had yet to be used in lessons, I had 'borrowed' the children from another class. She promised not to use anything embarrassing, so I let her continue. They did us proud. When she asked one boy, Greg, how he felt using the software he replied, 'Oh, it's so much better. You can work at your own pace and get help if you get things wrong.' He sounded as though he was fully familiar with every aspect of the course. Liz also wanted a shot of Anna walking, so we went to the lobby where two children were on the reception desk. Anna asked them if they had collected the registers and one replied without any prompting, 'Yes, and attendance is much better today.' I stopped holding my breath. The next day Liz's report was on all the local BBC news bulletins and Radio Leeds. I was interviewed on the Radio Leeds *Breakfast Show* and afterwards I heard them interview a parent, who said, 'My kids were suspended a lot before. Now, although they've been in trouble, it's been sorted out better and they get into less trouble.' The story was picked up by *Calendar*, the *Courier* and the *Yorkshire Post*; the front-page main headline of Friday's *Courier* was 'GIVE US A CHANCE, HEAD TELLS PARENTS'.

Our job advertisements were published in *The Times Educational Supplement* under our new mission statement, 'Together we can make the difference.' The same day, ITN arrived to interview us about the roles and the type of people we wanted to attract. They had driven up from Birmingham and were in a rush to get to Leeds to edit their piece. They wanted a shot of the advertisement, so I found myself on the pavement outside the school holding up a copy of the *TES* in the wind, so they could focus in on it. The interview appeared on the national news bulletins and had splendid coverage on *Calendar* that night. The *Guardian* talked to us, and the *Independent* featured an impressive photo of Anna. I felt we were managing the media interest more effectively: a widely seen promotional video and our job advertisements broadcast on national television in one week – and all for free.

Two conversations with staff reinforced my belief that our 'open' policy in dealing with the media was correct. During one of the more high-profile days, I moaned to Jo Clark, Head of Science, 'Is this still all worthwhile?' and was instantly told, 'Yes. Go for it! We need all the good publicity we can get.' Later, I was talking to Peter Bartle, Anna, Stan and other governors in a pub after a meeting. I knew that some members of the LEA thought I was taking too much credit for the changes and I had been criticized by one governor for courting publicity. 'Should we cut it down?' I asked. Peter was adamant: 'No. One day they will understand that this has been a tremendously effective PR operation – even though it happened by accident!'

18

PARENTS AND GOVERNORS

The PR campaign continued into half-term. I had never realized there was a BBC radio studio in Huddersfield Town Hall until I was interviewed for Radio Essex on the Tuesday of half-term – apparently, as I had attended Essex University and my wife was from Colchester, I was regarded as a local celebrity. My son David accompanied me, and we were surprised to be led down into the cellar underneath the building. I was apprehensive when I heard that I would have to operate the equipment myself, especially when I read the long list of instructions from the producer. It gives some idea of the level of technology to say that the advice started, 'Turn on the cooker switch on the wall.' It went on to say that the technician at the other end of the line would ask me to press the 'divert button', but the 'divert button' did not exist. The headphones didn't work either, so David and I shared the phone in order to listen to the programme whilst I spoke into the microphone. Not quite the same league as national television coverage.

We were due to start the second half of term an hour late on Monday 24 February, in order to train the staff to use the *ears* computerized attendance system. A large number of pupils had extended their holiday to include the Friday before half-term, so they missed our newsletter which, amongst other things, informed them of this. As a result, and much to their disappointment, they arrived on time – sufficient punishment, I thought. However, that was the only hiccup in the training session. The *ears* system, with its portable keypads that transmitted and received data from a central computer, had been installed just before half-term. One of the electricians had commented, 'I thought this was a rough school. Compared to a lot of schools we work in, these kids are pretty well-behaved. The last school we were at, they stole all our tools!' Another example of the unfair press the majority of our children had received, and of our success in improving behaviour.

With half an hour's briefing under their belts, all the teachers returned to their classes clutching their brand new toys.

We needed to improve not only the attendance of pupils, but also that of their parents at Parents' Evenings, two of which were held in the first week after half term. Barely a third of all parents turned up to the Year 11 event on Tuesday to discuss their children's potential for the summer GCSE examinations. Attendance was even worse at the Thursday event for parents to meet Year 10 tutors – barely a quarter turned up and one teacher had her car's back window smashed. We strongly suspected this was retaliation by one Year 10 pupil whom she had had to discipline repeatedly during the previous few days. On the evening of the Monday, the very first day back from half-term, he had sneaked in and ripped posters off noticeboards as part of his long-standing campaign to irritate the caretakers. The next morning, in a display of bravado, he had smoked a cigarette in a corridor. His response to being punished was, 'You don't like me 'cos I'm famous!' – a reference to his prominent coverage in the *Sunday Times* during the height of the troubles, which referred to his large collection of condoms.

We were also making steady progress in recruiting pupils as a result of the school's gradually improving image. Although the figure for the September 1997 intake had dropped slightly, the numbers were still forecast at 90 – and holding. We had also admitted ten children since Christmas, and six more were due to look round over the next week. The two Chris's, Binns and Short, were doing sterling work to show the school in a positive light to prospective parents. As Head of Upper School, Chris Short's line was, 'Look, we're the most inspected school in the country. We *have* to make it work!' Chris Binns was having a noticeable effect on the pupils of the troublesome Year 7 since stepping in when their Head of Year went on sick leave.

Over four months had passed since the school had re-opened, and we had settled into a familiar pattern of work, managing the school and laying the foundations for its future development. Our main emphasis was to support the work of the classroom teacher, and Anna had drawn up a timetable for senior staff who could be instantly called upon to intervene on request. The *ears* pads had an alarm button, which sounded in the main office and identified on the computer screen the class, room and teacher requiring help.

Responding to these calls, I came to know a small proportion of the pupils – and the staff – quite well. One or two of the temporary staff felt the need to use this device quite frequently – so frequently, in some cases, that you were tempted not to go, or at least not to rush. However, teaching at the Ridings was not easy for the most experienced teachers, never mind the least skilled, and all efforts were essential to restoring order and routine.

That weekend, I took part in a Sunday morning programme on Radio 5 about school discipline. I had a 15-minute telephone discussion with Nigel de Gruchy and Zoe Redhead, from the 'progressive' independent school, Summerhill. I agreed with Nigel's points about local councillors interfering in exclusions, but Zoe Redhead was very keen to put the blame for all the troubles of the state sector on the fact that, in her view, pupils were kept rigidly under control. At Summerhill, children are famously 'free range', living in an environment that aims to encourage them to develop at their own rate and decide their own priorities for study. In contrast, she felt that our pupils were treated like 'battery hens', rigidly confined to school routine with an over-emphasis on classroom discipline and the National Curriculum, and unable to express their individuality. I found her attitude inflexible and dismissive of the dedicated work of teachers who consistently strive to encourage children to express their individuality in extremely positive and self-disciplined ways. She seemed to ignore the many significant successes of state education such as the improvements in examination performance at 16 and 18, the greater numbers entering Higher Education, and more staying in education longer, and the wider range of vocational opportunities available, simply because they did not conform to her views. I know little about private education, but can quite happily accept that some children, especially if they are bright and self-reliant, can flower in a 'take it or leave it' school atmosphere. However, in my experience most young people achieve more if they feel secure within a caring and disciplined structure, one that deals consistently and fairly with the day-to-day problems that occur in all schools. They respond to high expectations and rewards for their effort and achievement, and that was the culture we were working so hard to establish. It gave me no satisfaction to learn some months later that Summerhill had also failed to impress the Ofsted inspectors with their academic standards.

At the school itself, we had become accustomed to a three-to-four-week cycle of media visits. On the Tuesday after half-term, we had a visit from Julie Etchingham of *Newsround* on Children's BBC; I was very happy to allow this, as we were still working to maintain our high profile in order to attract good children, and keep those we had. Greg (the star from the earlier OILS interview) and his friend were superb, talking honestly and openly about the horrors of the previous situation and the vast improvements that had taken place. The piece was transmitted the following day with two additional slots in the BBC's *Breakfast News* magazine programme. These interviews in the classrooms were not particularly disruptive, and they had two important benefits: they helped to generate a feeling of pride amongst the pupils – a very different emotion from the dispirited feelings they had previously – and gave them a chance to tell their side of the story.

The good publicity had helped swell the numbers applying for the staffing vacancies. We took confidence from the series of interviews held that week to select staff. There were good short-lists for most of the posts, and over three days of intensive interviews we appointed Heads of Special Needs, Design Technology, Humanities and Religious Education, plus a teacher of Design Technology. One or two of the candidates seemed in awe of the situation, and others had not appreciated the difficulties; one was so anxious to withdraw that he hardly had time to finish his tour of the school. We were looking for commitment and potential, and were delighted to find that for some of the jobs we had real difficulty in choosing because of the quality of the candidates. Most importantly, with a new Head of French appointed early the following week, we could look forward to being fully staffed from Easter.

A reporter from the *Daily Express* contacted me. I gave him the standard treatment, saying, 'Come round and see for yourself,' and he arrived almost immediately. As I took him round, I could see he was very disappointed with the relatively calm, purposeful atmosphere. Unlike all the other journalists, he seemed determined to write a negative story. When I mentioned that I was head of a grant-maintained school, he sensed a sensational scoop, asking: 'Are you going to opt out?' 'No,' I answered, 'it would be totally inappropriate, especially as the LEA has committed so much in financial and other support.' He kept pushing me and to finish the conversation I said, 'Anyway, I'm leaving at the end of summer term, so there wouldn't be time to organize an opt-out.' He said in surprise, 'Oh, aren't you permanent then?'

All in all, it was apparent that he was poorly informed about the whole situation apart from his main interest – exclusions. He let slip that he had just been interviewing a girl whom I had temporarily excluded at the outset, and who was absent from school having been recently discharged from hospital after a miscarriage. Her boyfriend had been permanently excluded. 'She's told me that she wants another baby and doesn't want to come back to school,' he told me, 'although she says the school's much better now than before.' He said that the boyfriend, who had been placed at the local College of Further Education with two of his friends, was happy. I was tempted to ask him what the problem was if everyone was happy. I insisted, 'I'm not prepared to say anything about the exclusions other than that, in co-operation with the LEA, we've done our best to ensure that those pupils involved have been found acceptable, alternative provision.' He finally left.

Next day the girl's mother rang, and angrily told me how her daughter had been photographed by the newspaper without her permission. She was even more annoyed after I enlightened her about my conversation with the reporter. It transpired that some people had visited her to discuss her daughter's exclusion and had also visited the mother of the boyfriend for the same reason. Believing they had been sent by the Education Department, she had thought little about it. Now she was suspicious. I later checked with all the obvious sections and no one had any record or memory of such a visit. Anxious to stop the story, because she felt it would put her and her daughter in a poor light, the mother asked my advice as to what to do. Was it right for her 15-year-old daughter to be interviewed and photographed without her permission, and to be quoted about such a sensitive medical situation? I promised that I would try to help and rang the paper. Within half an hour the reporter rang me back, and I told him how upset the mother was and gave him her phone number. I bought the paper every morning for the next few days; fortunately the story never appeared.

I discovered that parents of other excluded children were also upset at the protracted press attention. I mentioned to a couple of governors my worries about how potentially disruptive this attention was. They agreed that the exclusions issue needed to be dropped. Without my knowledge and, supposedly in an effort to support me, one of them contacted a councillor to ask to her to 'drop a word in the ear' of David Helliwell, the governor who most wanted to see the issue re-opened. A week or so later I met him in the Education Department reception area. We made polite conversation as he accompanied me to Peter Flower's office where I was due to meet Peter, Stan Brown and Peter Bartle to select the longlist of candidates to be interviewed for the Deputy Headship. Once there, however, he launched into a diatribe about me misrepresenting him, asserting that I had said he had visited parents to get them to appeal against the exclusions, and that I had organized a press campaign to 'bounce' everyone into doing what I wanted: I had, apparently, even informed Radio Leeds that this meeting was taking place.

Everyone was flabbergasted. 'I've not told anyone that you've been to see parents or talked to the press, but someone certainly has been to see them,' I replied. 'You've made no secret of the fact that you think the exclusions were wrong and have consistently argued that the rights of individuals, however much their actions disrupt the work of others, transcend the rights of the majority. I've not put all the connections together as you state them – you have! What's more, I don't know anything about Radio Leeds saying we're meeting – I certainly didn't tell them.'

We argued round in circles. David Helliwell declared the LEA was trying to 'stitch up' the forthcoming appointment of the permanent Headteacher by drawing up the personnel specification too tightly: it was all a disgrace; he would organize a splinter group on the governing body who would dispute every issue. I managed not to ask him what difference this would make, as he disputed every issue anyway. Refusing to be mollified, he said he would go public to expose how I was manipulating everything. At this, Peter Flower became agitated, and explained pretty forcibly that going public would be counter-productive. Peter Bartle suggested that David should put all his complaints in a letter to me and then consider my reply. I told him that I regretted that we were still at odds and I was sorry if anything I had said had been misinterpreted: I would write to him outlining my position. This I later did and the matter was never mentioned again. He left saying that he was sure he would meet a 'frosty reception' the next day at the committee meetings. 'Not from me,' I told him.

The councillors had delivered a staffing subsidy of £250,000 and I had to justify on radio why we should get the money, explaining that the funds came from the Council's contingency reserves, not from the education budget available to other hard-pressed schools: this was new money. I added that it was necessary to keep the school open, as its closure would result in the influx of our 500 or so students into other local schools. Some time later I was asked in an interview for Radio 4's *PM* programme, 'If there had been no problem, would you have got an extra £250,000?', to which the only honest answer was, 'No'.

These questions would have been irrelevant if education were funded adequately, but too many schools in areas like Calderdale are under-funded and unable to serve their pupils effectively. Sometimes this is due to the extraordinary complexities of the Standard Spending Assessment, which determines the grant paid to local authorities by central government, and sometimes it results from the priorities decided at local level. The budgets for schools of similar sizes and organization can vary significantly – often by more than £200,000, depending on the LEA in which they are located. In addition, some LEAs attempt to exercise more central control over spending than others, reducing the 'pot' available to distribute to schools to spend directly on pupils. In a sensible world, the priority would be to finance schools equitably, with the highest priority being to spend at the point of service delivery – school classrooms.

The good news about the appointments and the subsidy should have been the main business of the first full meeting of the Liaison Group on Thursday 27 February, which included the Chairman and Vice-Chairman of Governors, and at which we intended to agree future plans. Unfortunately we first had to consider a letter Stan Brown had written, outlining governors' concerns with the way the school was being managed. It cited lack of communication and criticized involvement with the press. I was sure most governors had not been asked their opinion and, although it was meant to be presented formally, no copy had been sent to Anna. To me, this undermined its validity: Anna was the Associate Head, as well as a governor and member of the

Liaison Group, and her role should have been recognized by those who were so keen to have their own standing and importance identified.

I exploded; all the pent-up frustrations of working with the muddled governing body flooded out, and I berated Stan for the failure of the governors, as a group, to focus on their targets and support the school. According to Anna, I wagged my finger at him as though he was a naughty boy. 'You all have to recognize that Anna and I are working like mad to cope with all the normal day-to-day problems of running a school with a very restricted senior management team. Between us we are Head, Curriculum Deputy, Pastoral Deputy, Head of Special Needs and Bursar, as well as coping with the press and the politicians, and trying to put right all the fundamental problems highlighted in the Ofsted Report. We don't always have the time to consult and meet with others. We're still fire-fighting. It's all right for some of the governors to criticize us for not giving them all sorts of background detail, but the only detail that exists is what we write. We're not consulted about the content of agendas for governors' meetings, so we have to raise things under Any Other Business and circulate documents at the meeting: and that looks like we're disorganized.'

I reminded the governors of the working group that the LEA had set up the year before to address the probability that the school would fail the forthcoming Ofsted inspection, and how little it achieved. 'Instead of bringing everyone together to face the issues and approach the impending inspection constructively, you and the councillors spent all the time arguing about who was responsible for what.' Since they were still not taking their responsibilities seriously, I repeated that the governors were the only group likely to fail to meet their Action Plan targets. 'I've said before that heads usually work closely with their Chairman of Governors, having regular meetings to keep you informed and organize the business for the meetings. We need to build a strong relationship based on trust and an understanding of the pressures that we face.'

Stan was clearly unhappy about having regular meetings, but eventually we sat down and set a series of dates. I couldn't understand why he was so reluctant, because he was very supportive of the school, and as far as I could see, supportive of me personally. I did wonder whether he was being heavily pressured by one or two other governors, who were pushing him into taking up positions against his better judgement, and I think that his anticipated move to a parish in Wimbledon helped him shake off these influences. Looking back, this meeting was a turning point both in my relationship with Stan and in the process of improving the effectiveness of the governing body.

The next week my confidence was reinforced with firmer estimates of pupil numbers, and, with the curriculum subsidy agreed, it was time to think seriously about the next year's budget. Unlike other authorities, Calderdale has not encouraged its schools to manage their own affairs and bank accounts. One of the most frustrating aspects of returning to an LEA school was to find that the incompatibility I remembered between the IT systems used by schools and those in the Finance Department still existed. Schools had to pay to use Finance Department personnel who had the necessary knowledge of the arcane procedures required for the labour-intensive task of monitoring the budget – siphoning valuable resources away from classroom provision. Proper financial procedures would have resulted in less work for the school clerical staff, together with better and more up-to-date information for the school and LEA – and at considerably less cost. However, it would have required treating schools as equal partners at the cost of their own authority.

Consequently I could not get access to the up-to-date information necessary for proper financial monitoring. I was beginning to suspect that the deficit would exceed the £50,000+ forecast and therefore we would need to find around £50,000 in savings or extra income. Or I could try to persuade the Education Department to allow us to set a deficit budget over the £250,000 subsidy. Apart from the fact that some of the expense of the 'rescue operation' had been borne by the school's budget, there were two reasons for this massive overspending. When setting the 1996/7 budget, governors had agreed to maintain the staffing levels by using most of the reserves to avoid the difficult step of making staff redundant. This was clearly an unsound strategy, as no steps were taken to resolve the over-staffing in the meantime. Using up all the reserves in this way only delayed the inevitable. At the same time, they had assumed that the school's income would be based on an intake of 150 pupils, whereas in fact only 100 children arrived while a significant number left. Perhaps the LEA's Finance Department, who approved the budget, did not have all the information on pupil numbers held by the

Education Department, who in turn might not have been aware of the financial picture. However, it is ultimately the governors' responsibility to set a sensible budget; they should have taken immediate steps to reduce the staffing costs.

When we had our first scheduled meeting with Stan Brown to discuss the business for the governors' sub-committee meetings, I outlined the details of our financial position. He seemed surprised, and I asked him how much information the governors had been given before they decided to use up all the school's reserves in the attempt to avoid redundancies. He implied that the decision was hedged around with talk of the incompetence of the LEA and the lack of information about intake numbers. In short, it was the story I was tired of hearing: blame everyone in an attempt to evade responsibility for managing the issues. I told him, 'You keep saying that you want examples of the statutory responsibilities that the Ofsted inspectors stated the governing body had failed to address. Well, this is one of them.'

The local papers had picked up on the latest, extremely supportive report from the February inspection and quoted it extensively, but the national press were mainly interested in the Ofsted report on Calderdale Education Department. There was a general belief that a hit squad would be sent to sort out the LEA, and the omens were not good. The *Mail on Sunday* and the *Yorkshire Post* echoed the criticisms made by the mother at the parents' evening about the LBA programme which some of the older Ridings pupils attended. The students were attending a snooker club as an incentive to behave – it taught them some basic mental arithmetic and practice in working co-operatively (and losing gracefully). The stories had all the hallmarks of a government briefing, uncannily anticipating one of the criticisms that would be made by the inspectors – a lack of alternative programmes for disaffected students.

If the Ofsted report was to be negative, I felt it important that we try to distance the school from the publicity that would surround its publication, so I turned down an offer to appear on breakfast television on Monday 10 March. Driving into work, I heard Ian Jennings on Radio 4's *Today* programme sounding confident, making the point that many of the original assurances given to the LEA by Ofsted had been ignored. His implication was clear: the report was largely a political exercise. More significant, and nearly making me drive off the road, was that

James Naughtie referred to us as the 'once-notorious Ridings School'. 'Once notorious'! It was official: we had passed the media test. Later, at her national press conference, Gillian Shephard didn't even mention the Ridings and I sensed that the focus of criticism had moved from the school to the LEA.

I thought the report on Calderdale was fair. It highlighted the climate of distrust between the LEA and its schools and identified ten recommendations which included:

- developing information systems to support schools and assist them to improve educational standards
- ensuring that officers had the power to fulfil their responsibilities and reducing their workload by cutting the number of sub-committees and working parties
- making the decision-making processes more transparent and accountable
- developing Service Level Agreements with schools
- devising an effective strategy for supporting pupils with behavioural difficulties.

Whether or not these criticisms can be made about all local authorities I do not know, but they must be typical of those LEAs that have fought against the devolution of responsibility to schools and striven to retain power and finance centrally.

I agreed to interviews on the understanding that I would not discuss the report, only our efforts at the Ridings. All the media coverage that day mentioned the Ridings, but in a positive light. An interview on Radio 5 went well, and we took the opportunity to feature some pupils working on literacy using the Global English computer software on YTV's *Calendar*. The one exception to the rule was the interview for the midday Radio Leeds news bulletin. Every question, despite previous assurances, was about the LEA – but I am proud to say that every answer I gave was about the improvements at the Ridings.

19

MAKING PROGRESS

As the second half of term progressed, we were consistently working to establish a tradition: putting good practice into place, so that the essential jobs would be undertaken as a matter of course in years to come. The staff had put considerable effort into producing an Options Booklet outlining the GCSE courses available for Year 9 students. I was taken aback when I found that they intended simply to hand the book out to pupils with no explanation. Yet again, I had to confront the staff about the right way to do it – or perhaps the 'Clark' way to do it. I felt it was paramount to explain how we were planning to organize the choice of options and introduce the students to the booklet. It was a Friday, and I wanted the booklets to go home before the weekend, so I got the year group together and 'busked' it. It was a routine talk I had given many times in the past: I was astonished when some staff said they were impressed that I could do it without preparation.

The Ridings staff had compiled handbooks for each department the previous year, knowing that the Ofsted inspectors were due in December. Although handbooks are not officially required, they are regarded by Ofsted as evidence of 'good practice'. However, I had been struck by the absence of a whole-school handbook; it would have been extremely useful, if not essential, to present all the staff with a coherent guide to the policies and procedures of the new school at the outset. School handbooks are considered an invaluable reference source, especially to new staff. We now had a Staff Handbook ready to be distributed to the staff and governors, although the presentation of the material, such as colour coding the sections for ease of reference, needed further work. It had developed into a fairly substantial document, collating all the papers distributed to staff over the previous months. It was heavily based on the policies of Rastrick and Todmorden High Schools, and would be an important element in the induction of new staff after Easter.

At the weekly staff meeting on Wednesday 26 February, Anna distributed certificates for attendance to the tutors of the forms with the best attendance record in each year group. In the weeks since the introduction of *ears*, we had seen the attendance rate reach the giddy heights of 82 per cent – well up from previous figure of around 70 per cent. There was some good-natured banter after one teacher admitted that he had marked some of his form as attending medical appointments by mistake, instead of recording them as being ill, but it was gratifying to see that the relationships between the staff were flourishing. Another indication of the positive attitude from the staff was that, now the teaching audit was in its final stages and teachers were feeling more secure, they were prepared to be critical of the 'knockers' – many of whom were now on sick leave or had resigned. The previously powerful anti-Karen clique had lost its power base and influence. We had clearly achieved Key Issue 8, 'improving the morale of the staff so they work together, sharing corporate responsibility for school policy'.

At the same meeting Joan Williams gave an insight into her work on the Furness Project, and explained the plan we had drawn up to re-integrate its first graduates back into school. Over the next few weeks, therefore, we would gradually build up the proportion of time they spent in school, starting with them eating lunch in the canteen just before the normal midday break. As they became more used to the school routine, they would begin to attend the most appropriate lessons until they were attending normally. Once they were back, we could identify a fresh group of pupils to work with on another programme designed to improve their ability to cope in ordinary classroom situations. It had always been our intention for the initiative in the Youth Centre to be short-term, and we were keen to measure its success once the youngsters were back in the normal school environment. Two had dropped out of the original group. One was moving, to the relief of all concerned. The other, who had transferred from primary school with obvious behavioural and emotional problems, had never even been assessed for a statement of special educational needs. He had now been 'fast-tracked' through the system with unprecedented speed and as a result had been found a place in a school outside the Authority which specialized in dealing with disturbed children – at a cost of over £20,000 a year. Without the crisis and our intervention, I doubt whether he would have received the help he needed, and the odds are that he would have ended up as the subject of an exclusions sub-committee.

When setting up the Furness Project, we had discussed at length whether or not to include one extremely badly behaved Year 7 girl. We had decided against it, as she would have been the only girl. Although she was a considerable problem to all staff we felt that, given the personalities involved and their previous relationships, she would react against the others and in all probability get worse rather than better. She was very difficult to control and regularly had to be retrieved from lessons when she had a tantrum or fell out with other pupils. Most days she spent much of the time sitting outside Anna's office. We had tried everything, but although her mother was very supportive, working with us to improve matters, there was little support from the stepfather. We tried to set up a contract under which, if she failed to behave reasonably, a referral to Beaconsfield would result. She did not improve and we began the procedures. Although her mother felt it was for the best, the stepfather was adamant that she would not go to Beaconsfield. He stormed out of my office shouting and swearing, vowing that his other two children would never return unless he got his own way, and he kept all three off school for about a month. After considerable effort from Anna and Bob Naylor, the EWO, we arrived at a point where he agreed to withdraw his objection to Beaconsfield if we gave her another chance. We agreed to admit her with three 'lives': three serious incidents of misbehaviour and it was Beaconsfield or permanent exclusion. Anna, Bob and I crossed all our fingers and her behaviour markedly improved.

That week we held two more Parents' Evenings and, although the turnouts were still disappointing, there were positive indicators. One Year 10 tutor looked depressed at the start of the evening, but had brightened up by the end. The turnout for parents of Year 7 and 8 pupils was better, at about a third – still less than half that one would normally expect. The new computer software was now well established in the curriculum for Years 7 to 9, so we encouraged parents to visit the 'OILS Room', and they were very impressed. One mother told me, 'He's been home late every night. He said he'd been working after school, but I didn't believe him. I thought he was in detention!' Anna and I talked to a number of parents. Without exception they were supportive and complimentary.

It was also a busy week at Rastrick. On Saturday my wife and I were in the audience for the school's musical production of *Camelot*. Once again I was reminded of the Reins Wood days: in December 1984, as I watched the Christmas productions of two of the Rastrick feeder schools and saw the talents on display, it had been brought home to me that I had the responsibility for ensuring that these children's potential was realized. Whilst watching that evening's performance, it was inevitable that I compared the Reins Wood of 1984 with the Ridings School of 1997. I felt positive about the future for the Ridings: what had been done a dozen years ago could be achieved again.

Tuesday 11 March was Open Day. Anna had written to the parents of all the children on our intake list inviting them to attend. That morning the school looked fantastic. The main event was to be held in the evening, starting with an introduction and welcome from Anna and me, and trips around the school to visit classrooms where children and teachers could answer any questions and demonstrate their work. Parents also had the opportunity to visit during the morning. Older pupils had volunteered, or, in some cases, been volunteered, as guides, and they proved to be slick and competent. The morning went smoothly – at least as far as our visitors were concerned. I was 'sweeping' in front of one of the first groups and arrived at one classroom to find the teacher busily stripping his noticeboards. The floor was covered with piles of ripped-up paper, revealing for all to see graffiti that dated back years, and his class were less-than-purposefully occupied sitting around in their coats chatting to each other. Aghast, I asked him, 'What are you doing? We've got groups of parents touring the school!' He looked at me uncomprehendingly: 'I was away yesterday – I didn't realize there were morning trips!' It was pointless to remind him that details of the day had been publicized for weeks. There was no deliberate attempt to undermine our work, in fact quite the opposite. He was doing his bit, he had just failed to plan effectively. I consoled myself with the thought that he was soon to leave, and managed to steer the visitors away until the mess was cleared up.

Over a hundred parents attended that evening. As part of the introduction Anna read extracts from the latest HMI monitoring report. There were many complimentary and positive comments, but some questions were difficult, especially as I was asked several times, 'What will happen after you leave?' My response was always, 'All the success is down to a team effort. There will be a seamless transition building on everything we have achieved. The school will go from strength to strength.' The next day Marian Partington, who co-ordinated admissions in the Education Department, rang to say that two of the parents who had appealed against a place at the school had withdrawn their appeal because they had been so impressed by the evening. Further success followed on Thursday, at the Year 9 Option Evening for pupils and parents. Attendance was up to over half the parents, who without exception voiced keen interest, commitment and enthusiasm for the future. Successful schools maintain good relationships with supportive parents, and it seemed that the tide had turned on this front as well. The emphasis on explaining our work and giving parents the opportunity to come into school was beginning to pay off.

Comic Relief Day also fell in that week. The students behaved admirably and there was a real team spirit. We held a Non-Uniform Day to raise money: Anna came dressed as Cruella de Vil, complete with a toy Dalmatian on the end of a cane. Two of the children from the Furness project saw her; they were amazed and sat with her, stroking her spotted fake-fur coat. In their restricted experience, they had seen nothing like it and reacted in much the same way as they had to the pantomime. It was a sad picture, yet at the same time hopeful: with proper support, inside and outside school, there were indications that they could learn to overcome the deprivation and lack of stimulus that had so far marked their young lives. If only they could have been caught earlier. Children from dysfunctional families need the security of school life. Unfortunately this is not always appreciated by the agencies involved with them; I have only ever known one social worker visit a parents' evening with a child who was in care.

The day was memorable in other ways. Jo Clark had organized the 'Hot Ice Show', a demonstration of explosions and pyrotechnics in the central courtyard that had the whole school amazed and enthralled. The two performances lasted about an hour each and held every pupil's attention. Lunch time saw a specially organized disco in the Youth Centre, with a well-trailed and eagerly anticipated Spice Girls Look-alike competition. The various Spice Girls, together with Anna dancing with Youth Tutor Denis Midwood, provided more footage for the in-house documentary using the Sky video camera. The event was a great success, the youngsters proving that they could now participate in unstructured activities in an enjoyable manner without getting over-excited and behaving badly.

My feeling that things were definitely getting better was reinforced when the IT Adviser, Tim Scratcherd, remarked that the behaviour in the corridors had noticeably improved since the school's re-opening. The LEA advisers were undertaking the teacher audit very professionally, but two staff were particularly unhappy about their final 'grade'. However, after talking it through, they accepted the verdict. I pointed out to one of them that he should be grateful, as without the high level of support he had received from the subject adviser since before Christmas, he would have been in danger of failing. In fact that adviser was doing a superb job, working with a group who had really lost their way, and successfully getting the teachers to rethink their approaches and relearn their skills. Unlike Ofsted inspectors, LEA advisers often perform three roles – advising, training and inspecting – and the best ones build good relationships based on mutual respect with school staff. We were lucky that the LEA had recently appointed advisers in some key subject areas, and they grasped the opportunity to develop their new roles.

In all this excitement we even found time to name a road. A local housing association was building an estate a couple of hundred yards from the school, and had asked us to organize a competition to name one of the roads. The natural wit and sense of irony that characterize English schoolchildren were evident in the hundred or so suggestions: Clark's Way, Great White Way and Panorama View were among my favourites, while Hope Rise expressed the optimistic spirit prevailing throughout the school. The winner was Buxton Way, in memory of Sue Buxton who had died in January. On top of all the excitement at the Ridings, I learned that Rastrick had had its Technology College status renewed for another three years. This was a major triumph for Paul Armitage, who had masterminded the bid.

Saturday was another good day. A week or so previously Geoffrey Levy from the *Daily Mail* had spent most of a day in school. He was different from the education correspondents I had met from the national press. I was wary after the snooker story in *The Mail on Sunday*, but he seemed to understand my concerns. His only knowledge of the school was from being a member of the press pack during the crisis, and he obviously enjoyed his trip round the school to see things at first hand. He spoke to many pupils, a number of whom impressed him as polite and intelligent, and we parted on a positive note. However, I became a little apprehensive about what he would write after I spoke to a Year 10 student the next day: he had phoned her the evening before (how do journalists get such easy access to people's telephone numbers?) to ask what she was studying.

'Nine GCSEs,' she replied.

'That many! What's your favourite?'

'English.'

'What are you reading?'

'Macbeth.'

'What do you think of it?'

She told him.

'Oh, you seem to know a lot about it.'

She and her mother were amused because they felt he was checking on how well she was doing. In the Ofsted jargon, I suppose he was 'triangulating', checking out his observations by questioning others.

I needn't have worried. The article made the Saturday *Today* programme's newspaper review slot, and was favourable and morale-boosting – apart from an amusing, but totally untrue, account about a girl I was supposed to have put in detention because she complained that I had pushed into the dinner queue. I was described as 'jovial and jowly' and quoted as saying, 'If we had come in with a rod of iron, it would have blown up in our faces' – a mixed metaphor which I had intended as a joke. In dealing with the press I found I had to be very careful to balance my desire to be open and get them on my side with keeping the less positive aspects of the situation out of the headlines. I always attempted to build up a relationship with the journalists, so I could only laugh at being caught out when my joke fell flat.

Levy also wrote, 'The last time I visited the Ridings, in late October, I described it as an odyssey of despair. Going back this week was a surprising introduction to hope.' He quoted Ian Calvert ('greying Head of English') as saying, 'It was a nightmare, but just look at them now.

They're keen; they want to do well. They are working. The whole culture is different because the pupils know what will be tolerated and what will not. It's a more comfortable and secure place for everyone.'

Monday 17 March began the last week of term. At the morning staff briefing, I outlined the arrangements for the HMI inspection due to take place on Thursday and repeated my now-familiar exhortation: 'The lessons need to be well planned, have a beginning, a middle and an end … You all need to have your IEPs available for all your pupils who are on the Special Needs register – and to be seen to be implementing them.'

On a day-to-day level we still had our ups and downs, and there was some trouble on Wednesday at lunchtime. A teacher had seen some pupils throwing something at a contractor's van. As he approached they had run away, but he noted the names of the culprits and escorted the workmen – understandably annoyed – to see me. I assured them that I would deal with the pupils responsible and asked them to let me know the cost of any damage. The driver said he had driven the van away from where it had been damaged to the car park, and would have to wash it before he could tell the extent of the damage. He left saying he would contact me.

The culprits played truant that afternoon, so I was unable to deal with them by the time Ian Jennings rang the next morning. One of the managers in Property Services at the LEA had sent him a long statement outlining the considerable damage alleged to have been caused to the van. The contractors had complained about a broken windscreen and wing mirrors, various dents and panes of glass carried outside the van being smashed. I was sceptical. How could they move the van and not notice it had a hole through the windscreen and a smashed wing mirror? The caretaker and I walked every inch of the area where they had been working, and we could not find a single shard of glass, apart from a broken pop bottle in the car park.

When the press rang about the story I explained what had happened. Most newspapers were fine and played down the incident, but the *Yorkshire Evening Press*, a Leeds paper, printed a fairly hysterical version of events, and in Saturday's *Independent* the headline was 'HORROR SCHOOL'. Although the contractors had been told not to say anything by the Property Services Manager, I was convinced that they had sold their story to the papers. They vehemently denied it, blaming the pupils for ringing the press. If that had been the case, I felt it was far more typical for the pupils to have rung the *Halifax Courier*, not a paper in a city 20 miles away. And the contractors' firm was based near Leeds... A single undisciplined act had been blown out of all proportion. A year before I would have had a week's sleepless nights worrying about the effects on the school's reputation. I explained to the LEA staff what I had done and told them that firm must not be given any more work at the school. I punished the children involved and arranged with the caretaker that no contractors should work inside the school during break or lunch time, unless we knew and trusted them.

However, Wednesday was constructive in other ways: six sets of parents came to the inaugural PTA committee meeting, Gill Hellewell's secondment from the Halifax to our administrative staff was extended until the Spring Bank Holiday, and the Careers Convention, which had been planned since early Autumn, attracted a good number of students and parents. We reviewed the progress we had made on achieving our Action Plan targets at a Liaison Group meeting, and could report that we had met all but a very few objectives within the timescale. For example, we had not yet undertaken detailed forecasts of future pupil numbers, as we had been unable to gain access to the appropriate information, and pressure of work had meant that we had had to postpone the surveys of pupils' and parents' attitudes to the changes that had taken place. On the other hand, we had improved behaviour, carried out the teaching audit, recruited new staff, re-timetabled the school and planned the curriculum for the future – amongst other things!

The best was yet to come. As I had come to expect, the whole school again pulled out all the stops for the next day's third monthly HMI inspection. Two colleagues accompanied Kath Cross, one looking predominantly at the pastoral system and the other at SEN. All three were complimentary, and when one said, 'It was a pleasure to walk round. It feels like a school – not like at the time of the inspection,' I was overwhelmed. He continued, 'I rarely give a one [Ofsted grade lessons on a scale of one to seven, where one is the best and seven the worst], but today at the Ridings I gave a teacher a one!' I was bursting with feelings of pride and vindication. I felt we had finally turned the corner.

Whatever technological developments take place in education, reading is the essential key to achieving success in all subjects, and a school's top priority should be its emphasis on reaching high standards in literacy as early as possible. One of the inspectors said, 'Forget the National Curriculum, forget Programmes of Study, get them reading.' They were critical of the fact that so many of the children had remedial problems, and that their poor reading skills did not stem from physical or psychological difficulties but were a reflection on earlier teaching. This view had also been expressed by an ex-primary teacher working in the school who said, 'I used to be very unsympathetic towards secondary teachers, but now I can appreciate some of their problems. Some of the teaching in some of these primary schools must be awful.' It is true that many of the children arrived at the Ridings way behind national educational targets: as many as ten per cent of them were 'non-readers' – what most people would understand as basically illiterate. How much of this was down to poor teaching and how much to truancy is another matter.

The HMI praised the progress we had made in literacy with the Global English software and the Corrective and Paired Reading programmes, and we discussed moving to a second stage. Anna had many ideas to encourage reading during form-tutor periods, for example by providing collections of books that pupils could read after the register had been called. We considered the notion of a 'buddy' system, giving older and better readers responsibility for helping poorer, younger readers; schools using this strategy have seen reading improve for both the weaker and the stronger 'buddies', with the added benefit of all involved improving their social skills. Another idea was to complement the reward system, currently based on credits and the regular award of certificates for effort and attendance, by giving material rewards, such as tickets in a free raffle for a mountain bike or Walkman. The prizes could be displayed prominently throughout the year, with raffle tickets issued for a certain number of credits earned, and the draw held at the end of the summer term. When one governor heard of this idea she immediately offered to donate a bike to start the scheme off at the beginning of the next year.

It was the end of the Spring term and we had made considerable progress. There was still plenty to do, but next term the new staff would be starting and we would only have to cope with two HMI visits.We had broadly achieved all the targets we had set ourselves, had three successful HMI inspections, tripled the intake from 30-odd to over 90 and successfully completed the teaching audit. There had been setbacks, but mostly these had been peripheral to our real job of improving the classroom experiences of the Ridings pupils.

One of the younger pupils who had formerly always been in trouble typified the positive relationships being established between pupils and staff. He was so intimidated by his father that he reported on virtually every minute in school to stop his father 'clattering' him. He had often been 'on report' to monitor his behaviour and had to achieve a minimum standard for his behaviour in each lesson. That week he received a low grade in only one subject, so to encourage him and to demonstrate that we wanted him to succeed, I changed it. On the last afternoon he told me that he had been 'strangled' by one of the builders when playing football with them at lunchtime, unfortunately without the guiding hand of a referee! He was unhurt and the story was garbled, but he said, 'Don't tell my Dad now or he'll come round. I'll tell him when I get home and that you sorted it for me, and he'll have forgotten it after the holiday.'

The celebrations for the retiring staff leaving at Easter started after school on the last day of term and continued into the evening with a buffet and dance at Elland Cricket Club. Chris Binns was in a local group who had been playing in the Halifax area since the sixties – 'Dino and the Travellers'. They had started out as teenagers, and although they had gone their separate ways, mainly into teaching and politics, still joined up for a number of gigs each year. Anna had a bet with Jenny Baker and some of the other staff that she could get me to dance – she lost.

20

THE SUMMER TERM

After enjoying a restful Easter holiday, I returned to the Ridings on Monday 7 April to meet the new staff and participate in a training day Anna had arranged to widen the teachers' knowledge of General National Vocational Qualifications, or GNVQs. The Sixth Form was very small and offered only A levels in English and Art and GNVQs in Health and Social Care. As part of our curriculum planning, we wanted to expand the courses available – at both A level and GNVQ – to provide relevant, high-quality programmes of study that would encourage more of our Year 11 students to continue their education at the school. The new staff started an ad hoc induction process, including the inevitable photo opportunity. With our increased confidence, I was now happy to allow it to take place on the infamous steps.

The Liaison Group meeting that week was much more business-like than those of the previous term. For once, we were able to concentrate on normal school issues. The planned extensions to the school agreed earlier in the year seemed to be under threat, as the finance was by no means secure, although we tried to be optimistic. We made more progress on filling the next round of staff vacancies, getting permission to advertise the jobs and discussing our plans to restructure pastoral care. In the last few months, a much more effective pastoral system had evolved, and it was time to formalize it. This gave us the opportunity to re-examine other posts within the school, assigning some staff to positions more suited to their skills and interests. For example, one teacher who had been made Head of Department was unhappy in this position, preferring a pastoral role to which he was more suited. Another still felt aggrieved at being passed over for Head of Department initially, and an ex-Head of Department could fill a vacancy caused by a resignation. I wanted to take this opportunity to eliminate as many of the old sources of conflict and disillusionment as possible, allocating people to jobs they felt confident in undertaking and removing some of the problems and jealousies caused by the original appointments. We also discussed our plans to create Heads of Year to take responsibility for the progress and behaviour of each year group and manage teams of form tutors. Anna suggested that we should advertise the posts internally to avoid possible dissension but, apart from the new posts, I disagreed. I argued that we could only achieve our objectives if we ourselves chose certain people for certain posts. If we explained why we were doing it, I reasoned, the staff would see that it all hung together and was an attempt to be fair, leading to a more effective and efficient structure.

On Thursday we had two sets of visitors. Despite repeated invitations, only three councillors had visited us during school hours in the six months since we had been open (even though we were such a high-profile item on the Education Committee's agenda). So I was happy to welcome the Mayor of Calderdale, Councillor Dawn Neale, and her consort in the last weeks of her mayorality. This was a welcome change from the media visits. I felt they both enjoyed their tour and they were certainly impressed by the standard of work displayed, especially in the art area.

Later that morning, we met with a group of three officials from the DfEE led by Simon James, our main link with the School Effectiveness Unit, which oversees work with schools in special measures. It was a constructive visit, but when we went round after lunch some of the classes were not working as purposefully as usual, although there was no obvious misbehaviour. This showed that there was still a lot to do, but Simon was very supportive and passed on the best wishes of Robin Squires, the Education Minister responsible for schools. I sensed that in the DfEE's eyes we were doing all right.

When I left to attend a governors' staffing committee at Rastrick, Anna took the visitors to a rehearsal for our Global Rock Challenge entry. I had first heard about this initiative some months before – I thought it was about rock climbing and ignored it. I was mistaken: it was actually an initiative developed in Australia to help combat their teenage drug problem. The idea was to give kids the chance to experience a 'drug-free high' by conceiving and performing an eight-minute dance routine to highlight a social issue. Jenny Baker, Ian Calvert and Maggie Binns offered to take on the task and enlisted the help of

Joanne Whalley, a Support Assistant with our Furness Project, who was a trained dancer. They were supported by a police inspector seconded by the Hampshire police to popularize the initiative. He was accompanied by an experienced dancer who was on the Bishop of Winchester's staff, who had been instrumental in introducing the idea to this country. It seemed an ideal opportunity to build on the growing corporate spirit; there was no shortage of volunteers from the students who, inevitably, decided to base their entry on the 'troubles'. The visitors were very impressed with the commitment of the 40-plus children taking part – and Anna herself was very touched by the kids' enthusiasm.

The next day Carol and I travelled to a hotel on Lake Windermere, where I was to speak at a course for the Funding Agency for Schools. The FAS is responsible for monitoring the financial aspects of all grant-maintained schools, and the course was designed for its staff involved in the planning aspects of the Agency's work, specifically for those schools judged as failing. I was not sure exactly what they wanted to hear, so we arrived early in order to listen to the other speakers.

As I listened to the other contributors I began to clarify my ideas in the light of my last few months' experience. I knew I was not alone in my frustrations with the inadequacies of the system for improving schools after they failed Ofsted inspections. Although the inspection process takes into account the past history of a school, it is essentially limited to a report based on less than a week's observation. This can be effective in normal circumstances, and has had a positive effect on school improvement, but limited if fundamental problems are identified without a mechanism for helping the school to rectify them. There are many well-rehearsed criticisms of a lack of real professional understanding and expertise in some Ofsted inspectors, and concerns about the loss of the old relationships between heads and HMI, which had allowed for more constructive criticism. My experience had taught me that the mechanisms for working with inadequate schools lack power and effectiveness. Merely publishing bad reports and requiring a school to draw up an Action Plan tends to condemn the unfortunate pupils of the school to a drawn-out process with little guarantee of long-term success.

All schools may have staff who are not well-regarded by pupils, but one of the speakers got it exactly right when she highlighted two symptoms of a failing school: disillusioned staff, who walk away from issues which require their intervention and rarely smile and, crucially, children who are not bothered by their presence. As I listened to the description of the steps taken in other failing schools I could not understand why the role of the HMI was being criticized until I realized that the Ridings had not been treated as a 'normal' failing school. Most schools did not have the benefit of the close involvement of inspectors at an early stage and were very much left to their own devices, seeing the HMI as monitors rather than mentors. We had now had six formal visits by HMI, three of which had been mini-inspections, and had only had 20 days to map out our plan for action – this pressure dictated the momentum for change. We simply did not have the time to react like other failing schools, which often made excuses of feeling hard done by or attempted to justify the school's poor performance in terms of spending cuts, inadequate pupils, or whatever (although some of our staff, governors and others had tried to do just this). In addition, Anna and I were 'new brooms', able to distance ourselves from the previous regime.

I am convinced this is a valuable lesson for dealing with failing schools in the future. The policy certainly should not be centred around merely 'naming and shaming'. There should be a clearly structured response to helping schools that are failing their pupils, through identifying the crucial problem areas and helping senior staff and governors to plan effective strategies to overcome them. Leaving it to the schools to take the initiative is more likely to result in weak action – or inaction. After all, those managing the school must take most of the responsibility for its problems. Should they then be trusted with the vital task of drawing up, and implementing, an Action Plan designed to put the situation right? Schools also need access to additional finance to pay for the agreed course of action and an agreed strategy to ease the transition back to normality. This is especially important if on coming out of special measures a school loses financially, for example if the LEA withdraws any additional funding allocated because it was failing.

I talked about my experience in 'the school from Hell'. To put the situation in context I outlined the Ofsted report's Key Issues and tried to identify the pressures on the school: the difficulties surrounding the amalgamation, the lack of decision-making, political incompetence and interference, the high level of exclusions, the lack of co-operation from a small but influential minority of the staff, the all-pervading presence of the media – all factors that had contributed to the loss of control as the kids were allowed to make the running. I explained that it never had been the school from Hell, but nevertheless was a school with real problems, exacerbated by being in an LEA with weak relationships with its teachers and insufficient facilities to support schools in dealing with disaffected and disruptive pupils. In outlining the steps we had taken, I emphasized that most of the success in turning the school round was due to the hard work and commitment from the staff and children who had all pulled together in response to our initial challenge. They perfectly illustrated our new maxim: 'Together we can make the difference.'

By contrast, Monday 14 April brought a more prosaic aspect of school routine. In the early months of the school, the behaviour in the canteen was very poor and lacked effective supervision because most teachers refused to participate in midday supervision. There had been numerous examples of theft, together with abuse of the dinner ladies, who were attempting to operate a cash cafeteria system. Consequently, the School Meals Service had reintroduced the more traditional set meal, paid for with dinner tickets. This reduced its popularity, so that the majority of children patronizing the canteen were on free meals and were recorded daily in a register. All schools experience difficulties with the administration of free school meals, as families have their entitlement regularly assessed and consequently are repeatedly put on and taken off the register. For this reason the position of each name in the four or five registers required was not in any logical order, but depended mainly on when the child had been granted free meals. Lynne Sharp, who marked the registers, knew which children stayed to lunch and their place in the register. Unfortunately she was absent, and her stand-in had to check and look up every single name, dramatically slowing up the queue. When I noticed that the queue was hardly moving I helped, but it was an impossible task for us to move the children through at anything like the usual rate. So the start of afternoon school was delayed.

This was another example of the overly complicated nature of many of the school's basic administrative procedures; they only worked because of the expertise of specific individuals. They had often evolved from tackling problems in an ad hoc way without ever reviewing the basic operation. The difficulty was compounded by a general distrust that the students could cope with systems common in other schools. A list of names in alphabetical order, with the marks transferred later to the registers, quickly solved the problem and lunchtime proceeded smoothly for the rest of the week.

However, such a small irritant could not take precedence over the main business of the day: the regional heat of the Global Rock Challenge. The staff, students and volunteers had worked very hard on Sunday to polish their performance to a backing of three records which reflected the phases they wanted to express: Chris Rea's 'The Road to Hell' and 'Working On It', and Labi Sifre's 'Something Inside So Strong'. Other staff were dragooned in to help provide costumes for the characters representing the press; and Gordon Dickson, the Community Constable and governor, organized the West Yorkshire Police coach to transport everyone to Bradford. To complete the preparations, Jenny Baker and her students painted the most photographed image of the school, the front entrance, on two large sheets of MDF.

The competitors in the regional heat were from Bradford, Leeds, Kirklees and Calderdale schools; they filled the auditorium. The contestants had been in Bradford most of the day rehearsing their routines and working with students from the other schools – a key aspect of the project – and our staff looked shattered. The event was sponsored by a number of businesses, including YTV and the local station Pulse Radio, and was supported by the West Yorkshire Police. The atmosphere was buzzing and, although the event was competitive, the hundreds of school pupils were well behaved and appreciative of each others' efforts – but loud! Carol and I sat with some of the parents and staff and watched the entries, gauging them against our school's performance.

Each entry was introduced by the compere and a school pupil. The Ridings School entry was introduced by Michelle Foster, a Sixth Former, who was far and away the most articulate and professional school representative, and far more self-assured than the professional compere – in my opinion. Our piece expressed the problems of the initial amalgamation, the press reaction and interference, and the final coming together to get the best out of the school. The press and camera crews were all represented, as were the pupils themselves, who began by behaving badly and finished as model students, praised by Ofsted and the journalists who had exploited them by bribing them to misbehave. The audience were gripped – perhaps wondering how they would have reacted in a similar situation – and I was impressed by their grasp of the realities of the situation and instinctive desire to conform to society's expectations.

The reception from the other schools and the judges was overwhelming, and we won the heat. The award was presented by the Mayor of Kirklees, Councillor Alison Harrison, who said that she would have been very proud if the youngsters had attended a school in her area. Pupils, staff and parents alike were thrilled. The next morning the school was in a state of high excitement. The result had been broadcast on Pulse Radio, and by the time the school opened Jenny had displayed the certificates and plaques that the group had won in the entrance hall. You could see the children expand with pride. The Ridings School had won against competition from other schools with untarnished reputations, and had been praised publicly. People who had no connection with the school had acknowledged the strong, creative effort that had resulted in the winning performance. The pupils had faced their past shortcomings, and in doing so many had made a significant step towards maturity.

However, winning meant that we had to return that day to work with schools who had won regional finals from the rest of Yorkshire and Humberside and compete against them in a second evening performance, to be recorded by YTV and broadcast as a special Sunday afternoon programme a couple of weeks later. Ian, Jenny, Maggie and the rest spent the day rehearsing in Bradford, and we all met up that night for part two. It was perhaps too much to hope that we could pull it off two nights running, and unfortunately we lost out to a school from East Yorkshire; but the event had been hugely successful, and I know it taught the children important lessons in winning and losing. Anna had missed both performances, as she was busy preparing for her interview for Headteacher on Tuesday and Wednesday.

I ended that week back in the basement of Huddersfield Town Hall being interviewed by Vincent Hanna for Radio 4's *Medium Wave*. We were delayed because the IRA had exploded a bomb in Leeds railway station. Vincent asked me about the 'black arts' of media management:

had I deliberately made up stories in order to cover up potential bad publicity? No, I hadn't. He finished his questions by asking me what advice I would give another headteacher facing the media circus; I replied, 'Get them on your side!' When I listened to the piece on Sunday morning he rounded off with, 'Peter Clark, the man who became a spin doctor without even knowing it.'

21

THE HEADTEACHER IS APPOINTED

During the spring half term I had a meeting with Peter Bartle, Peter Flower and a member of the LEA's administrative staff to draw up the personnel specification for the posts of Headteacher and Deputy Head, which were shortly to be advertised. We talked through the requirements of the Headteacher post, and decided that it was essential for candidates to have had at least managerial experience in SEN and to show that they had achieved significant improvements in a school or department. Unfortunately this last was translated in the personnel specification as requiring that candidates should have worked in a failing school.

There had been fewer applicants that we had hoped for the post of Headteacher – but Anna was one of them. I had been surprised to learn that applicants had to send 80p postage: one of the Education Department clerks decided to add it to the instructions because applicants usually sent self-addressed envelopes complete with a first-class stamp, which made it difficult to operate the franking machine. I found that annoying, but when Gill Hellewell received a call from a clerk in the Education Department telling her to place an order to re-advertise the job in order to attract more candidates, I was incensed. Why even consider the idea in the first place? What did they think they were doing communicating it to a member of the school office staff without any discussion with the governors? And why should we pay for it? After all, the LEA had responsibility for personnel issues: they should pay all recruitment costs. I rang back to say we were not paying and demanded to know what was going on. Apparently it had been decided to re-run the advertisement 'in case' the councillors and governors on the short-listing panel decided to re-advertise; it could be withdrawn if it was not needed. It was felt that potential candidates might have been dissuaded from applying because the personnel specification had been too rigidly defined.

My view was that the interviews should go ahead, as it was no secret that Anna had applied for the post – to re-advertise now would undermine her position. I also felt the panel's decision should not have been pre-empted in such a clumsy way, but it had happened, and I broke the news to Anna. She saw clearly that she might as well withdraw if the officers and members had so little confidence in her so soon after offering her the post on a temporary basis. To Anna this was another test of the LEA's support. She told me, 'Your test was the exclusions. This is mine.' When they made their monthly visit at the end of the spring term, the HMI team expressed concern about any delays to the headteacher recruitment process, and I learned later that Ian Jennings had been contacted by someone from the DfEE expressing similar worries.

Although I had initially been told my presence would be appreciated, I was not in the end invited to the short-listing meeting for the Headteacher appointment. I found out that all four of the applicants were to be interviewed, but there had been an attempt by one councillor to restart the whole process. However, the three governors on the panel had presented a solid front, and the other two politicians had supported them.

Our list of a dozen candidates for the Deputy Head post had been circulated to the appointment panel, which met during the Easter holidays at Halifax Town Hall to agree a shortlist of people to interview. I had been included in these discussions and chatted with the three governors and Liberal Democrat and Conservative councillors whilst waiting for Councillor Helen Rivron (Labour) and Peter Flower. Finally they arrived with another senior officer who, we were informed, was to ensure that we complied with the Council's Equal Opportunities Policy. Once started, there was little disagreement on whom to interview, but the councillors were not prepared to carry out the interviews until 7 May, after the general election on 1 May. This was some weeks away, and I was worried that the better candidates might accept other jobs in the meantime. In order to start in September, the successful applicant would have to resign his or her current post before the end of May; if we did not appoint because other schools had scooped up the better candidates during our self-imposed delay, and had to re-advertise, it would be almost impossible to guarantee appointing someone to take up post from the start of the academic year, losing the opportunity for a smooth transition to a new management team.

Councillor Rivron was adamant that the usual method of dividing into groups to question the candidates on specific issues, such as curriculum, management and pastoral care, could not be followed, insisting that unless everyone involved in the final decision was present at every stage the procedure would contravene the Equal Opportunities Policy. This highly subjective understanding of the Council's policy rendered the process less rigorous by limiting the opportunities to question the candidates thoroughly on a wide range of topics. However, I kept quiet – fortunately, as the late start was the result of a long discussion as to whether I should be present at all. Although I had originally been told it was important that I should be involved in the selection of both the Head and the Deputy Head, the fact that Anna had applied for the post apparently meant that my involvement contravened the Equal Opportunities Policy. This astonishing interpretation implied that I could never be present at any internal appointments or interview anyone I knew – and presumably that councillors could never promote any officers. However, those involved with local government soon realise that 'Equal Opportunities' is often used to justify courses of action which may not reflect common sense.

Things did not improve with the start of the summer term. At the end of the Liaison Group meeting in the first week, Paul Leach, the Vice-Chairman of Governors, showed me a copy of the Education Department's *Weekly Bulletin*. It contained a re-advertisement for the post of Headteacher. Although the clear majority of the appointment panel had agreed on the withdrawal of the advertisement from the national press, someone had forgotten to remove it from the LEA's own publication, so the difficulty in attracting candidates was no longer a secret.

The interviews for the post of Headteacher were to be held on Tuesday 15 and Wednesday 16 April, a week or so into term. I received a number of phone calls from the LEA, but most seemed to be concerned with the catering arrangements. I decided to brief the four candidates after they arrived at the school on Tuesday morning, then give them the opportunity to talk to the staff and children. Everything started according to plan, and I spent the first couple of hours with them before letting them go round on their own. One asked to speak to me around noon: he thanked me for my time, but said that on reflection the job was not for him. He had 'other irons in the fire' and felt the school would not be supported by the LEA. He had not met anyone from the authority yet, and I assured him that Calderdale Council was firmly committed to the school – otherwise why spend so much money on keeping it open? – but he left.

The other two candidates and Anna spent the afternoon talking with groups of senior staff before attending a tea time session with the governors, officers and interview panel. During this, Stan and I had a heart-to-heart talk. He felt it was a pity that we had not managed to work together more effectively. 'We never really fell out,' I replied. 'We just never got to grips with the relationship. I'd been told to get on with the job and ignore the governors, and you hadn't been told anything.' He had been dumped with the chairmanship at short notice and, as a result, had had to take responsibility for the governors' lack of action, while at the same time trying to support Karen when she most needed it. I was under considerable pressure to turn the school round and, although I understood the governors needed to be closely involved, I kept coming up against political infighting and lack of time. I don't really know why we had waited so long to get our relationship straight – probably because Stan was such a nice bloke and made allowances for me. We parted with understanding and respect for each other's point of view and a shared dismay at the antics of some of the politicians. 'How can they attempt to snatch disaster from the jaws of victory?' Stan wondered.

During the reception, the three remaining candidates circulated and were quizzed by the representatives of the school and LEA – in the case of the external candidates the quizzing was two-way. I heard one of the LEA governors saying that the interview process should be halted because so few people had applied. The main reason for the overall lack of interest was the original poor publicity and the perception that the school did not have a future – but I am sure my analysis would not have been accepted.

I am surprised at how often the people charged with making these important decisions lack confidence in their own judgement: they need to go through rigidly set procedures to reassure themselves that they are acting correctly. Justifying decisions on the basis that all the prescribed procedures were followed, so the outcome must be correct, seems to me an excuse to avoid responsibility. Some people seemed to want to stop the interviews; Anna could not help but pick up this dissatisfaction –

although I always felt the critics were very happy for her to have the job – and was worried about the outcome, however much I reassured her. She reckoned her main rival lived in Crewe, and fortunately when I rang her to give her the Rock Challenge news I was able to say, 'Don't worry about tomorrow's interview, the omens are good. I've heard the football results. Bury [where she lived] have beaten Crewe in a top of the table clash.'

Next morning, just before the Wednesday staff briefing, the phone rang. One of the candidates informed me that she was unable to attend as her mother had been taken seriously ill and was in intensive care. At this point, I somehow knew the phone would soon ring again – and it did. The other candidate rang to explain he had withdrawn because, after talking to the councillors and officers over tea, he was not convinced that they understood the situation and would continue to back the school. I asked him if it was anything I had said, as I knew that his withdrawal would create a problem if Anna was left as the only candidate. But he was anxious to reassure me. He told me that I had been fair in my briefing: I had given the candidates every opportunity to find out about the school, and had been very positive about Calderdale's support. It was just that he had not received the responses he was looking for from the councillors, officers and governors. I was sure he was telling the truth. There were plenty of other excuses he could have given if he were simply looking for a way out, and no one would have reproached him. If those to whom he had spoken had been confident about the school's future and had convinced him that the LEA would continue to give its support, I am sure he would have attended the interview.

I immediately rang Ian Jennings. He was well aware that not making an appointment that day could mean the school would be without a headteacher until after Christmas. I also passed on the information to the interview panel, which comprised three politicians: Helen Rivron (Labour), Peter Cole (Liberal Democrat) and Bill Carpenter (Conservative); three governors: Stan Brown, Jill Wilson and Anne McAuley; and three officers: Ian Jennings, Clem Rushworth and Lin Stebbins, an LEA adviser. Lin had replaced Peter Bartle, who, like me and Peter Lloyd, was excluded from the process in the interests of Equal Opportunities. I was ineligible because I worked with Anna, Peter Bartle because he had written her reference, and Peter Lloyd because he had been so involved in our work to turn the school around. My cynicism grew when I realized that the Council's Equal Opportunities Employment Procedures did not apply to councillors. Presumably they could always be relied on to act in a fair and proper manner – even if they acted outside their own procedures!

I was having a cup of coffee in the library with some of the panel when Helen Rivron entered with Ian and Clem. She was obviously agitated at the news. She accepted an offer of coffee, saying, 'This is a two-coffee problem,' and shooed me out. I told her I would send in the rest of the members of the panel as they arrived. 'There's only Peter Cole. He's coming.' She had completely forgotten Anne McAuley, the parent governor on the panel. I met Peter on his way in and had a chat whilst we waited for Anne. As she walked through the door, Mrs Rivron ran down the corridor and herded them into the library.

I had imagined that it would be a relatively quiet morning and had arranged a meeting at the Ridings with other LEA secondary heads to discuss the size of the LEA schools' budgets. Meanwhile the selection process was to start with a short presentation by each candidate. They had drawn lots the previous day, and Anna was to have performed first. When she arrived, I told her what was going on. She took the situation calmly and over the next hour, whilst we waited for the panel to make their 'two-coffee' decision, David Scott, the Head of Calder High, and I chatted with her and listened to her presentation in between participating in our colleagues' discussions.

Councillor Rivron departed, and some of the others engaged in a flurry of phone calls. She told the *Halifax Evening Courier* later that day that she was unhappy with the interview going ahead as she felt that it would be 'unsound' to make an appointment when there was only one candidate – an amazingly imprudent comment for the Deputy Chair of Education to make. However, the rest of the panel decided to proceed without her and had a short break while I set up the overhead projector and screen. Two were very scathing about the morning's proceedings and about their departed colleague's part in it.

It was agreed that the presentation and interview should be run together. Anna entered the room with the attitude 'It's not my fault I'm the only one!' and remained for just over an hour and a half – half an hour longer than we had planned. Ironically, given all the fuss that had been made about the catering arrangements, she was interrupted by the catering staff obeying to the letter the exact time 'the Office' had instructed them to deliver the food. 'Well,' Ian Jennings said, 'we've thrown everything at you now!' Anna came out and we chatted.

In education, you don't go home after a job interview and wait for a letter: you find out then and there whether you have the job. There is the small caveat that the appointment will have to be ratified, but this is generally a technicality: appointments are always ratified unless something extraordinary happens. So Anna went to talk to Ian, Clem and Stan to try and find out where she stood. She had to press Ian Jennings to tell her whether or not they were recommending her appointment. This in itself was unusual, but it was even odder that he was heavily criticized at the sub-committee meeting for telling her that they were.

I also collared one of the councillors on the way out, and he told me they would recommend Anna's appointment to the Ridings sub-committee, saying, 'That was the best interview for a headship I've ever attended, and I've interviewed dozens of secondary heads and over a hundred primary heads. Everyone agreed that it was an outstanding interview and that she was right for the job.' One of the governors told me she had said to Councillor Rivron, albeit guiltily, 'Your procedures are not as important as the future of the kids and the school.'

Although the councillor had warned me that the appointment might be blocked, I was fairly certain that the committee could have no grounds to do so: if they did, we would be back on the front pages. However, to be certain of the facts I rang John Sutton at the SHA, who had been supportive in the exclusions conflict before Christmas, and asked if he could think of any reason why the appointment should be blocked. All we could think of was forging qualifications or bribery.

Predictably, the sub-committee postponed making a decision on the grounds that Councillor Rivron's absence from the interview meant that the panel was inquorate: legal advice must be sought. Talking to Anna on the phone that night, we agreed that she would stay away from school to avoid answering the inevitable questions from the staff. The next morning I told them that everything would turn out all right, trying to ease their strong suspicion that the Council would let us down again. I then took a quick assembly, using as a theme the problems Robbie Fowler had caused his Liverpool team-mates by being sent off in a game that week. I needed to impress on them that it was vital to work together as a team – and not mess the builders about, so that the sports hall and the five-a-side court would be completed on schedule. Later I learned that wiser counsel from senior politicians had prevailed, and the sub-committee had ratified Anna's appointment. From September, the school would have a new, permanent Headteacher: one with wide experience and knowledge of the school and the qualities to lead it out of special measures.

The LEA released the news of Anna's appointment, and she spoke to various newspapers. The story, complete with some stunning pictures, appeared in the national papers on Friday. She gave a powerful interview on Radio Leeds that lunch time, although the report on the front page of the *Halifax Courier* quoting Councillor Rivron as being unhappy did somewhat detract from the general satisfaction felt by everyone at the school. She had obviously not persuaded anyone of her case, however, as early the next week there was an extremely positive editorial in support of Anna's appointment. That the school had a new Headteacher was brought home to me when I took a call from a reporter from the *Times Educational Supplement*, who was clearly most disappointed to speak to me, saying, 'I thought Anna White was the Headteacher.' Six months on from 'Superhead' and I was 'yesterday's man'. It was also interesting to see that Anna was described as 'thin with an infectious smile' – how unfair to be called a grey, jowly man.

When Stan and I next met, not only did we continue our better relationship, but as we chatted with some governors it became clear that the debacle had unified the majority of governors. Councillor Rivron now withdrew from the interview panel for Deputy Head, to be replaced by Michael Higgins, and Anna began planning a proper interview process with panels on different topics. As far as Jill Wilson was concerned, she had now definitely decided to stand for Chair of Governors. I also talked to Brian Garvey, the NASUWT Officer, who on Friday informed me that – crucially for the future success of the school – the staff were very happy with Anna's appointment. He would relay their concerns about the political interference to the union's headquarters.

I was warned by some friends with political connections that I was held responsible for the way Anna's appointment had been handled and should watch my back. To say I was perplexed would be an understatement. My involvement in the whole process had been in the open. Admittedly I had never disguised my view that the appointment of Anna would be the ideal solution – it would ensure a smooth transition when I left – but that was because she had proved time and time again that she was extremely competent and totally committed to the school. I had imagined, naïvely perhaps, that I was doing the job asked of me by the councillors and officers – the very people who had promised to back me up, and who repeatedly extolled Anna's qualities to me. I was by now thoroughly bored and disillusioned with the senseless political games played by some of the councillors and their supporters. I ignored the politics and focused on my next goal: harnessing everyone's efforts to fulfil the remaining promises in the Action Plan.

The following week the politicking continued. As Stan had resigned, we started with an election for a new Chairman. When Jill Wilson was nominated, David Helliwell objected, claiming that there was no precedent for a governor like Jill, appointed by the LEA under special measures, to become Chairman. This odd objection was swiftly dismissed and Jill's appointment overwhelmingly endorsed. Next, he blamed me for Councillor Rivron's remarks quoted in the *Courier*, and went on to criticize me for defining a code of school dress for pupils but not for teachers. He also claimed he was continually obstructed in trying to discuss the staff handbook – although we had asked him twice for a copy of his objections. At one point he wondered aloud, 'just to clarify the position', whether I should be sent back to Rastrick now that they had a 'proper head' in Anna – this immediately after arguing that Helen Rivron had been correct in pulling out of the appointment process. After complaining that everyone else failed to follow procedures, he introduced without notice an investigation he had made into the secondary school destinations of primary school children from the local area, implying that we were doing nothing to counteract the 'pull' of the grammar schools and the well-established 11–18 comprehensives. Thankfully, the staff governor attending her first meeting – as the previous one had retired – interrupted to put him right on this, highlighting the success of Anna's visits to primary schools and our press campaign.

When Anna asked David to come to the forthcoming parents and teachers Quiz Night he said it was 'inappropriate' for him to do so because he, like Jill, was a 'special measures' governor. 'Come as a friend then,' she suggested, and he finally agreed to this. Afterwards, we decided that he must see his role as being to monitor the head and governors in order to keep us all on track, and that was why he thought Jill should not chair the meetings – she should be neutral, like him. Everyone else felt the two were appointed to strengthen the governing body and actively support the school until it fulfilled its targets.

However, I felt it had been a good meeting overall. We had a new Chairman, the majority of the governors were united behind Anna and the school, the budget for next year had been accepted 'on the nod', and we had agreed to organize a governors' training event.

22

The Pastoral Deputy

I suggested to Anna that it would be sensible for me to be more involved with the day-to-day pastoral problems for the rest of the summer term, whilst she took on a higher profile in the key areas of staff appointments and planning for the next academic year.

My short career as a pastoral deputy brought me into closer contact with the children. The examples of poor behaviour could often be extreme, but they were now down to a small hard core and a few hangers-on. The first problem I had to tackle involved a number of pupils provoking the catering staff during lunch time: for example, pushing a piece of wood through the handles of a double door so that it could not be opened from the inside, and some incidents of stone throwing. I enlisted the support of a Year 11 student, who undertook a covert surveillance operation in the art room, and placed a video camera the back of the kitchen. A combination of this surveillance and Jeanette Wallace's vigilance identified those children involved in the more trivial incidents. We called in their parents, who gave their total support, and after a fairly substantial dressing down the problems with the kitchen staff ceased. I did have to exclude one boy for damaging a dinner lady's car and a girl for swearing at a teacher. However, there were more positive notes. A group of Year 7 pupils who had been working on a musical project with Barry Russell, a lecturer from Bretton Hall College of Higher Education, were acclaimed for their performance at a music festival in Halifax, and the behaviour of the Year 9 students taking their National Curriculum Standardized Attainment Tests (SATs) was far better than the previous year, when it had been totally unacceptable.

By May, we had excluded a total of only three or four children for a few days each since the original exclusions. We wanted to maintain that record – partly because the political reaction to a permanent exclusion would be predictable and tiresome – but also to make the staff realize that exclusion was not the easy solution to discipline problems. It was important to give the most difficult pupils every chance to mend their ways, and we had little chance of gaining access to the limited support available from the LEA to help schools cope with disruptive pupils unless we exhausted all possible internal sanctions first.

In one instance, warning the parents of a boy of the consequences of any further disruption and placing him 'on report' resulted in an immediate and significant improvement in his behaviour; I eventually counted him as one of my successes. However, a second boy arrived very late next day to his first lesson 'on report', so for the rest of the day I followed him from lesson to lesson to ensure his attendance. Obviously we could not maintain that level of supervision, and sadly, he failed to behave acceptably; however, because we had tried this strategy, he was accepted into Beaconsfield without question.

These two problems were typical. The first pupil was badly behaved because he thought he could get away with it, and clear boundaries and sanctions regularly reinforced by praise for his good behaviour let him know how far he could go. The behaviour of the other boy was much harder to manage because, like a number of the most difficult children, he lived in a short-term 'now' of no more than five minutes. With the ability to dismiss what had gone before, and little concept of the consequences of his actions, he would absolutely deny being involved in any bad behaviour and feel aggrieved when sanctions were applied. When I took him step by step through his actions, he might grudgingly accept some involvement, but he would often continue to deny being involved in incidents even when he knew he had been observed. Such problems are compounded by the readiness of parents, not to mention those community workers who see their role as supporting children's rights, to believe implicitly everything a child tells them. This gives children the wrong message, leading them to think that they can always avoid the final consequences of their actions and giving them no incentive to conform or control their behaviour. Inevitably, they will become ineffective parents of a new generation of disruptive, underachieving pupils.

Many of our children were also deeply insecure, and as a result were often more than ready to accept they were in the wrong – even when they weren't. Good comprehensive schools (like Rastrick, I hope) may contain many children who lack social skills through poor and inconsistent parenting, but these schools are able to establish higher expectations because of the presence of other, more confident children acting as role models. Of course, many of the Ridings children came from disadvantaged households, but I have never accepted that one can excuse poor behaviour on the basis of poor family circumstances. We need to understand the problems the children face and try to support them so they can grow into responsible adults. Although I appreciate the enormity of the problem, I am sure more could – and should – have been done by the agencies working with their families and the primary schools. It was a privilege to see the more experienced Ridings staff work with these children to widen their horizons and gradually modify their behaviour, but with many pupils they were trying to make up for a decade or more of lost opportunities.

Every school has pupils who misbehave, and often much more seriously than by committing the average misdemeanours at the Ridings. Describing incidents of poor behaviour out of context only sensationalizes problems. What is important – what we should be looking at – is how schools address these problems when they arise. The intervention system introduced by Anna earlier in the year meant that now I was more often called to help colleagues. In comparison with the previous autumn the majority of the problems were now much more easily solved – a radical improvement. But although there were far fewer serious problems, there was still a constant level of disruption in some classrooms and from several of the younger pupils. However, I was conscious that we were short of a deputy head to take responsibility carrying forward initiatives on behaviour.

One teacher complained to a union official that things were getting back to the poor state of the previous autumn, but her view arose mainly out of confrontations with students which, although not caused by her behaviour, were exacerbated by it. I took the teacher to one side and pointed out that if she had problems with the pupils she could come to Anna or myself, and to my surprise she burst into tears. Anna raised the matter at a staff meeting, demonstrating the right mix of hurt, concern, humility and steel. I thought that she used the opportunity to make her mark and the staff obviously respected the way she handled the situation.

My involvement with the pastoral work brought home to me the inadequacy of the record system; when I saw a parent it was sometimes almost impossible to obtain an accurate history of the child's behaviour. One member of staff tried to tell me that everything would be fine if we computerized the system. I was a bit irritated by this focus on the surface rather than the underlying problem. 'The introduction of an IT database isn't the point,' I said. 'If we can't recognize the importance of doing the job properly in the first place, it won't make any difference if we computerize it!'

By now the monthly HMI visits were almost routine, and the May inspection passed off well, although a couple of teachers had forgotten the basic classroom management rules that we had been drumming into them and received unsatisfactory reports as a result. However, the level of satisfactory or better lessons was up to around 90 per cent and we had another target to aim for – setting meaningful and achievable learning objectives for each child. Although the inspectors acknowledged that excellent progress had been made in assessing the pupils' level of performance, and we were improving our mechanisms for estimating their potential, they felt we needed to work out individual strategies for each child's overall academic improvement. One of the inspectors highlighted the need for a policy to ensure progression – keeping up the pace and challenge in courses – which set another target for us: ensuring that each subject area had a clear policy for monitoring pupils and improving their attainment.

Thursday 1 May was election day, and one of the school classrooms became a polling station. The voters came and went without any fuss, and the clerks left with a radically different view of the school from its public image. Later that week we held a Sixth Form Taster Day; it attracted plenty of interest, although some of the current Sixth Form, who resented the prospect of sharing their facilities with more students, had their noses put a bit out of joint. The Year 11 students were very positive about their future plans, and the staff continued with the plans begun on the training day at the start of term for the extension of courses.

With the reward of the May Day Holiday and the prospect of a four-day week, I returned on Tuesday 6 May eager to meet the candidates for the Deputy Headship. As I had feared, the long interval between the shortlisting in the Easter holidays and the interview date had resulted in the frustrating situation of only three from the original six candidates arriving to look round the school, before being interviewed the next day.

By the next morning another had dropped out because she felt taking the job was not sensible at this stage in her career. After the panel interviews we unanimously decided it would be best to re-advertise the post, even though the appointment would probably now be delayed until January 1998.

During a meeting of the Ridings sub-committee that evening, Councillor Rivron reiterated the idea that, now Anna had been appointed, it was time to let her stand on her own two feet and send me back to Rastrick. By now I could cope with the criticism, but it was a great pity that all this was said in front of Liz Lord, from the *Courier*, who dutifully wrote it up, quoting Rivron's and Higgins' view that it was inappropriate for me to have a mentoring role during Anna's first months: they needed an LEA Headteacher. The papers submitted to the committee had again highlighted the report of our achievements at the last HMI inspection, but this was buried in favour of the councillors' unhappiness with my continuing presence at the school. I had agreed to be interviewed for the BBC's *Look North* television news programme to emphasize the good news, but the interview ended with the inevitable question, 'Why do you think they want to get rid of you?' I fudged the answer – there was no point in making the situation worse.

The councillors' actions did not win wide acclaim: the *Halifax Evening Courier* described their 'heavy-handed move' as a 'shirty way (to treat) a man who did so much to turn round a local authority school in crisis'. I believed that the many assurances of support from councillors representing all parties were sincere, but my store of goodwill towards Calderdale was by now in overdraft. No lessons seemed to have been learned: there was the same lack of understanding concerning the consequences of councillors' actions, putting posturing and rhetoric before the future success of the school. Ofsted's criticisms of the LEA – that politicians were too involved in the day-to-day workings of the Education Department and that their behaviour sustained the 'climate of mistrust between schools and the LEA' – were neatly exemplified by this behaviour.

Ian Jennings came to see me, and he was as usual very supportive, promising to smooth things over. However, I got the impression that some politicians felt that their elected status gave them licence to treat mere appointed staff like puppets. The underlying problem was that they evidently felt I was taking all the credit for what was going on and resented it bitterly. I was amazed. 'I give them credit in every interview, it's not my fault if it's edited out. And to avoid the "Superhead" label I always give maximum credit to Anna, the staff and the pupils. If they really want me to go, I'll take "garden leave" until my contract ends in August. They chose me to do the job: get them to leave me alone to get on with it!' I returned to my other theme. 'They promise to support us but they take little interest in what we're doing. The reality is that Anna and I are on our own, doing two or three jobs each! You've got to understand that to cope with all the work we can't always be expected to do everything in line with the bureaucratic minds of some of your officers. We need to be supported – not overseen.'

Thanks to Ian's diplomacy, my relationships with the councillors improved afterwards, and I had a long conversation with Michael Higgins at an awards ceremony for Brighouse Adult Education a week or so later. Once again he assured me that I had his full support and promised that the Education Committee would tackle the wider problems in the area, leaving us to get on with running the school. Further declarations of support came from Councillor Pam Warhurst, the Leader of the Council, and Paul Sheehan, the new Chief Executive, after they visited the Ridings School. They had both been sympathetic and helpful from the outset. 'I want them to see chaos in order to make the point that everything hasn't been solved,' I urged the staff, but they failed me – everything was perfect.

With the governors' acceptance of their need for training, we could look forward to progress in this area as well. Ron Hill, Assistant Principal of Calderdale College and a newly co-opted governor, had volunteered to help organize the two governors' training sessions and started with a SWOT analysis (Strengths, Weaknesses, Opportunities, Threats) on the governing body. We organized the governors into groups based on specific categories – LEA, parent, co-opted, staff – to facilitate general discussion and encourage those who felt reticent about making a contribution in the face of the few who tended to dominate discussions.

Unfortunately, the training session clashed with another meeting at the school. Since it was obviously more important for Anna to stay with the governors, I left after the beginning. I discovered the next day that I had missed an eventful evening. One of the governors had constantly muttered that it was all a waste of time and walked out, although he later returned and worked very effectively – until he had a row with Jill about her links with private education. He told Anna that she was the only competent member of staff – all the rest should be sacked – and, saying he was resigning, he walked out for the second time. Despite this petulance, which would not have been tolerated from a pupil, the session went on and a good start was made on developing a coherent vision and agreeing a strategy to improve the running of future meetings. The follow-up session was also constructive – although the discontented governor (who by now had 'reconsidered' his resignation) was absent, refusing to attend any more meetings whilst I was at the school because I was a 'self-publicist', an excuse that conveniently ignored the fact that his outburst originally had nothing to do with me. Without him, the governors were more united, and I found it easy to produce a set of recommendations which was agreed at the next governors' meeting.

The first half of term ended on a high: the Ridings School was not amongst the 18 worst schools in the country named by David Blunkett that week. I slept through most of Friday evening and pretty much all day Saturday.

23

THE END (FOR ME) IS IN SIGHT

I had been invited to appear on *Kids Behaving Badly*, a live, hour-long Granada television programme presented by Richard Madeley and Judy Finnegan during the Spring Bank Holiday. After closely questioning the researcher about the content of the programme, I agreed to take part. They failed to organize the promised train tickets – an omen of what was to come, as it turned out – but at least there was a red Mercedes to get us to the studio. I had understood that I was part of a six-person 'expert' panel who would discuss the behaviour of young people, but when we got to the studio we found that the hospitality room was overcrowded, and it turned out that numerous people had been booked to speak as part of the audience.

As the transmission time approached, the panel were taken off to a tiny storeroom to have our make-up applied, a stark contrast with Richard and Judy's much larger room, where they were relaxing in front of *A Question of Sport*. The camaraderie that develops when strangers sense that together they are facing a potential disaster was very evident. For my part, I was able to make a major contribution to British television, averting one disaster by noticing that Richard Madeley's shoelace was undone. However, others were to follow. The programme was too ambitious: it was over-scripted, too many 'experts' sitting in the audience had been promised they could participate, and panel members had no opportunity to comment freely (although some of us considered that an advantage). Consequently, many important and nationally recognized people were ignored, and the programme focused on the sensational.

Unsurprisingly, 75 per cent of viewers voted in a phone-poll that parents should take responsibility for their children's actions. (Although, in my experience some parents only hold that view about other people's children.) The viewers were then told that the studio audience disagreed, but the audience had been asked a different question: 'Would you imprison parents for their children's crimes?' The vote had followed an emotional interview with a mother jailed for her son's anti-social activities.

Violent and nasty extracts from closed-circuit television footage were shown, with the justification of 'shocking' children into behaving well and highlighting the plight of socially excluded children, which concerned Richard and Judy. However, the youngsters with a record of offending who were sitting in front of my wife just lapped it up, getting quite excited at the violence. Richard and Judy were out of their depth; in the last break, the audience was in uproar and nearly revolted against the programme's manipulation and bias. The presenters vanished at the end, to be replaced by a team from Group 4 Security who turfed us all out of the studio onto the street. The expert panel didn't even get tissues to wipe our make-up off. The researchers, the only members of the production team brave enough to face their contacts, were besieged by angry people who had given up important engagements because they had been promised an opportunity to participate in a serious programme. A group of us piled into a minibus and returned to the hotel bar to relive our experience. So far, Richard and Judy have not repeated this experiment with the peak-time, hour-long, live format.

With the Spring Bank Holiday behind us, I felt I was in the home straight. I was amazed at the number of pupils who had seen me on the *Kids Behaving Badly* programme. They had been impressed by the fact that I had said they had behaved well and my street cred rose considerably. I was pleased that my short contribution had registered, as I think I had been the only contributor to say that extremely badly behaved children were in a minority and that rewards were just as important as sanctions.

However, just when you think things are moving along nicely, along comes reality. The caretaker was very concerned about the starlings nesting in the eaves of the school, and the builder who came to block up the holes discovered that the stonework on the front facade was falling off. Then, as work to remove some lagging took place during the Spring Bank Holiday, the contractors had discovered that the ceilings of the boiler room and the adjacent classrooms were full of asbestos insulation; the Council's Health and Safety staff immediately insisted that we stop using the three affected rooms. Unfortunately these included the food and textile teaching areas. They also wanted us to vacate all the rooms above, which included the main IT room, the library and our offices. What had started as a weekend's work expanded into four weeks and rising, so I refused. We would move out of the affected rooms, but the work to remove the asbestos had to be delayed. The two staff mainly affected, Karen Dean and Margaret Williams, responded with true Dunkirk spirit, quickly relocating the essential equipment with minimal disruption to lessons, although teaching programmes had to be changed to allow for a heavier concentration on microwave cookery, as the electric and gas cookers were marooned in the closed-off rooms. The cost of rebuilding and clearing the asbestos was estimated at over £50,000, but fortunately it was the LEA's responsibility. At the same time, bright yellow notices appeared stating that the Education Department was seeking planning permission for the Science and Expressive Arts extensions.

Problems with buildings occurred right up to the end of term. In the final week, the builders – with no consultation or notice to us – started to dig up the roadway, blocking an important access route for pupils. This disruption, combined with the discovery of a bees' nest in one of the roofs, meant that the site was almost at a standstill as virtually every route around the school was blocked. The builders were prevailed upon to re-organize their work, but why were they given permission, and why were we not consulted in the first place?

I had been meeting with a group of staff from Youth and Community Education and Calderdale College to draw up a plan for possible community use of the school. A public evening meeting was organized which was well attended, and there were many takers for the various courses. We also managed to attract around £1,000 of Prince's Trust funding to operate homework clubs in conjunction with the Youth Club and a local primary school. With the go-ahead on the Expressive Arts block, the future for community involvement looked bright.

We had arranged an Open Day for the providers of the Global literacy software, Systems Integrated Research, to demonstrate their software to teachers from other schools in Yorkshire and Lancashire. Some outstanding improvements had been achieved in reading skills and attitudes to learning since we had been using the computer-aided learning materials. The major gains had been achieved by 21 pupils in

Years 7 and 8 who had worked in the Global English groups, whilst also participating in the Corrective Reading programme. The average gain was about seven months in reading age – significant, as these pupils had made little progress since starting primary school – and three students had made gains of over two years, with one improving his reading age by three years. Only three of the pupils involved in this intensive part of our programme failed to make any progress: they had sporadic attendance records and missed too much of the work. We could also point to improvements in those Key Stage 3 pupils who had concentrated on OILS in place of French.

This proved to be a real boost, combined with the results of the surveys into the attitudes of pupils, parents and staff to the changes that had taken place. All three groups expressed increased satisfaction with how the school had changed since the crisis, although we had some way to go in totally fulfilling our promises in terms of homework.

The following week saw the last HMI monitoring visit of the year on 16 and 17 June. The first day of the visit was not our best, particularly the afternoon. It was an inspection too far: the staff and pupils had had enough and it was the wrong time of year. Nevertheless, the vast majority of lessons were satisfactory or better, with some encouraging comments about the staff who had been observed. The key finding was that learning had not improved as much as teaching. Given the history of the school, this was not really surprising; old habits die hard, and some of the children had been so neglected during their time in the education system that they were unable to change their attitudes to education as quickly as the experienced teachers. The tragedy of the Ridings School was that it became a scapegoat for the inadequacies of so many who had for years failed in their responsibilities to the young people of the area, blaming their own poor performance on the disadvantaged community.

The same week, Chief Inspector Adam Briggs masterminded a visit of the dance group to perform at the Association of Chief Police Officers' Conference, held in a luxury hotel. The youngsters thought it was another world. One of the Year 10 girls said to me, 'We're not supposed to be in a place like this. This is too good for us.' 'Rubbish!' I replied. 'This is what you should be aiming for.' Michelle was once again eloquent in her introduction, and the dancers were superb. The audience of hard-nosed police gave them a standing ovation. During the morning coffee break, I had attended a reception and drunk a couple of glasses of champagne with some senior officers from the Intelligence Services and Customs and Excise. I felt guilty at drinking whilst the rest of the staff were working, rehearsing the dance routine, so I invited them to join us. They got it into their heads that I had drunk their fair share of the champers, and I suffered later when they regaled Anna with an exaggerated version of the event. After a presentation by Chief Constable Keith Hellawell of some glassware and an aerial picture of the Ridings School, we posed for photographs before lunch and the return journey. It was a valuable opportunity for the pupils to see how the outside world appreciated their hard work and creativity, and it made a real contribution to raising their self-esteem.

On my return, I discovered that there had been moves to manoeuvre me out of the second attempt to appoint the Deputy Headteacher. I told Jill Wilson and Anne McAuley, 'It's not a problem. I'm tired of all the backbiting and at least I'll be able to keep an eye on the school during the interviews.' However, I was moved by the depth of support for me from the governors who insisted that I be involved. The 'silent majority' on the governing body was as tired of the silly games and grandstanding as I was; I went into the final governors' meeting feeling proud to have belonged to the group. First there was a reception to thank Stan for his labours as Chairman, then they presented me with a framed photograph of the infamous steps and a chocolate football to remind me of my constant complaints that the dates of meetings clashed with notable football matches. I was genuinely sorry to give up the comradeship we had developed. Unfortunately, two governors arriving late for the reception but early for the meeting had to wait in the lobby, as they were unable to get past the security locks on the entrance doors, and they broke the mood by tetchily saying, 'Well, if you don't want us to come we'll go home!' – but to be fair, I think they were more bothered about having to wait with each other.

Anna, Jill and I had met with Eileen Shea from the Education Department to sort out the agenda for the final meeting, and I had taken responsibility for ensuring that the paperwork was spot on. Each agenda item was supported by a précis of background material or a short paper, and carried an indication of the type of outcome expected.

It worked like a dream, although we had to suffer one governor's sotto voce swearing and discourteous remarks – mainly directed against me or the political associate with whom he had been trapped in the lobby. It became clear that he, like the councillor governors, was being briefed by an LEA officer before each meeting. I had disagreed with this practice for some time, as I felt it created two categories of governor, and it was clearly not succeeding in its objective of ensuring that the meetings ran smoothly. From the looks on the faces of the other governors, they agreed with me.

There had been almost 50 responses to the Deputy Head re-advertisement, which was better written and larger than the original. In addition, the material sent to candidates was more informative – and no postage was required. The stages were arranged within a sensible timescale, and all the shortlisted candidates turned up this time; from a strong field, the successful candidate was Andy Pugh who was working at a school in Kirklees. Tragically, Anna arrived home after making this significant appointment to find out that her father had died.

Unfortunately, the self-imposed delays meant that we had passed the 31 May resignation date, and Andy's headteacher and governors refused to release him until Christmas, despite the pleadings of Ian Jennings and Jill Wilson. This meant we had to look carefully at an interim arrangement. Some days were difficult even with Anna and me working closely together, so it was too much to ask for Anna to cope alone whilst the many new staff were also finding their feet. Chris Binns, Head of Lower School, and Ian Calvert, Head of English, were appointed to take on additional responsibilities and the two deputies from Ovenden, David Bond and Jeanette Wallace, now both retired, agreed to share the job of bursar.

Anna worked hard organizing a series of prize-giving assemblies for the first week in July, to reward the pupils for their efforts. There were awards for pupils who had excelled in particular subject areas, higher awards for those who had been commended in several subjects, and further awards for attendance, sport, the Rock Challenge, and so on. As the timing of the assemblies clashed with the funeral of Anna's father, I led the first, and Stan Brown and Paul Leach presented the certificates. Although the events took place in the morning, about a dozen parents attended. The second event also went well, with certificates awarded by

Jill Wilson and the Deputy Lieutenant of Yorkshire, who talked about the problems the students had faced without patronizing them, emphasizing the importance of leadership and responsibility. Afterwards as we talked with the parents who had attended, Jill said that she had seen Stephen Byers, the Minister of Education, announce that the school was being granted £650,000 towards the costs of constructing the planned Science and Expressive Arts blocks, and congratulate everyone for their achievements. Sue Julian had been lobbying the DfEE to grant this money for the last few months and, together with the LEA's matched funding (which they had to find as part of the terms of the deal), it meant that we had £1.3million, enough to complete the extensions.

Anna returned to school but suggested that I officiated at the remaining awards assemblies. These were followed by my final school assemblies, in which I recalled the difficulties we had faced together and congratulated the pupils on how they had responded to the challenge: 'I will always remember you and wish you every future success.' After the Upper School assembly I even got a round of applause, which gave me a real buzz. Never mind the Ofsted reports and figures or the public plaudits, this was what really made my time as Head of the Ridings School worthwhile.

The final week started with a visit by John Price Jones and a group from the Northern Ballet Orchestra, who illustrated the various sections of an orchestra and left the younger pupils animated and excited by the performance, setting the right note for the week. Anna made her final staff appointments, finished the next year's timetable and organized an Induction Day on 11 July for the new pupils on whom the long-term future of the school would depend. The new staff came and met their new forms in a structured and productive day which they all enjoyed.

The media were drawn by my departure and the end of the school year, and after completing a taped interview for Radio Leeds to be transmitted on my last day, I 'minded' Jill Wilson through a live interview. True to form, the equipment didn't work, and I had to hold a transistor radio, turning the volume up and down to give the presenter her cue. As we switched from the live element, involving Jill and the presenter, to the taped sections, I concentrated fiercely on my vital task. The interview made every bulletin, but no one realized the crucial role I had played.

It was a strange week, tying up loose ends – I'm not sure I ever tied them all. As so many of my colleagues seemed to be retiring, it felt like the end of an era. It was strange to think that such a tremendously challenging and fulfilling phase of my working life was over. I was pleased to think of the exciting opportunities that faced the staff and slightly envious – although, of course, I was delighted at the prospect of a six-week summer holiday and the thought of returning to Rastrick High School. Then came the last day. I was pleased that Michael Higgins came with Ian Jennings to mark the occasion; we had a friendly chat about the previous months. Fittingly, Liz Lord, the *Courier* reporter who had been present from the outset, interviewed us. Anna and I both spoke of the hard work that everyone had put into the enterprise, and then went outside to have our photograph taken. Anna forgot the ground rules and stood at one end – she was cropped.

The farewell from the staff was not as bad as I feared. The goodbyes for the other leavers took some time, inevitable given the relationships that had built up over the years; mine was the shortest. Anna and Jenny Baker said some very nice things, interspersed with some very unfair character assessments, and presented me with various mementoes including a tee-shirt with a picture of me holding a mop and a bottle of Jif, to illustrate my real skills as a caretaker – the best job in a school.

Then it was time for the final, inevitable television interviews and – unfortunately without the added piquancy of a sunset – Anna and I did our last walk for the cameras.

24

LESSONS FOR THE FUTURE

So what lessons has my year at the Ridings taught me about education? The Ridings' initial Ofsted report was damning, but it did mention many instances of positive teaching by staff and good behaviour from pupils. Unfortunately too often the mismanagement of the behaviour of a minority of the pupils allowed small problems to escalate. This was highlighted more than once in the report:

> Good relationships exist between some teachers and pupils and between pupils themselves. In too many lessons minor instances of misbehaviour led to relationships deteriorating rapidly and to serious disruption of lessons...The behaviour of pupils is very good in well-taught lessons, but in other classes and in public areas of the school it was, at times, completely unacceptable. The disorderly conduct of a significant minority of pupils continually disrupts many aspects of school life.

From the start, I sought to build on the report's positive aspects, with the first priority being the restoration of discipline and morale. In those first assemblies, I read out extracts that emphasized effective teaching and exemplary behaviour to stress to the whole school that everyone had been involved in the crisis, and therefore everyone had to work together to restore normality.

Restoring basic discipline was the most immediate and fundamental objective, but in many ways it was the easiest. Having no past history at the school – and with the media tag of 'Superhead' – I was regarded by the teachers and pupils alike with some circumspection, and the exclusions episode reinforced the idea that pupils could no longer misbehave with impunity. After 'drawing my line in the sand' with the exclusions it was vital to put in place a fair, consistently applied policy that encouraged good behaviour, rather than merely punishing misdemeanours. The demise of the hated DFL policy symbolized to the pupils that their concerns had been recognized, and gave the staff the message that good discipline comes from common-sense application of sound educational practice inside and outside the classroom. This in turn was supported by establishing a coherent pastoral system with distinct roles for staff and, more importantly, clearly defined referral structures.

Much of the disorder occurred at lunch time. From the outset, every teacher volunteered to staff 'social bases' for each year group, equipped with games, music centres and, in the case of the Year 10 and 11 students based in the youth club, pool and snooker. Even so, there were still incidents of disruptive behaviour, especially among the younger pupils. Most occurred in the last 15 minutes of lunchtime, with the ramifications often extending into afternoon lessons. Simply shortening the lunch time to 45 minutes markedly reduced the problem.

Attempting to build on these initial stages was frustrating in an LEA where provision for 'difficult' pupils was so limited. Working within a system that encouraged and supported schools, instead of denigrating them, would have enabled us to be much more creative in dealing with the disaffected pupils in an open and collaborative way. Sometimes exclusion is the only answer as a last resort, but it must be accompanied by a fresh start in appropriate alternative provision. In other failing schools, a far greater number of children have been permanently excluded in an attempt to restore – and maintain – control. Without a clear structure to deal with disaffection and disruption, pupils end up being placed outside a formal school environment, severely limiting their education, or drop out altogether, especially in their final years. Without a coherent framework, cases are dealt with in a piecemeal manner that often leads to large amounts of money being spent on giving children a sub-standard 'token' education. Lessons could be drawn from the good practice developed in the Furness Project and the successful re-integration of our excluded pupils.

Failing schools face major problems when additional children with significant problems are imposed on them. I believe that schools that fail to meet the Ofsted criteria should be protected from taking on additional problem cases for at least two years. It is unreasonable to expect staff and other children in institutions already struggling with their own difficulties to cope with the pressure of more disruptive or disaffected children – sometimes two or three per month – whilst trying to establish normality and improve standards.

It is fundamental that pupils can only learn if they are in school on a regular basis. Given that truancy was such a severe problem at the Ridings, we needed a sound strategy to boost attendance. The average figure for the first half of the autumn term 1996 was 76 per cent, and during the inspection it was only 65 per cent. Pupils chose which lessons to attend: the inspectors found considerable internal truancy, ranging up to 75 per cent – but also down to zero in effectively run lessons. At the same time, they found that 20 pupils in Year 11 had not attended a single session that school year, and that a third were regularly absent from school. The improved pastoral structure, more effective classroom discipline and the introduction of the Bromcom *ears* system to record attendance all helped to reduce internal truancy radically, but it continued to be a serious problem. By January, attendance was still only 78 per cent, and on the day of the first HMI inspection of 1997 it was only 72 per cent. With considerable effort on the part of the EWOs and pastoral staff working with them, the easiest cases – those who missed lessons occasionally – were successfully targeted. We then tackled the more intractable problem pupils, especially those aided and abetted by their parents, with whom we had much less success. Gradually attendance improved, until by the summer it was around 85 per cent. However, in areas where a number of pupils live in dysfunctional families with little structure to their lives, it can be almost impossible to achieve targets which would be the norm for other schools – simplistic comparisons that do not take these factors into account are failing to perceive the underlying problems.

It is essential in these circumstances that the various local authority support agencies representing Education and Social Services work coherently with each other and with agencies of the Health Service and the judicial system, all focusing on the needs of the child and family. Too often, in my experience, the concerns of the family or child are seen as a lower priority than whose budget bears the cost, or protecting demarcation lines in the face of professional sensitivities. Schools can play their part by operating as focal points for their communities. This is not just by offering extra opportunities to pupils through acting as a base for local educational and recreational activities and improving contact between parents and the school.

Our major objective was to address the quality of teaching. Poor teaching starting in the local primary schools contributed significantly to the low levels of attainment. Consequently, 75 per cent of the pupils had below-average reading ages, and 40 per cent of the pupils in Years 7 to 9 had reading ages more than three years below their actual or chronological ages. The obvious first step was to concentrate on improving basic literacy by introducing paired reading (with adults listening to children read for a short period each day) and corrective reading, a daily intensive course for small groups. The effectiveness of these methods has been well-documented in many schools over the years. That these strategies were not already in operation reflected badly on the school.

On this foundation we started using the Global English Learning Programme, which was introduced to the weakest pupils in Key Stage 3. The room full of computers was a visible statement of the school's wholehearted commitment to improving standards of teaching and learning. The programme was an outstanding success: reading improved dramatically, and children responded enthusiastically to the challenge. Teachers were also encouraged to widen their expertise in both teaching and monitoring progress, and these skills were obviously used across the curriculum. Other methods of increasing achievement were planned for the next school year. These included more emphasis on reading throughout the curriculum and during form time, use of the 'buddy' system – in which older students helped the younger ones, simultaneously improving their own reading and social skills – and encouraging parents to monitor their children's reading and help them to read.

The inspectors found that pupils also had poor verbal skills:

> Pupils are often unwilling to engage in meaningful conversations and discussions. [They] do not speak confidently or sustain their point of view. They listen well at times but quickly lose interest.

Regrettably, drama had been dropped from the curriculum, losing an important stimulus for talking and expressing emotions, further limiting the ability of the school to compensate for this weakness in the pupils. In the short term, we encouraged teachers to use approaches that promoted speaking in lessons – giving presentations, using role-play, and so on. The appointment of a specialist teacher, re-introducing drama to the curriculum and including the provision of the drama studio in the building programme were medium-term solutions. Over the longer term, the drama studio was intended to provide further impetus as well as emphasizing the importance of a high-quality physical environment as central to enhancing learning and modifying extreme behaviour. The Ridings students had so little faith in the 'system' that they would not believe that the new sports hall being constructed at the rear of the school was for them. 'It'll be like the swimming pool,' they would say, 'we'll never be allowed in!' This cynicism gradually broke down as they saw improvements to the fabric of the building and it became apparent that that the new sports hall would be followed by extra science labs and an expressive arts studio. This visible proof that they were considered worthy of the best facilities fostered a pride in themselves and the school.

By the spring it was clear to me that improving learning would be more difficult than improving teaching. Many pupils had little interest in learning, due to the absence of a proper school routine, compounded by a lack of structure in their home lives. Too often, teachers did not identify these weaknesses and provide remedial action, failing to challenge or enthuse pupils. They tended to occupy students rather than stimulate them, and dampen rather than raise their expectations. Children were presented with work that did not challenge them. Consequently, the Ofsted inspectors found very poor results in some subjects. By contrast, in other areas of the school, whilst there was evidence of under-achievement, there was good teaching, especially for more able students; and many experienced teachers were working hard to raise pupils' horizons.

It was vital to change the culture of the school for both students and staff. We reviewed all programmes of study, re-organizing and re-timetabling the curriculum, and introduced homework with a published timetable. As a result, the quality of the planning and delivery of lessons improved quite markedly. However, improvements in learning lagged noticeably behind those in teaching. Too many pupils lacked the skills necessary to seize this new opportunity; they had never learned how to learn. This lag between the improvement of teaching and that of learning had to be carefully managed, as the immediate reaction from the staff was 'What's the point? We've put in all this extra effort and nothing has changed!' We had to explain to teachers the importance of continuing to work hard to improve their output, since it must always be much easier to change the behaviour of intelligent professionals than develop the skills of children, those whose previous experiences had left them with such an immature grasp of how to acquire any skills.

Demoralization was a major problem. Staffing dilemmas often result from teachers on long-term sick leave. Under current conditions of service, teachers are eligible for six months on full pay followed by six months on half pay. Consequently, their classes can be condemned to temporary replacements for a year, while continuity is lost and the school's budget is stretched. If the LEA or the DfEE helped pay for a permanent replacement and underwrote the additional cost that would occur if the teacher returned, schools could more quickly establish stability. Short-term sickness, as well as being a telling indicator of staff morale, can often lead to worse disruption as it is difficult to forecast. The level of short-term absence at the Ridings grew from 3.9 per cent in September 1996 to 7.2 per cent in October – the average figure for other Calderdale comprehensives was 2.18 per cent. The Ridings had changed remarkably by July 1997, with levels dropping to 1.1 per cent – well below the LEA average. A positive ethos sustains morale.

'Naming and shaming' a failing school can further demoralize competent staff and drive pupils away if used as a stand-alone policy. If 'naming' is seen as an essential spur to ensure that schools pursue the highest standards, the policy should be 'naming and supporting'! Much has been achieved in recent years through rigorous inspection and monitoring processes, but comparisons need to be accurate and based on more objective data than they are at present. Working with schools to make real improvements towards achieving agreed goals rather than arbitrary targets would be far more effective.

Our experience suggests that those who believe that failing schools can close, be re-staffed and quickly re-open do not appreciate the difficulties in recruiting staff at short notice and arranging secondments from other schools. A short break during which everyone can reflect on their actions can be salutary, but good staff simply cannot be obtained in such a short time, and if a school is to be closed until they can be found, it might as well close altogether. However unsatisfactory an option, 'working with what you've got' is usually less disruptive to children's education, though clearly incompetent or obstructive staff should be removed quickly. Failing schools do require an injection of new, enthusiastic staff, keen to make their mark; and current ideas for paying new staff higher salaries are a possibility. However, it is a mistake to think that the prime motivation is money. A more powerful incentive can be the challenge of working in a rewarding and stimulating environment.

Our teaching audit was a great success. Not only did the positive outcomes raise the self-esteem of teachers, but Heads of Department had the opportunity to monitor and assess their colleagues. Our in-service training programme was based on the high input from the LEA's support staff developing into longer-term professional relationships, regular staff meetings with occasional outside speakers, and a mentoring programme. Teaming departments at the Ridings with 'mentor departments' in other schools was a promising concept. However, staffing shortages and the lack of time to plan the links meant that fewer staff participated than I had hoped.

Keeping up the momentum was another problem. At first I was faced with a group of demoralized people united in saying 'Tell us what to do!' so initial success was relatively easy. But people need the encouragement of regular signs of success in order to sustain performance and bring about long-term change and improvement – milestones by which progress can be measured and celebrated. Our milestones in those first months included re-opening the school, removing the intrusive media, managing the exclusions, completing the Action Plan, HMI acknowledging that discipline had been restored, changing the image of the school in the eyes of the media and the community, completing the teaching audit, introducing the successful OILS initiative, winning – and then losing gracefully – in the Global Rock Challenge and appointing the new Headteacher.

Successful management of schools requires effective middle managers who take responsibility for managing their teams and achieving their objectives. At Rastrick, I have sought to develop an ethos that encourages continuous staff training and a shared commitment to and understanding of the aims of the school. Achieving 'Investor in People' status gave us the incentive to plan training priorities that are embedded in the school development plan, and to introduce procedures such as annual personal development interviews for all staff to enable them to understand the contribution they need to make to achieve our agreed objectives. The changes we made to the management structures at the Ridings, giving staff more involvement in planning and organizing the curriculum and pastoral care, started the process of creating strong middle managers who would become the 'engine room' of the school, taking initiatives and making decisions.

As long as they achieve the desired outcomes, management structures can be adapted to reflect the nature of the organization. Of course organizations will not do well if staff roles and responsibilities are inflexible, collapsing when one vital member leaves. Structures need to reflect the experience of the staff as well as where the school is on its developmental continuum. As schools move along this continuum, they are able to become more responsible for monitoring their progress and taking charge of their improvement.

Our success in the early stages was in part due to regular and frequent monitoring by HMI, coupled with having only 20 days to complete the Action Plan. This created a climate which encouraged change, keeping up the pressure on staff and the LEA to focus on and meet their targets. The lead inspector's many days in school, visiting the lessons of all the staff, gave her an insight into the successes and failures of the first few months – and the potential for the future. The discussions at the end of each visit were extremely constructive, as was the willingness to bring in specialist inspectors to target the specific problem areas we identified.

The secondment of two experienced staff from other schools meant the Action Plan could plot a far more objective approach than if it had been drawn up solely by those held responsible for the failures of the past. If the staff had been left to their own devices, the consequences could well have been a slower pace of change and a failure to face up to the reality of the situation. The school's high profile ensured that we were focused on our objectives, but nevertheless the discipline of regular and intensive monitoring would enable any school in this situation to be managed much more effectively. It was a good model, far better than the 'You get on with it your way, and we'll tell you if you get it right' approach.

I was once told by an accountant that firms do not fail because they make the wrong decisions; they fail because they make no decisions at all. The same is probably true of many organizations, and certainly of schools. During the school's early history, the governing body seems to have had little sense of urgency, resulting in a paralysing lack of decision-making. If the ideal governor is defined as a 'critical friend', perhaps Karen's problem was that many of her governors were 'uncritical friends', who accepted everything they were told without question. I know from experience how difficult it is to find the right sort of governors, and in some areas, where parents have problems simply coping with their own lives, it can be virtually impossible.

The majority of the Ridings governors wanted only to support the school, though a minority pursued the inevitable private agendas, point-scoring and the like. It was unfortunate that the quick fixes and cosmetic changes we introduced to improve the morale of the school community and our image outside were seized on as indications that the job had been done. Governors are like a company's non-executive directors, in that their major role is to consider the strategic aspects of school life, with the headteacher being responsible for the school's management. However, it can often be difficult for governors to gain sufficient knowledge and professional expertise to establish this ideal relationship. In practice, a more flexible partnership needs to be developed, where mutual trust allows a free exchange of ideas and information and an atmosphere exists where all governors feel they can make a contribution.

The relationship between schools and LEAs – both councillors and officers – is also crucial. The role of Local Authorities in the management of schools has changed radically since the 1988 Education Reform Act. Local management is one of the major successes of the recent educational reforms: it allows schools to decide their priorities and realize them with the minimum of bureaucracy and the maximum value for money. Councils that managed this transition best were those who handed over responsibility to schools and were prepared to compromise where necessary. They understood that the devolution of responsibility to others often increases the chance of achieving your own objectives. The climate of distrust between Calderdale LEA and its schools lay in Calderdale's refusal to concede power. When organizations and individuals act in this way they emphasize their own insecurity, and the result is usually inaction.

LEAs that are genuinely committed to improving their schools should delegate a high proportion of the education budget to the schools themselves and offer cost-effective and high-quality services rather than imposing the use of their agencies. These should be overseen by a slim bureaucracy made up of officers with a sound professional understanding of school management who are able to monitor effectively schools' self-evaluation.

The growth of one-tier Unitary Education Authorities taking over the responsibility for education previously held by county councils and metropolitan authorities has increased the number of small LEAs like Calderdale. Small authorities often lack the resources and expertise necessary to assist schools properly, as they do not have the economies of scale to make the provision cost-effective. It is also often easier for objective decisions to be made away from the considerations of prospective voters. In my opinion the Police Authority is a good model. We could improve strategic planning by removing the parochial influences on decision-making – as decisions taken by small authorities can be heavily influenced by vociferous but unrepresentative local groups – whilst still maintaining a regional identity. Larger authorities would also be able to provide higher-quality professional support services, which could become involved with failing schools at an early stage. Such a system would also remove many of the inequities and inconsistencies of locally based school funding, as the financial allocations to schools in neighbouring LEAs can vary by several hundred pounds per pupil per year. Like most heads, I would welcome a fair, national funding formula based on the costs of delivering the National Curriculum.

An exciting way of bringing together the partnerships and co-operation necessary to achieve improvements in groups of schools is the government's idea of an Education Action Zone. A number of schools, working in partnership with industry – which would bring in additional resources and expertise – could create an environment designed to encourage schools to be innovative. Collaboration between a group of schools managed independently of the LEA, but working in a genuine partnership with it, seems an excellent idea. It could maximize the use of existing local resources and have enough clout to ensure that other agencies working in the community operate in a coherent and consistent manner.

However, these advantages could be lost if enmeshed in the bureaucracy and committee cycle of a local authority. Putting back the clock to the days before local management, where decision-making was limited by constant reference to LEA officers and committees, would have nothing to recommend it. Nor should private enterprise be allowed to manage an Action Zone in such a way as to make a profit: little enough money is available for education, so skimming money from school budgets for private profit is totally unacceptable.

The identification of schools with similar problems to the Ridings should be an opportunity to encourage local businesses to rally round. One of my most disappointing experiences at the Ridings School was the attitude of the business community. Aside from the Halifax Building Society, which seconded extra staff at a time when the school's administration was most stretched, and the Calderdale and Kirklees TEC, which managed the delivery of vocational programmes, most of the promises of help never materialized. At the outset local firms were keen to help, perhaps prompted by their concern over the effects on the local economy – at least one firm had rejected a relocation to Calderdale because of worries from their employees about education in Halifax: 'They thought their kids would have to go to the Ridings!'

We also had to reject some offers because they diverted us from our objectives or led to expenditure that we could not afford. Firms often only want to give you what they want to give, or what they think you should want. I found myself repeating, 'What we want is an IT support hotline and money for extra computers, extra staff and proper college links.'

Some commentators have cited the existence of two grammar schools and numerous grant-maintained schools in Calderdale as a major contributory factor in the Ridings problem. It is true that many children who could have joined the Ridings preferred to attend other LEA schools, as well as grant-maintained schools. I happen to believe that all secondary schools should be comprehensives, but I accept that if parents perceive that a local school is not delivering an acceptable quality of education they will vote with their feet and take their children elsewhere, whatever the organization.

Many parents did see both Ovenden and Holmfield as poorer alternatives to the other schools within easy travelling distance. The emotional response of one teacher caught up in the turmoil – 'They should have let Holmfield die out and concentrated on Ovenden' – was entirely understandable, but if the amalgamation had not taken place, would things have been better for the pupils? To be a pupil or a teacher stranded in an atrophying institution, with the school roll continually falling, the curriculum inevitably narrowing and morale fading, cannot be an acceptable answer. Amalgamation is always preferable. Nevertheless, the LEA's failure to ensure that the Ridings School got off to the best possible start and to nurture it in its early years was a major – and expensive – error of judgement. Children have one main chance for education, and this consideration should have outweighed all others.

Anna said in an interview shortly after her appointment, 'The Ridings is a generic term, like Hoover. It will be included in future dictionaries.' However, I cannot conceive that there will ever be another Ridings – it is almost unimaginable that such a combination of poor decision-making by the LEA, governors and the school's staff could recur. There have been many failing schools, many reorganizations of schools that have gone wrong, and many more where relationships at all levels have been tense and unproductive. In a number of these cases, the unions have become involved and media interest has been aroused, but none have generated such world-wide interest and become part of the nation's consciousness as the Ridings did.

It would have been understandable if we had tried to keep the press at arm's length after the sensational and biased reporting that described the Ridings School as 'the worst school in Britain' and 'the school from Hell'. The stress of trying to work normally with the world's press lined up outside, some of them encouraging pupils to misbehave, is difficult to imagine. However, I felt it was better to manage the media interest, and build positive relationships with journalists. In the end the good news story ran longer than the negative crisis publicity and helped improve the recruitment of pupils and the morale of the whole school. I also have to admit that in many ways it was the rollercoaster ride of a lifetime, and I enjoyed it tremendously.

It was a unique situation in terms of managing change. The circumstances demanded the achievement of significant improvements in an extremely short time; we were faced with the stark alternative of closure, resulting in sacked teachers and pupils transferred to other schools, with the consequent wide-scale disruption to the education of all involved. In retrospect, I am struck with how much easier it often was to deal constructively with the pressures of the high-profile media presence, constant inspection, union scrutiny and national political interest than to work effectively with the LEA and governing body. However, I have to admit that my personal approach – to get the job done at all costs – sometimes led me to take action which cut across the roles and responsibilities of others within the LEA.

Almost from the outset, people suggested I write about my experiences at the Ridings School, and my daughter, Joanne, persuaded me to keep a diary. I felt it was an important story to tell and I hope it will be of some use to those who read it. Obviously it is the story seen through my eyes, rooted in my experience and philosophy, and I am sure others might place greater significance on some aspects or interpret events differently.

Towards the end of my time at the school, I attended a conference for heads who, like me, had been 'parachuted' into failing schools, and I realized that the other headteachers, about 40 in all, had coped with the same types of situation in broadly the same way. For me, the following priorities emerged:

- Developing a fair and consistent approach to discipline
- Devising strategies to improve individual pupils' teaching and learning
- Promoting a team approach, taking steps to improve staff morale, and emphasizing the importance of training middle managers to take responsibility for achieving the school's agreed objectives
- Planning for change and maintaining the momentum to achieve it

- Improving literacy, oral and basic skills and developing pupils' self-confidence
- Working with committed and well-informed governors
- Working within a coherent LEA-wide approach to disruptive pupils, based on a professional assessment of the needs of pupils and schools
- Enlisting the involvement of other agencies to support families in order to attain high levels of attendance and motivation
- Building links with parents, business and the local community
- Providing a high-quality physical environment
- Establishing good relationships with the press, but not believing one's own publicity
- Understanding that 'quick fixes' – often seen by others as a reason for doing nothing more – need to be replaced by long-term solutions.

During the Millbank media circus I stated that my objectives were to restore discipline, improve teaching, gain the confidence of parents, get the cameras off the streets and see the appointment of a good headteacher. With remarkable good fortune and teamwork, I feel these basic objectives were achieved. But no failing school can be transformed overnight. Genuine improvement comes from the accumulation of small steps over a number of years.

I am confident that the Ridings School will develop into a stimulating school serving the needs of its pupils and improving its reputation, working with local parents and their children over the exciting years ahead. It was never the 'school from hell', but it had real problems. For a few weeks in autumn 1996 it was hell for the staff and many of the pupils, but over the next few months 'together they made the difference', building a secure foundation for its future success.

INDEX